Whole-Being-Embrace ™

Wholeness as a path to Self-Love

By Zeb Lancaster, Ph.D.

Whole Being Books

Published by Whole Being Books

Dedication

For the individual heart rediscovering its worth, for the human family relearning how to love, and for the Earth remembering our gentle touch; may this work support our reunion with the unchanging ground of wholeness we all share.

Acknowledgment

I owe the deepest gratitude to Teresa Neptune. She listens to me and advises me with a presence that is both remarkably insightful and unwaveringly kind. The way she shows up—engaged without ever intruding, supportive without ever abandoning—embodies the very principles at the heart of this book. Her presence partly inspired this book and allowed me to share this approach with far greater clarity, honesty, and heart.

I thank Judith Blackstone for her development of the Realization Process® meditation method. The material presented in this book occurred while I was deeply involved in practicing and teaching this approach. Judith's understanding has greatly influenced my yoga, my counseling practice, and my life.

I cannot express enough gratitude for the very engaged community of participants who show up for my guided online meditation gatherings and workshops. I learn so much from you. I deeply appreciate how we grow and heal together in such meaningful ways.

Thank you, Kailash Shankara. Your scholarship and personal understanding of the spiritual journey in relation to emotional growth have been precious to me.

Renne Provost and Bill Hunter have been tremendously supportive of my experiential guidance, and now as initial readers of this book. This has been a rich exchange that I value very much.

Table of Contents

INTRODUCTION..6

    My Story..6

    Meditation & Trauma Guidance............................8

1: NOT TWO ROADS, BUT ONE 11

The Heart of Healing 12

Bonding With Oneness Within..........................15

Facets of Oneness 18

A New Paradigm of Healing and Awakening 21

    Why Embodiment Matters for Healing................23

    Why the Body Is Central 25

    Body as Sanctuary..................................28

Spirituality, Psychology & Wholeness.................30

2: WITHOUT EARTH, THERE IS NO HEAVEN............. 33

    Spirituality's Mind Over Body........................34

    Eastern Spiritual Materialism 37

    Cosmologies of Participation........................39

    Cosmologies of Control 39

    Two Stories, Two Selves 40

    Meditation as Participation 41

    A Return to the Original Instructions 42

    A Cosmology for Healing 43

Psychology & Eastern Spirituality in Conversation.............43

Nurturing Nature of Nondual-Qualities of Self.................46

The Effortless Dance Between Two Selves.........................50

3: ENTANGLED TRUTHS 53

Meeting in the Dance of Love.......................53

The Unwavering Presence of Oneness 57

    Nurturing with Happiness & Knowledge................63

I See You – I Am You 69

Existential Trust 72

Not Bypassing & Feeling What is Real 73

Effortless Truth 75

How Healing Unfolds in Meditation 76

A Paradox Emerges 81

Stillness Within the Movement 85

4: COPING – HOW WE LEARNED TO GET ALONG 93

Oneness & Separateness at the Same Time 95

The Dance of Becoming 96

Survival Responses 99

How We Cope - Types of Attachment 101

Avoidant Attachment 101

Ambivalent Attachment 102

Disorganized Attachment 104

Reflections About Insecure Injuries 105

Secure Attachment 106

Whole-Being-Embrace in Action 108

5: ALLIES & ENEMIES 114

The Good Intentions Behind Ego 114

Respecting Our Ego's Fears and Fixations 115

Fragmentation as a Body Experience 116

Awakening to Personal Truth 118

Injury, Selfhood, and the Loss of Inner Guidance 120

Filling the "Hole" 123

6: PERSONAL TRUTH & WISDOM 125

What is Personal Truth? 125

Wisdom 128

Oneness as "Good Enough Parent" 131

The Capacity to Be Alone 136

Timelessness 137

Living in Grace 140

7: QUALITIES OF ONENESS... 142

Quality Rich Oneness 142
A Match Made in Heaven..145
How the Light Gets In..148
    Inner Alchemy of Wholeness 151
Unconditional Love 155

8: IT'S NOT OUT THERE, IT'S IN HERE 160

Embracing Impermanence..160
The New Spirituality of Wholeness & Boundaries............161
    Holographic Body 166
Being Held 169
    Washing our Five Senses Clean 172

9: PATHS TO WHOLENESS... 175

The Indirect and Direct Paths of Yoga 175
What is Whole-Being Meditation? 179
    General Practice Guidelines 183
    Open Witnessing...185
    Continuing the Meditation 188
    Three Primary Stages of Perception.........................190
Your Personal Event-Horizon 193

10: THE NONDUAL MIRROR... 197

Earth's Cry & Heaven's Smile 197
The Dance of Attunement..201
Aligning with What has Always Been Whole 202
    Contactful Presence..203
    Our House of Mirrors 206

11: WHOLE-BEING-EMBRACE™.. 208

The Three Phases of the Healing Journey 209
    Healing the Cycle 213
1. Being Nurtured..214
2. Uncoupling 217

Uncoupling Fear from Intense Experiences 218

3. Authentic Expression 223

Nurturing Expression into Authenticity 224

Letting Go of Effort & Finding Spontaneity 227

The Promise.. 229

Healing our Sense of Vision 231

12: BONDED TO WHOLENESS 233

From External to Internal.................................... 233

From Inner Bond to Collective Responsibility 237

CONCLUSION 244

Rethinking the Goal of Spirituality........................ 245

When Self-Love Awakens 246

A New Spiritual Paradigm 247

Living From Wholeness.................................... 248

Where Now? 248

Introduction

My Story

For as long as I can remember, I've been fascinated by the mystery of consciousness, how a physical brain can produce the living experience of *me*. Science calls this the "hard problem," and while researchers map neural networks and measure brainwaves, I've always felt that the deepest truths about being alive are discovered from the inside out. Mystics and meditators have explored this inner landscape for centuries, sensing directly the unity that underlies everything.

But before I ever understood consciousness, I was only a youth longing for what we all want: to feel safe, loved, and fully accepted. I wanted closeness, real closeness, the kind where you can show your hopes, your fears, your softness, and still be held. But I also needed freedom. I guarded my independence, my pace, my inner space. The fear of being controlled or swallowed up made intimacy confusing.

These two desires: *come close* and *please don't overwhelm me*, lived inside me like two tides pulling at the same shore. They shaped my relationships, my conflicts, my hesitations. Sometimes I opened deeply, then pulled away just as quickly. This push and pull followed me everywhere, into friendships, family dynamics, even how I handled chores, money, and daily life. Eventually, I went to therapy and learned how early relationship injuries shape our attachment patterns. Therapy helped, it gave me tools, language, boundaries, but the ache inside me didn't fully soften.

Then I discovered yoga and meditation. Non-attachment felt like a revelation. It promised peace without possession, love without fear, connection without losing myself. At first, it felt like a superpower: I could step back from chaos and find a still center. But slowly, I noticed something troubling; I wasn't just creating space, I was creating *distance*. I was using spirituality to avoid pain rather than heal it.

When heartbreak or betrayal happened, I'd tell myself I was "letting go," or "transcending the drama." I floated above my feelings like a witness, but the truth was simpler: I was bypassing my own heart. I wasn't healing. I was hiding.

I began to see this pattern not just in myself but everywhere, in clients, in spiritual communities, in the quiet ways people use "clarity" to avoid vulnerability. Peace built on avoidance is fragile. And detachment that silences the emotional body is not maturity; it is fear wearing spiritual clothes.

The turning point came when I stopped treating my emotions as illusions and started treating them as *messengers*. When I let myself feel, fully, honestly, without spiritual shortcuts, something opened. I realized that healing doesn't come from floating above our humanity but from embracing it with tenderness.

That's when the practice I now call whole-being-embrace began to take shape. Whole-being-embrace™ is the meeting place between the evolving-self (the emotional, vulnerable human within us) and the unchanging-self (the spacious, unified awareness that holds everything together). When these two aspects finally stop polarizing and begin to relate, something extraordinary happens: self-love blossoms.

Not the self-love of affirmations or achievement, but the kind that rises naturally when we hold ourselves the way we always needed to be held, with presence, compassion, truth, and care.

Whole-being-embrace taught me that spiritual awakening isn't about distancing from life but deepening into it. It showed me that my longing for closeness and my longing for freedom were never opposites, they were invitations. One asked me to open my heart; the other asked me to stay true to myself. Together, they formed the foundation of a more joyful, authentic, and free way of relating.

I learned that when we bring our emotional injuries into the presence of our unchanging-self, something reorganizes inside us. Old patterns soften. Fear loosens. Our relationships become clearer, kinder, more honest. Whole-being-embrace makes space for love, real love, the kind that is unconditional, spacious, grounded, and alive.

This book honors the role of non-attachment, but it insists on going further. It invites us not to transcend our humanity but to integrate it. It shows how the unchanging-self gives our emotional life a safe home, and how our evolving-self gives our spirituality depth, warmth, and meaning.

Throughout these pages, we will explore how unity and attachment, presence and vulnerability, spaciousness and intimacy meet within the body. It is here, in the gentle convergence of our wounded places and our deepest wholeness, that the true path of awakening unfolds not above life, but within it; not beyond the heart, but in the very space where it finally learns to open.

Meditation & Trauma Guidance

Meditation is an important part of cultivating mental and emotional well-being. Research consistently shows that meditation supports emotional regulation, focus, and self-awareness, and even produces measurable changes in the brain, such as reduced activity in the amygdala (the brain's "fear center") and increased volume in regions involved in emotional processing and attention.

But while meditation can be truly transformative, it is not a complete or sufficient approach for healing complex trauma. In fact, for trauma survivors, meditation can sometimes be overwhelming. Practices that invite stillness or inward focus may trigger flashbacks, disorientation, or emotional flooding. Even the calm states that meditation produces can feel unsafe, because trauma teaches the nervous system to remain hypervigilant. For someone stuck in chronic fight-or-flight, conscious breathing or relaxation practices may not bring ease, they may actually amplify distress.

Dissociation presents another challenge. It is common for trauma survivors to dissociate to some degree. But it makes it difficult to stay present with oneself, which is a core component of most meditation practice. This can create internal conflict or confusion during meditation, without the person fully understanding why they feel unsettled or "blocked." For these reasons, trauma healing requires a comprehensive, integrative approach, one that includes psychotherapeutic guidance that address both the physical and psychological dimensions of injury.

Transcendent forms of meditation may help temporarily ease symptoms or soften the intensity of memories, but in my experience they often do not reach the underlying emotional wounds, which makes it difficult to shift deeply embedded patterns of fear, shame, or disconnection.

Working with a trauma-informed therapist is essential whenever working with severe trauma. Skilled support provides a safe relational field in which emotions can be processed and old coping strategies gently replaced. Within this context, meditation can be adapted in ways that truly support healing. In fact, I believe that when we carry unresolved trauma, we need some form of contemplative practice to help us cope and integrate our experiences. Without this, sustained true emotional growth is unlikely.

Whole-being meditation is a trauma-sensitive meditation approach. It emphasizes grounding, presence, and safety rather than forcing deep introspection. Instead of withdrawing from the body, it helps us return to the body at a pace that feels manageable. It is more active and participatory than many forms of meditation, integrating mindful awareness into everyday movements, sensations, and relational experiences. Still, meditation is only one part of the healing process. Complex trauma often calls for a combination of therapies to support genuine, lasting change.

Chapter One

Not Two Roads, But One

Early in my work as a psychotherapist, a client said something that has stayed with me: "I know all the right things to think and do, but I still feel like a scared child inside." She had been meditating for years. She could access profound states of unified consciousness and clearly recognized her mental and emotional patterns. She felt like she had done everything "right." And yet, in moments of conflict, something deep would take over. Her body would tighten, her voice would fade, and she would collapse into the same old fear.

This reflects a common dilemma for meditators: we can touch clarity, even oneness, and still find ourselves overtaken by the parts of us that were never met, never completely understood, and never fully healed.

Her words echoed something I had felt in my own life. Meditation helped me find calm, but it didn't resolve the emotional injuries woven into my body. Psychotherapy helped me understand my past, but it didn't reconnect me with the spacious, loving presence I touched in meditation. I began to wonder: *"What if real healing requires both?"* That question became the seed of what I now call *Whole-Being-Embrace.*

We stand at a threshold. Many Eastern paths have sought to escape the body in search of pure awareness. Much of Western psychology has tried to heal the self without touching the deeper ground of unity (except Transpersonal psychology makes a good effort). Both approaches leave something essential out. The truth is that healing emotionally and awakening to unified consciousness are not two roads but one: a living integration where body and spirit, self and world, meet.

Whole-being-embrace is the communion of our ever-changing "evolving-self" and the wholeness and stillness of our "unchanging-self" in the temple of the body. This unchanging aspect of ourselves is the primary ground of our being, a very subtle, undivided consciousness and sense of wholeness that can be felt to pervade our body and the environment.

Whole-being-embrace is more than a practice; it is a revolution in how we inhabit life. When we reclaim the body as sacred, we reclaim the Earth as sacred. The qualities that restore our inner life, attunement, empathy, and presence, are the very ones that can mend our broken world. This is the invitation before us: to live as though our bodies and this Earth are holy ground, and to let that knowing change everything.

The Heart of Healing

Living in our bodies is a relational experience. We are born in relationship. From the very first breath, the way we are held, or not held, begins to shape us. Our deepest wounds happen here, in the space between self and other. Yet it is here, too, in that same sacred space, that our deepest healing can unfold.

At the heart of healing lies the experience of emotional bonding, but bonding can take many forms. When it includes contact with our experience of wholeness as a body experience of unchanging-self, the central theme of this work, healing reaches far beneath the surface of emotion into the ground of being itself. Before we explore this broader and deeper dimension of bonding,

12

we must first understand what bonding means for our evolving-self.

Bonding in a relationship is not simply an emotional event. It is a living dance between connection and separation, choreographed in the body long before we have words to express it. To bond in a relationship, with a person, a place, or even with an aspect of ourselves, we need to feel a sense of connection: the warmth of being seen, the safety of belonging, the comfort of being felt and understood. This satisfies our fundamental need for safety and support. Without this felt sense of attunement, we experience isolation and insecurity.

Paradoxically, bonding also depends on our capacity to separate. Separation is not disconnection. It is the quiet strength of knowing where I end and you begin. Healthy separation creates space for our uniqueness and individuality, and for us to have room to explore and manifest what feels personally meaningful. This allows us to establish the foundation for developing emotional autonomy as the capacity to make choices that arise from presence rather than from habit, fear, or old survival patterns. We stay true to our own center.

Without connection, we wither in isolation. Yet, connection without separation leads to fusion or enmeshment; we lose ourselves in the other, which can feel safe at first but becomes suffocating over time.[1] If we lose touch with what we feel to be true, there is "no one home" and authentic and intimate contact is not possible.

Healthy bonding thrives in the fluid movement between connection and separation. This dynamic allows us to experience

---

[1] "Other" here means not only other people, but also the situations we engage in, the environments we inhabit, and the broader world we move through. "Other," in this sense, includes anything we relate to beyond our immediate sense of self: intimate partners, family, and friends; workplaces and communities; as well as places, routines, and life circumstances. It also extends to how we relate to experiences themselves, challenge, change, uncertainty, and even opportunity.

13

intimacy without sacrificing autonomy, and independence without sacrificing belonging. Bonding, in this sense, is about attachment. It is also the ongoing dance that gives our experience depth, texture, and meaning.

How we make contact with others and how we learn to separate, shapes our relationships, as well as the very core of who we understand ourselves to be. From our earliest moments, the ways we connect and disconnect form the foundation of our personal identity (Bowlby, Ainsworth, Winnicott). They influence how we relate not only to people, but also to situations, substances, ideas, and to our own thoughts, emotions, and sensations. Both how we connect and separate compose how we bond in relationship to what is meaningful for us in life, whatever that is. Real authenticity and intimacy breathe in the rhythm between the two: belonging without losing self, freedom without breaking the thread of connection.[2]

Our bodies remember this rhythm. They carry the imprints of every embrace and every absence. At its core, bonding is cellular, kinetic, and emotional. In the slope of our shoulders, the depth of our breath, the tilt of the head, whole histories of relationships are stored. In this sense, bonding is far more than a mental concept; it is a deeply embodied experience. It encompasses how we physically orient ourselves toward others, the space we allow ourselves to occupy, the subtle muscular patterns of tension and collapse we maintain, and the way we listen and respond to others. These embodied memories silently influence how we show up in every new interaction.

In meditation, we uncover the stillness that allows us to feel these subtle traces, the tightening that accompanies fear of rejection, the collapse that comes with shame, the hardening that hides vulnerability. As we sit in stillness, we begin to feel the

---

[2] By "intimacy," I refer specifically to emotional intimacy—the felt closeness and connection in a relationship that allows us to share our inner world with openness and vulnerability.

subtle layers we've come to embody that reflect our relational history. We may notice physical sensations (tension in the belly, a tight jaw, a slouched back) that correspond with old roles or dynamics we've taken on.

As awareness softens these physical constrictions (and the collapse and numbness they can lead to), the body remembers a different way of relating: openness grounded in safety, strength that doesn't harden, love that doesn't dissolve. We recognize that these patterns of constriction, once intelligent adaptations born of necessity, will continue to quietly run our lives until we learn to meet them with awareness and love.

A relationship, fundamentally, is commonly understood to be a dynamic interplay of physical, emotional, and behavioral mannerisms and attitudes. Each person's response reflects and shapes the other, creating a relational field in which safety and support or further wounding can occur. When we begin to view bonding not just as an emotional or conceptual event, but as a full-body process, our understanding of healing deepens. The body becomes both mirror and teacher, revealing the truth of our emotional life.

The body reveals how we have learned to love and where we've learned to hide. Even our habits with food, work, or technology echo these patterns (attempts to recreate connection or control where trust was once broken). We rediscover that connection and separation are not opposites but partners in the dance of being alive. Through the body, we learn again how to belong without losing ourselves and without leaving anyone behind.

Bonding With Oneness Within

This book is an invitation into a new inner relationship that involves bonding with the realization of wholeness, the body's experience of the primary ground of our being, the unchanging-

15

self. Wholeness is not a far-off, abstract, or ethereal state, but an unwavering presence that pervades flesh and bone. It is the steady ground that does not flinch when we falter, the stillness and inner openness or spaciousness that can hold our most human grief. It is our deepest contact with ourselves, with others, and with the living world. Awakening to this essential dimension of existence is, I believe, the basis of a "spiritual" life.

Although the unchanging-self can be experienced in a variety of ways, many experience this as unconditional love and access it as a heart-based consciousness that connects us to all that is. This love is a luminous presence in the heart rather than something we have to create or "do;" it arises naturally when the heart remembers its own nature. The embodied wholeness of our unchanging-self is available to each of us and is crucial for healing emotional injuries.

This unchanging-self that most of us first discover in meditation offers a steady, reliable ground within the body that, with practice, we can learn to turn to when we feel lost, disconnected, or overwhelmed. Just as a child needs a nurturing caregiver to develop secure attachment, the emotional injuries we still carry as adults need the steady, unconditional presence of inner wholeness to heal. Wholeness becomes the consistent, caring inner parent we may never have known, listening without judgment, embracing without condition, never turning away. Rooted in an inner sufficiency rather than how we respond to external circumstances, this presence restores a profound peace.

In this state, we no longer feel separate from our surroundings; instead, we experience our being as continuous with everything around us. Wholeness becomes both the ground of the feeling of unity within us and the living recognition that we are inseparably one with life.

Wholeness provides a profound sense of connectedness. It is also accompanied by a felt openness, an experience of vast, unlimited space both within the body and throughout the environment. This is not the ordinary spaciousness of physical distance but a primordial openness, a boundless expanse of being that includes connectedness, which allows our evolving-self the autonomy to breathe and move with ease. Within this feeling of openness and spaciousness, we discover radical acceptance (as an inner freedom that supports our evolving sense of sovereignty and autonomy) in how we connect and separate in all our relationships.[3]

Our experience of connectedness and spaciousness associated with the felt wholeness of unified consciousness, speaks directly to our two deepest relational wounds that threaten healthy bonding in relationships: the pain of emotional abandonment and the fear of being imposed upon. With abandonment in our body-mind system, we seek contact, and with feelings of being imposed upon, we seek room to move and find our own initiative. When we experience profound connectedness and infinite space within our body, where abandonment once left us feeling isolated, wholeness restores our sense of belonging. Where intrusion once threatened our boundaries, infinite space now provides the breathing room necessary for freedom.

Together, these virtues of wholeness offer a living experience of balance: we feel both deeply connected and profoundly free, capable of intimacy without losing individuality, and able to remain authentic while fully engaged with life's challenges. When we bond with this unchanging aspect of our being and existence, we create the conditions for profound healing. This bond gives our ever-changing, evolving-self a new source of information: stillness, openness, timelessness,

---

[3] Part of this experience comes from discerning two complementary dimensions of space: the infinite, unbounded space of oneness and the familiar, limited space of everyday life. When these dimensions meet, our whole way of inhabiting the body and the world changes. As infinite space and unconditional love coexist with ordinary space and conditional human experience, new possibilities for responding to life's pressures emerge. We are freed from the frustration and disappointment that arise when expectations go unmet — in ourselves or in others.

spaciousness, pervasively universal, and unified (sometimes felt as unconditional love).

With this information within our body and mind, our old survival strategies begin to dissolve. Instead, they can become pathways to self-love, spiritual realization, and wholeness. Relationship is no longer a place to hide our wounds. It becomes the very ground where wholeness reveals itself.

When the wholeness of unified consciousness enters our relational life, our connections with others are no longer only social or emotional. They become sacred. They become part of a living spirituality rooted in the body, in presence, and in the possibility of authentic connection.

To understand how this embodied, relational wholeness differs from traditional spiritual views, we must look at how various traditions have defined the nature of the self and the meaning of nonduality. Where we turn to next is an exploration of those differences: how the quest for transcendence in many Eastern traditions, while offering profound insights into freedom, often leaves out the relational and embodied dimensions of wholeness that bring awakening fully into life.[4]

Facets of Oneness

Across most Asian nondual spiritual traditions, there is broad agreement that the true nature of existence is ultimately *unified*, and that this unified reality appears to express itself through two fundamental dimensions of consciousness: duality and nonduality.

"Duality" consciousness is the everyday state of awareness in which we perceive life through separation and contrast, self vs.

---

[4] The term "transcend" here is used in the theological sense, meaning to be above and independent of the material universe (rather than simply moving it into a new, more organized state of being).

other, good vs. bad, mind vs. body. It's the operating system of our "evolving-self." Duality is essential for navigating the world, making choices, and developing individuality, but it can also lead to overwhelm, conflict, and suffering when we over-identify with it.

"Nondual" or unified consciousness is an awareness that exists before ego creates a sense of separation between us and others. When we access this state in meditation, we recognize that all things are interconnected and arise within a unified ground of being. Distinctions like self and other still appear, but they're no longer experienced as absolute separations.

The experience of nonduality is a recurring theme across traditions like Taoism, Mahayana Buddhism, Advaita Vedanta, and the nondual Tantra of Kashmiri Shaivism. It can be said that it even shows up in Judeo-Christian traditions in the form of God as the creator. To say that consciousness is nondual means that it is "not two," not divided. In this experience, the apparent multiplicity of the universe is recognized as a manifestation of one essential reality.

Yet despite this shared experiential ground, philosophical disagreements about the nature of the self and the meaning of nonduality abound. These divergences often stem from ambiguities in ancient texts and the evolving interpretations of key concepts over time. They are also shaped by the limits of human perception, how easily we mistake a partial truth for the whole, or a single aspect of reality for its entirety.

In many Eastern spiritual traditions, the highest goal of human life is seen as liberation from the earthly realm, freedom from suffering through transcendence. This is often achieved by cultivating detachment from the body, emotions, and personal identity, and abiding instead in pure, formless awareness, often referred to as *atman* or pure nondual consciousness.

To experience the transcendent state, these spiritual traditions propose methods of distancing or withdrawal from ordinary sensory and mental processes. The core premise is that our embodied, sense-based perception is a filter that limits our awareness of the unified dimension of existence, so transcending this limitation requires non-sensory practices. Practices such as Transcendental Meditation, many Buddhist meditations, or classical yoga meditations aim to quiet our ordinary mental noise and sensory input. By detaching from the stream of thoughts, emotions, and sensory perceptions, we can reach a silent, pure awareness.

As a result of transcendent practices, we can undergo a process of profound detachment from the mind and body. Emotions, thoughts, and sensations (those things that make us human) are often treated as obstacles to spiritual realization, rather than integral aspects of it. Our humanness is not embraced, but is understood to be temporary, and due to its impermanence, therefore unreliable and untrustworthy. It is the functional aspect of human experience that organizes our perceptions. In this sense, our evolving-self is considered to assume a secondary role that is subtly or overtly minimized. The goal is to detach from our evolving-self to experience a voidness or emptiness that is pure consciousness, devoid of individual form. While the intention is to achieve a state of unified consciousness, it is based on separation from the human experience.

Conversely, Western traditions, particularly those shaped by modern psychology, are based on a different kind of separation. Mainstream psychological thought, despite its numerous contributions to healing and human development, primarily operates within the framework of the individual as a separate self, defined by ego, shaped by history, and bounded by personal identity. The therapies most widely used today for treating trauma and emotional injuries focus almost exclusively on the evolving nature of the *self*, with little to no recognition of the deeper, unchanging dimension of our being.

Western religious traditions, for the most part, reinforce this separation by maintaining a division between the human and the divine. God is seen as external, distant, and fundamentally other. The divine is something to worship, but not something to embody. Our intrinsic wholeness is rarely affirmed. Instead, we are often taught that redemption lies outside of ourselves, in grace bestowed from above, rather than awakened from within.

In both Eastern and Western traditions, something essential is missing: a deeply embodied, relational path to wholeness. What is absent is an inclusive view that honors our full humanity while simultaneously awakening us to our inherent divinity. We are in need of a new paradigm, one that goes beyond the split between transcendence and our humanness. A paradigm in which healing is not found through separation, but through integration.

A New Paradigm of Healing and Awakening

Whole-being-embrace offers an alternative approach, a living synthesis. It proposes a new paradigm where healing does not come through separation from humanity, but through integration. The multiplicity of human connection (the dance of self and other, love and loss) is not regarded as part of the dream to be awakened from, but rather the ground in which awakening to unified consciousness blossoms. Our sense of wholeness is not far away; it is the inner dimension of life itself. The body is the very vessel of spiritual development.

From this perspective, the path of awakening is not about leaving the body behind, but about coming home to it more fully. A truly integrated spiritual experience merges the material with the transcendent, matter with spirit, flesh with consciousness. To live spiritually is not to bypass our humanity but to consciously uncover and awaken to our wholeness through the body. In this view, body and spirit are not adversaries but two entwined dimensions of a single reality, inseparable facets of existence itself.

Embodiment becomes a living practice: the act of breathing with awareness, walking with presence, feeling our deepest emotions, or tending a garden as though each touch of soil is sacred. These simple, grounded actions reveal the extraordinary within the ordinary. Through them, awareness awakens within the body, rather than pulling away from it.

In this integration, we discover something revolutionary: healing our emotional life and awakening to unified consciousness are not two separate paths. They are one and the same journey toward becoming fully, authentically human.

As mentioned, I generally use the terms "unchanging-self," "unified consciousness," "ground of being," or "oneness" to point to this ineffable essence, a still, unshakable presence of wholeness within us. Traditions have called it by many names: Buddha nature, Christ-consciousness, Tao, saguna Brahman, and ishta-devata, Divine Mother, Source, the universe, universal consciousness, Presence, Great Spirit, God. Carl Jung called it unus mundus, a single world where mind and matter are two faces of one reality. Physicist David Bohm spoke of an "unbroken wholeness." Teilhard de Chardin called it the "within-ness of matter." Whatever the name, it points to the same fundamental consciousness. Each description is powerful in its own way, so in reading this book, choose the term that works best for you.

Where some traditions regard the ultimate state as leaving our evolving-self behind, the approach I'm offering embraces our most authentic expression of our evolving-self. Moreover, unified consciousness is not a remote cosmic event or a fleeting mystical high. It is a lived experience in which the body itself allows us to know unity and wholeness. This is where our deepest emotional injuries can be embraced and healed. The body is an active participant in awakening, as well as an expression of, the divinity of existence.

Why Embodiment Matters for Healing

In summary, most forms of the transcendent model, so popular today, tell us that our experiences, our evolving-self, and even the body itself are mere illusions (maya). But here's the paradox: while our perceptions may be transient and carry distortions, they are also deeply real to the nervous system and psyche.[5] Dismissing them as illusions can feel confusing and even invalidating, especially when we are dealing with emotional injuries or trauma. In alignment with two traditions found in Hinduism, it can be said that both truths stand side by side [6]:

> Yes, everything temporary is an illusion (*mayavada*) when we are in a transcendent state.
> And yes, everything is real (*satvada*), duality and nonduality, when we are in an embodied nondual state.

These are two distinct views of the nature of reality and the relationship between the individual and the divine. Both play a valuable role in helping us navigate life on Earth. Depending on our state of consciousness, each view of reality is true. In this sense, it is possible to simultaneously hold both views as true even though their foundational principles are in direct opposition. Yet, if we want to integrate spiritual awakening with emotional growth, recognizing that everything is real is vital.

---

[5] The Tantra sage Abhinavgupta explains that Advaita Vedanta's understanding that half of existence is not real creates a polarity that amounts to dualism (Tantraloka, 111:404). He further points out, "how can it be unreal when it is manifested... An entity that appears clearly and creates the whole universe must be something real and substantial and should be described as such." (Ishvarpritabijna 111.80).

[6] As Wendy Doniger (1986) notes, the real illusion is believing that either duality or nonduality (*turiya*) is the whole truth. It seems, the deeper reality is that both dimensions of self co-exist in dynamic relationship as a "whole-self"— what some call *turiyatita* or One Taste. Our experience of unified consciousness shifts depending on where we place our attention.

While emotional growth can occur with a transcendent approach, it is often limited, especially when we harbor unresolved injuries (Lancaster, 2023). Healing from emotional injuries happens most profoundly when we honor the evolving-self in a relationship of intimacy and attunement with oneness. Here, in this whole-being-embrace, both dimensions, the changing and the unchanging, coexist in what I call the "whole-self."

This is a radical reframe. Rather than an "either/or" approach, where we must choose between duality or nonduality, this book invites us into a "both/and" reality, a unity that includes diversity. Here, the evolving-self and unchanging-self don't compete. They communicate, like two lovers in a paradoxical embrace. What is communicated in this Tango is based on the feeling of profound connectedness and infinite breathing room, addressing the core bonding injuries.

The apparent contradiction between disembodied and embodied approaches resolves when we look more deeply into the nature of unified consciousness. Oneness is both *immanent*, completely present within the material body, and *transcendent*, beyond all form. The body, then, is not an obstacle to overcome, but a manifestation of the same unified ground that gives rise to stars, rivers, and galaxies. We are the bridge where the eternal meets the temporal.

The paradox is glowing: we can taste the transcendent precisely by inhabiting the body with the stillness of unified presence. We awaken oneness not by abandoning the flesh. The universal is not "out there" beyond us; it is within our breath, heartbeat, and sensation. By honoring the body as both immanent and transcendent, we recognize that awakening and healing do not come from fleeing life, but by fully entering it.

Why the Body Is Central

This integration cannot happen in the mind alone, and it involves more than awareness. Trauma and emotional injuries do not live only as concepts; they live in the body as tension, numbness, dysregulation, and survival patterns encoded in the nervous system. That is why talk therapy or insight alone often fail to resolve deep wounds.

Healing primarily requires a bottom-up process, where the body informs the mind. This is why yoga, somatic therapy, and embodied contemplative traditions are so essential: they help us reconnect to sensory experience and restore nervous system regulation (Kolk). In whole-being-embrace, when our presence as nondual consciousness enters into relationship with our body and evolving-self, something profound happens:

> We gain access to a ground of safety.
> This begins to reorganize our physiology.
> Our wounds, long cut off from love, finally find a place of belonging.

And here's the key: this is not just personal. How we orient spiritually and our relationship with our body shape not only our inner life, but also our relationships, culture, and even our ecological future.

Giving preeminence to the body is not just a philosophical issue; it is deeply political. Beneath the ferment of our time lies an impasse in our personal and cultural evolution, an impasse that cannot be resolved by incremental change alone. It demands a fundamental shift in how we construct our relationship with the body, with other people, and with the planet. How we relate to our body and ourselves determines how we relate to the world.

Our attitudes toward the body ripple outward, shaping how we perceive others, our participation in society, and how we inhabit the Earth. These embodied patterns are not abstractions;

they are lived, sensory realities that begin forming in early childhood and silently govern our behavior throughout life.

Stripped to its essentials, both personal and social transformation revolve around the human body. From birth onward, our bodies become the sites where social norms, cultural values, and power dynamics are enacted. Our earliest lessons about relationships, what is acceptable, what is shameful, what is controlled, and what is free, are learned through bodily contact.

If, in our formative relationships, we are conditioned to believe that control over our bodies is the best way to manage life, we end up overriding our communication and relationship with our bodies. This pattern becomes deeply ingrained within the tissues of the body. We unconsciously replicate formative relationships in our adult relationships, in the workplace, and in society at large. On the other hand, if we experience respect, attunement, and caring in our early bonds, these qualities become the foundation for relationships that resist systems of hierarchy and control. In short, the politics of the body begins in the nursery.

Many spiritual traditions have not helped this situation. For centuries, Eastern and Western paths alike have cast the body as a problem to overcome, a vessel for spirit, but not sacred in itself. (In some instances, the body is regarded as evil in its weakness.) In such frameworks, the body and emotions serve primarily as tools for navigating worldly existence, organizing life, and testing reality. When the body is a tool for transformation, it serves as a medium through which negative patterns can be purified and consciousness refined; however, it is not a divine expression of consciousness itself.

Yet, in the orientation of this book, the body is more than a tool. It is a sacred participant in the very fabric of existence. The body is not something we merely use to *reach* spirit; it *is* spirit in expression, in communion with our evolving-self. The body itself is a divine revelation, a living spark of cosmogenesis (*jīvanmukti*): the ongoing creation of the universe made flesh.

From this perspective, enduring psycho-spiritual transformation is not possible without bodily transformation. As we uncover and stabilize an embodied experience of oneness, we become living expressions of the formless, carried into the world through form. In this way, our breath, our gestures, and even the way we stand or touch another can radiate the presence of wholeness.

The goal here is not simply to dissolve back into an ultimate state of unity, leaving behind the richness of our individuality. It is not about merging with unity *to the exclusion of all else*. Rather, it is to awaken to the fullness of our whole-self, the lived recognition that both dimensions of our existence, unity and individuality, co-exist within us.

True awakening is the dynamic embrace of both the timeless ground of being and the ever-changing flow of life. When we rest in this whole-being-embrace, we discover that unity does not erase difference; it illuminates it, allowing our uniqueness to come into authentic expression. Our evolving-self, with its emotions, stories, and desires, is no longer an obstacle, but a vital expression manifesting through us.

This integration has profound implications for the healing process. Healing begins when we allow our evolving-self's fears, griefs, and longings to be embraced with the luminous presence of oneness. In this relational communion, pain is not bypassed, nor is wholeness abandoned. Both are given their place.

In relationships, the same principle applies. We do not heal by losing ourselves in fusion with another, nor by defending ourselves in rigid separateness. We heal in the dance between connectedness and autonomy, when the "I" and the "We" coexist in mutual recognition. Just as our inner wholeness grows by holding unity and individuality together, our outer relationships flourish when love honors both connection and difference.

To awaken to our whole-self, then, is to live a life of paradox and balance. It is to know ourselves as both the ocean and the wave, both the mirror of timeless stillness and the dancer of time-bound movement. In this awareness, authenticity blossoms. Our choices increasingly arise less from fear or compulsion, and more from the resonance of what feels true and alive in the moment. The result is a life that is not only more peaceful but also more vibrant, more creative, more fully human.

Awakening to the coexistence of unity and individuality is not the end of our journey, but the beginning of a new way of living, a way where healing deepens, relationships thrive, and every moment becomes an opportunity to experience the miracle of being both infinite and uniquely ourselves.

Body as Sanctuary

Another thing to consider about a transcendent worldview is that it fosters hierarchy: spirit is superior, matter inferior. The body becomes a servant of the spirit, and Earth becomes raw material for human use. Such assumptions do more than shape theology; they lay the template for all superior-inferior rankings, including gender, class, race, and species hierarchies.

Religious asceticism has historically reinforced this paradigm by training the body to accept control. Likewise, authoritarian child-rearing conditions us to sensorily obey authority, not merely attitudinally but bodily, through habits of posture, breath, and movement that normalize submission. Spirituality becomes another arena where control triumphs over participation and communication. In such a worldview, democracy, trusting the body's innate wisdom, becomes unthinkable, for the body is deemed too flawed, too wild, too dangerous to guide us.

Our current crises, relational, social, and environmental, are rooted in this fundamental split between spirit and matter, and consequently a split between our perception of self and the world. We objectify what we most directly experience: the body, emotions, and the living Earth. We reduce them to instruments, resources, and obstacles rather than divine expressions of intrinsic value.

If our body is not seen as sacred, neither is the Earth. And if the Earth is not sacred, domination and exploitation become inevitable. This is why healing our culture and our planet begins with healing our own split, the split between the evolving-self and unified consciousness.

Both what we consider sacred and our relationship with our body are defined very differently in societies oriented primarily toward partnership rather than control over our bodies, emotions, and the planet. For it is through these foundational relations involving contact and the body that we acquire many of the building blocks for later patterns of either partnership or control in our lives. The aim here is to show a way that can take us into a partnership rather than a control direction.

This book is an invitation to repair the fracture between these divergent approaches. It proposes a new paradigm in which the body is no longer a battleground but a gateway to unity and wholeness, a living bridge between psychology and spirituality, between healing and awakening. Here, I present a paradigm in which bonding, mirroring, and autonomy (the same principles that help a child develop a healthy sense of self) become the foundation for spiritual awakening. Where the state of oneness is not found through dispassion, disidentifying, discounting, or distancing from life, but an embodied intimacy with all of life

Whole-being-embrace transforms the body into a sanctuary where our most wounded parts receive what they have always needed: safety, attunement, unconditional love, and the presence of wholeness of being. From this embodied perspective, nondual awakening is an intimate, incarnate knowing that transforms how we live, love, and create. It is the foundation for a new way of being human, one that reconciles spirit and matter, self and world, unity and diversity. Whole-being-embrace is not only a meditative practice; it is a template for how we inhabit the world. It teaches us that healing is relational, awakening is embodied, and the body is our most immediate expression of the divine.

Spirituality, Psychology & Wholeness

From the view of whole-being-embrace, we move beyond the binary of attachment versus detachment. Instead of separating from experience, we open into it with refined awareness. This is the essence of *nondual wholeness* that has been called *turiyatita* or *One Taste* (explained later). Here, duality and nonduality are not opposites but expressions of the deeper unity of our whole-self.

The unchanging-self is not apart from our evolving self but is the very ground from which it arises. When we refine our inner perception, we begin to recognize that every emotion, thought, and sensation contains the spark of oneness. Nothing is outside of it. Every particle of experience is both form and essence, movement and stillness, personal and universal. This makes Teilhard de Chardin's descriptive term "within-ness of matter" particularly appropriate.

This is echoed in both mystical insight and quantum understanding. What physicists call "entanglement," mystics recognize as interbeing. Just as duality arises within nonduality, so too does the formless show itself within form. As David Loy puts it, we encounter the "quality-rich emptiness" (*sunyata*) of our essential being. This emptiness is not a negation but a fullness, a vibrant presence known in the Sanskrit phrase "*sat-chit-ananda,*" being, consciousness, and bliss.

In meditation, we often progress through perceiving various states: from gross to subtle, causal, witnessing, and ultimately to formless unity. As our senses refine, we learn to perceive not only the objects of our awareness but the space between them, and finally, that even the objects are suffused with space. What we discover is this space is not an absence or a void but a conscious presence of unity. As we uncover and awaken unified consciousness as a body experience of wholeness, we remain aware of both dimensions of our being. When meditation is grounded in whole-being-embrace, we do not seek to escape the body or emotions, but to include them as spontaneous expressions emerging out of this conscious presence of unity.

When we bring wholeness into contact with the evolving-self, even old wounds can become openings for deeper connection. Rather than transcending attachment altogether, we turn toward it with unified awareness. We open to the emotions, thoughts, and sensations that arise, not as problems to be fixed or distractions to overcome, but as gateways to deeper connection.

In this light, attachment becomes a teacher. Our longing for love, our yearning for meaning, our sensitivity to rejection, all carry the blueprint of our original wholeness. By listening rather than controlling, by respecting rather than overriding, and by including rather than distancing, we nurture an inner secure base from which we can fully explore, feel, and evolve.

Bonding with unity is about being able to meet whatever life brings, joy or loss, ease or difficulty, without losing contact with the unified presence that pervades it all. This is where the healing of the self and the awakening of consciousness meet. This is where the journey begins.

Throughout the book, I utilize the concepts of relationship, attachment, and bonding as an archetypal framework to guide readers through a process of growth and spiritual awakening. We explore a spirituality that grounds us in the world, and a psychology that honors wholeness. While the dialogue between Western psychology and Eastern spiritual traditions is still emerging, this approach introduces a return to a natural balance. This balance can be observed in the way nature expresses the most fundamental elements that form the foundation of life. We awaken a deep peace when we resonate with nature. We discover what it means to be still yet active, flexible yet strong, silent but eloquently expressive. This balance reflects the leading edge of where I believe spirituality and psychology are growing today.

This terrain is not widely mapped. Very few have traveled the path where nondual realization meets the raw material of our psychology through direct contact within the body. This work is not only philosophical and psychological, but also a practical manual for healing relational wounds and reclaiming authenticity. Each chapter offers approaches to tailoring meditation practice for emotional growth, inviting you, the reader, to walk your own healing path with awareness and grace.

Chapter Two:

Without Earth, There Is No Heaven

We did not invent this split. We inherited it. We inherited a holiness that floated upward, toward purity, toward heaven, away from flesh. We inherited a sentence that crowned thought as king: *I think, therefore I am.* Together, they trained us to doubt the senses, to discipline the body, to treat feeling as noise and matter as lesser. The result is everywhere: a spirituality that privileges distancing or objectifying over nurturing, control over communion, transcendence over life. This chapter is about that inheritance, and the cost of keeping it.

When mind rules from above, the body becomes a problem to manage. Sensation is treated as suspicious, emotion as interference, desire as threat. The meaning we associate with what we experience is objectified. We learn to leave ourselves to find the divine. We call this "growth," even as our culture rehearses the same choreography of objectification: of the self, of one another, of the Earth.

The Cosmologies That Inform Us

Cosmologies are the great origin stories of a people. They are living myths that shape our identity and orient us in the universe. They tell us who we are, where we come from, and what

33

our role is in the grand web of life. Whether we consciously believe in them or not, these foundational stories influence how we relate to the world, to each other, and to ourselves. Cosmologies also reflect our cultural values, ethical frameworks, daily practices, social interactions, and our relationship to the environment. Significantly, they influence why we meditate and, most specifically, whether we control and transcend or embrace and nurture our evolving-self and our body.

Broadly speaking, it seems we have two primary types of cosmologies: those of control and those of participation. These two worldviews reflect contrasting ways that cultures make sense of existence and their responsibilities within the cosmos. They are embedded not only in traditional beliefs, but also in our science, spirituality, politics, and healing practices. Western and Eastern societies each have their own form of cosmology and worldview.

Spirituality's Mind Over Body

In the West, Christianity carried a powerful ideal: the hope of restoring humanity to a state of original innocence, a return to the pristine condition before the "Fall," a catastrophe traditionally blamed on Eve. This narrative of regaining purity intersected with another historical force: René Descartes's radical redefinition of human identity. His assertion, *"I think, therefore I am,"* cemented the supremacy of rational thought as the foundation of existence. In elevating thought as the ultimate proof of being, Descartes dethroned the body and the senses, relegating them to a secondary, unreliable status.

René Descartes's worldview did more than influence philosophy; it reshaped spirituality and culture. It reinforced Christian ideals to create a paradigm where the mind was elevated as the seat of truth, and the body became suspect, at best a vessel for the soul, at worst a source of temptation and sin. The result was a profound alienation from the body as a source of wisdom and guidance. We still live with the consequences of this split today.

When the mind is enthroned above the body, we learn to distrust what we feel. Gut instincts, heartfelt discernment, and intuitive insights are sidelined in favor of abstract reasoning. Yet the body is our first language. It speaks through sensation, and these sensations give rise to emotion. When we ignore, or become neutral to, the body and the message it carries, we ignore the signals that inform our emotional life. Our perspective narrows, our inner world loses depth, and imbalance sets in.

The cost of this denial is immense. It breeds internal conflict, even self-hatred, an inner warfare where the mind tries to control or override the body, and the body resists through stress responses, illness, or trauma symptoms. We obsessively set goals based on rational constructs rather than lived experience, and when those goals fail to bring fulfillment, we push harder, fueling cycles of burnout and despair. Dissociation from the body, a hallmark of emotional injury, became embedded in the very foundation of Western culture.

As Christianity was usurped by science during the Renaissance, it lost its power to serve as a cohesive communal guide. As a result, the rational, isolated self emerged as the new spiritual center. In this transition, knowledge shifted from being grounded in divine revelation to being grounded in reason alone. Without God, Goddess, or the body as our guide, Descartes opened the door for alienating substitutes, forms of control, consumption, and addiction, to take the place of authentic connection.

These substitutes act much like what psychology calls a "transitional object," such as a teddy bear or security blanket, a child clings to for comfort when separated from a parent. Severed from the body as a reliable source of support, the disconnected mind seeks security in compulsions, consumerism, and systems of domination. But these external props cannot satisfy the deeper longing for wholeness. Instead, the anxious mind drives the body

35

into cycles of hypervigilance and stress, perpetuating a culture of disembodiment.

Carl Jung saw this cultural wound clearly. He argued that Christianity's alienation from the body had severed our connection to its own symbols. Religious symbols, at their core, are meant to carry the mystery of the unknown and herald the transformation of consciousness. But symbols only have transformative power when they are experienced viscerally, when they resonate in the body as living realities.

As a culture, we have largely lost this capacity. We may retain the conceptual frameworks of Christian symbols, but without embodied experience, those symbols become hollow abstractions. Under the influence of modernization, individualism, and a production-driven, consumerist culture, the deeper meaning of ritual has largely been forgotten. Rituals and ceremonies no longer nourish the soul or catalyze inner change. What once served as a bridge between the personal and the sacred has been reduced to routine or discarded altogether. As a result, many modern individuals find themselves adrift, disconnected from collective memory, tradition, and the grounding sense of belonging that symbol and ritual once provided.

Yet the human need for meaning, rhythm, and shared participation remains as strong as ever. Beneath our striving for progress, we still long for the ceremony of connection, the gestures, symbols, and moments that remind us of who we are and where we belong. Jung warned that what we repress doesn't simply disappear; it returns in distorted, often destructive ways.

This is exactly what happened. By exiling the body from spiritual life, we turned it into a problem to be managed rather than a revelation to be embraced. The body became a site of shame, suffering, and objectification. We see this not only in the commodification of bodies, especially women's bodies, but in the widespread alienation from our own felt sense. When we objectify the body, we also objectify emotions and how we relate to the planet, fragmenting the wholeness of being human.

36

In short, our cultural flight into the mind, rooted in both religious and philosophical traditions, has left us estranged from the very ground of our existence. This estrangement is more than a personal issue; it is woven into our systems, our relationships, and our spiritual practices. To heal, we must reclaim the body and its emotional life not as an obstacle to transcendence but as a sacred gateway to unity and wisdom.

Eastern Spiritual Materialism

Since the 1950s, disillusioned with Western religion, a significant portion of Western youth has begun to turn to Eastern spirituality, seeking answers. However, like Christianity, Eastern spiritual traditions embrace absoluteness and the lucidity of complete transcendence. This is motivated by a return to an unblemished, pristine state, before the messiness of our "illusory" duality-based evolving-self emerges (prior to suffering on Earth). I have referred to this as a transcendent state of pure unified consciousness only (*turiya*).

The emotional impulse of longing to return to the safety of the womb is strikingly parallel to the religious longing to return to a pristine state, such as the Garden of Eden or the transcendent state. Though they arise from different frameworks, they express a deep yearning for safety, security, and the release from the burdens of responsibility and anxiety that evolving and growth bring. This longing reflects a desire to retreat from the complexity and uncertainty of life, returning to a condition of simplicity and protection. The pristine state serves as an archetypal symbol of origin, a place of belonging where one feels connected, whole, and free from fragmentation.

Importantly, none of these Eastern versions of returning to a pristine state suggest a literal return. Instead, they point to a symbolic or existential desire to reclaim a state of consciousness that carries the qualities of that original condition: innocence, unity, and an unbroken state of wholeness.

When we emphasize returning to a pristine state, separation and control, rather than communication and participation, are the dominating forces. We turn to them to resolve the suffering and conflict in our relationship with life. This denies the importance and bypasses the depth of meaning found in our evolving, lived experience. When this is the primary solution to our suffering, we limit our sense of self in life, and in relationship. Most importantly, we limit our ability to overcome emotional injuries. We can weaken our ability to relate to ourselves and others with empathy and cooperation.

As mentioned, transcending our changing nature of experience gives us a crystal-clear perception that can feel like a peak experience. Yet alone, transcendence of body-felt experience is limiting. In embracing unified consciousness that is beyond body experience, we eliminate the potential for the body to be an expression of what is divine and the location of our cosmogenesis. When we harbor unresolved emotional injuries, transcendence too often leads to a spiritual bypass of our evolving-self's emotions, wisdom, and sense of wholeness. Transcendence of body-felt experience does not recognize how the subtle sensory-based nondual qualities of the unchanging-self (qualities of oneness) can help us resolve emotional injuries.

Yet, when we refine our senses, we recognize unified consciousness as having qualities of being, such as stillness, timelessness, spaciousness, universal pervasiveness, unconditional love, and the essential qualities found in each chakra, etc.. Each quality of oneness is a potential that is experienced to be luminous by nature. This potential and luminosity have an integrating and unifying effect on our evolving-self that is tremendously healing.

Tantra yoga recognizes the presence of qualities of oneness within our being, as expressed in each chakra's qualities of oneness. (This is described in my book, *Nondual Chakra*

Awakening, 2024.) Yet often Tantra yoga's ultimate goal is to transcend our body and mind, which is not the focus of the whole-being-embrace approach.

Cosmologies of Participation

Indigenous cosmologies across the globe offer a strikingly participatory model of existence. In these traditions, humans are not separate from nature, but part of an intricate and sacred web of relationships. The Earth is alive, responsive, and intelligent. Rivers, mountains, and animals are kin, not resources. The cosmos is not a machine to be mastered, but a mystery to be honored.

These cosmologies teach reciprocity: a give-and-take relationship between humans and the natural world. Participation is not passive; it is embodied through ritual, stewardship, ceremony, and direct relationship. Children raised within these worldviews grow up knowing in their bones that their well-being is interwoven with the Earth's well-being. The land itself becomes a teacher and a relative.

Cosmologies of Control

In contrast, many modern and Western cosmologies are rooted in control. Since the Enlightenment, Western thought has often positioned humans as separate from, and superior to, the natural world. Nature became a resource, something to be studied, mastered, and exploited. This worldview gave rise to industrialization, colonialism, ecological degradation, and alienation from the living world.

Modern scientific cosmology, though brilliant in its capacity to measure and model, often reinforces a non-participatory stance. The universe becomes a dead backdrop to human activity, with consciousness reduced to a byproduct of the brain, and subjective experience seen as irrelevant or illusory. In this cosmology, we are observers, not participants.

The Judeo-Christian tradition has also been associated with cosmologies of hierarchy and dominion. In the Genesis story, Eve is banished for her curiosity and hunger. She becomes an exile, cast into a wild world, burdened by labor, told to subdue the land. This exile story shaped a cultural mindset that sees the Earth as fallen and dangerous, something to be redeemed or conquered.

In contrast, many Indigenous stories describe the first woman (Eve) not as exiled, but as gardener, a co-creator of a generous and living world. One story leads to estrangement: the other, to belonging. This is described beautifully by Robin Wall Kimmerer in her book, *Braiding Sweetgrass*.

Two Stories, Two Selves

These cosmologies shape not just how we treat the land, but how we treat our own bodies, emotions, and sense of self. Richard Tarnas, in *The Passion of the Western Mind*, describes how Western culture has been driven by a heroic impulse to carve out a separate self from nature. This separation, while giving rise to individuality and science, also led to a rejection of the body, nature, and the feminine, as sources of wisdom.

Even in psychology, these split cosmologies appear. Freud's focus on ego control and repression reflects a control model: order is achieved by subduing inner chaos. Jung, in contrast, emphasized the importance of participation with the unconscious. His path to wholeness required engaging the shadow, the irrational, and the forgotten. In Jung's view, healing is found not by dominance, but by relationship.

Eastern spiritual traditions also reflect both strands. Many Hindu and Buddhist teachings emphasize control of our senses, encouraging withdrawal from the world to attain detachment and transcendence. These practices, such as *pratyahara* in Yoga, neutral witnessing (*sakshi*), or disidentification from the ego in Buddhism, can be profound tools for achieving clarity. Yet they can also reinforce subtle forms of duality by controlling the senses and distancing us from embodied life and the meaning we attach to it.

A spirituality with a cosmology that distrusts sensation, trains citizens to accept control; a spirituality that restores sensation, rehearses democracy in the nervous system. As mentioned, the politics of the body begin in the nursery, in how breath and posture are met, and continue in how our practices teach us to listen and open, or not, to what we feel.

Meditation as Participation

Our approach to meditation is not immune to these cosmologies. When meditation is based on control, the goal often becomes detachment, transcendence, objectification, or elimination of certain experiences. This "exclusive nonduality" subtly discounts, disregards, or even rejects emotion, sensation, memory, and the evolving-self as distractions to be overcome.

But in a participatory approach to nonduality, something else becomes possible. Rather than trying to transcend the evolving-self, we enter into deep contact with it, bringing a compassionate, unified awareness to its every movement. In this space, we do not objectify our pain or bypass our history. Instead, we recognize the evolving-self as a valid, meaningful expression of life, one that longs to be met, integrated, and healed.

This whole-being-embrace communion between the evolving-self and the unchanging-self is not about simply witnessing, discounting, distancing, or dispassion towards what is human. It is about reclaiming our humanity as sacred. It is not about disappearing ego into emptiness, but fully arriving into our most authentic nature. It is not about concentrating the mind to get to what lies beyond form, but about opening to the unified continuity of all of life, the changing and unchanging in sacred communion.

In this approach, the meditative space (as a body experience of any nondual quality) becomes a new kind of "holding environment," a living potential space where we can awaken to unity and wholeness. The original holding environment, as first described by Donald Winnicott in 1953, was the parents' presence, which, ideally, created a safe, nurturing space that the child could return to when in need of both physical and emotional support. This holding environment leads to a sense of security, trust, and emotional autonomy in relationship with others.

In a similar way, embodied nondual meditation, unified consciousness is not just a backdrop of awareness, but a relational presence of wholeness that touches, holds space, and transforms by its mere presence. When wholeness is a nondual body experience of who we feel we are, it parallels a holding environment, offering our learning self a safe location and supportive room to grow. When the same dynamics that shape a healthy relationship with another person are applied inwardly, between our evolving-self and unchanging-self, a new kind of spirituality is born.

A Return to the Original Instructions

The participatory cosmologies of our ancestors are not relics of a lost past. They are instructions for the future. They remind us of how to be in relationship, with the land, with each other, and with the sacred. They offer a compass not just a map. The work of living is to walk the path ourselves, guided by the wisdom of relationship and reciprocity.

Even in today's urban world, these instructions remain alive in the soil, in the breath, in the body, and in the stories we carry. Ceremonies, rituals, and meditation help us remember to remember. They reconnect us to the original instructions embedded in our bones. Participation lives beneath the pavement. It grows through cracks in the concrete. It rustles in the leaves, calls in the wind, and pulses in the heart. It reminds us that we are not exiles on this Earth, we are participants in her unfolding story.

A Cosmology for Healing

What we need is not another technique or ideology, but a cosmology of connection. A way of seeing that heals the fractures in our stories. A way of being that honors the body, the Earth, and the sacred in all things. When we know ourselves as both evolving and unchanging, both human and divine, both local and infinite, we become the bridge. We live as communion.

We need a spirituality that roots us in the world, not away from it. A psychology that embraces wholeness, not just a focus on fixing or control. A cosmology that welcomes us home, not to dominate, but to care. This book is an offering of that path. A path of embodied nonduality, rooted in the Earth, woven with breath, prayer, and presence. A path of remembrance, relationship, and return. And in this remembering, we may yet learn how to live well, together.

Psychology & Eastern Spirituality in Conversation

Psychology and Eastern nondual spiritual traditions often approach the evolving-self from very different starting points. Sometimes it can feel like they're speaking completely different languages. In Western psychology, particularly in Humanistic, Developmental, and Attachment theories, developing a strong, healthy sense of self is considered essential for emotional well-being. We need a stable sense of self and identity to function, to grow, to form meaningful relationships, and to navigate life's inevitable challenges.

However, many Eastern spiritual traditions invert this idea. They teach that clinging to a separate self is actually a key source of suffering. From this perspective, our sense of separateness isn't just problematic, it's an illusion. This difference boils down to two distinctly different ways of understanding reality and human development.

Psychology focuses on helping us build a strong, individuated self, one that's confident, resilient, and capable of forming healthy attachments. A solid sense of self gives us an anchor. Without it, we can feel fragmented, powerless, or lost. Much of psychotherapy is about strengthening this foundation, challenging negative self-beliefs, fostering self-acceptance, and cultivating an empowered, authentic self.

On the other hand, Eastern spiritual traditions like Buddhism and Advaita Vedanta invite us to question whether this separate self actually exists at all. In Buddhism, this is the teaching of *anatta*, or "no-self," the idea that what we perceive as "me" is merely a constantly shifting process, not a fixed identity. In Hinduism, we attempt to focus beyond the plurality of what our evolving-self experiences, so all individual expressions are simply one (Advaita Vedanta). In these views, holding tightly to our evolving-self only deepens our suffering because it keeps us locked in the illusion of separateness.

Instead of strengthening the personal self, these traditions encourage us to loosen our grip on it. Through mindfulness, meditation, self-inquiry, and contemplative practice, we're invited to observe our thoughts, emotions, and sensations as passing phenomena, not as who we really are. Over time, this can open the door to experiencing oneness, where the line between self and other begins to dissolve. We begin to see through the feeling that we're separate individuals to something much vaster: the seamless unity of all existence.

At first glance, psychology's focus on building the self and Eastern spirituality's focus on dissolving it might seem to clash. One approach builds the house; the other invites us to see that the walls aren't actually there. But maybe these two views aren't as incompatible as they seem. In fact, many contemporary thinkers, especially in Transpersonal Psychology, suggest they can beautifully complement each other. Transpersonal Psychology bridges these worlds, integrating the psychological work of building a healthy self with the spiritual journey of moving beyond it. It recognizes that we can both heal the personal self and awaken to something larger.

Philosopher Ken Wilber's spectrum model of self-development puts it simply: you need to have a self before you can transcend it. Trying to dissolve the ego too soon, before it's fully formed, can lead to confusion, emotional instability, or what's often called spiritual bypassing. Building a strong, healthy sense of self actually prepares us to safely explore the vast, transpersonal dimensions of consciousness.

This book is closely aligned with this integral perspective, but it also takes it a step further. When unified consciousness is a body experience, it isn't just a distant spiritual goal. It's a resource we can tap into right now, in our bodies. Oneness is available in our relationships and in our healing. It is available even though we suffer from chronic symptoms, like rampant thinking, anxiety, and depression. Due to this fairly easy and direct access, unified consciousness can immediately support our emotional growth and spiritual awakening. This is not something we have to wait to experience after years of meditation, purification, or transcendence. It shows up as a presence of being that is still, timeless, unconditionally loving, inner wholeness, and the deep safety we need to heal old wounds that is always available.

Moreover, as mentioned, the goal of our contemplative practices is not the dissolution of our evolving-self, but instead the co-existence of both dimensions of our being. Because of this, we don't have to choose between psychological well-being and a spirituality that simply transcends our psychological processes. They can inform and enrich each other. Psychology gives us the tools to make sense of our evolving-self's process of developing a healthy identity, one capable of autonomy, connection, and authenticity. Eastern spirituality offers us the path to our own wholeness as a way to soften our rigid attachments and open to a vast, interconnected reality.

When these two perspectives come together, something beautiful happens. Our evolving-self gives us the container to hold expansive, even mystical, experiences. And those nondual experiences can soften our defenses, deepen our compassion, and help us lovingly integrate even the most painful parts of ourselves. What emerges from this is a resilient, authentic evolving-self, free from the constraints, attachments, and habits that sabotage us. Together, they offer a more comprehensive and compassionate approach to realizing our full human potential. One that honors both, our personal journey of healing through communion, with the profound unity of all life.

A unique advantage of uncovering and awakening oneness as a body experience of our self is that it is powerfully nurturing. Exploring what this means, in light of not "dissolving" or discounting our evolving-self, is where we turn next. To highlight and orient the importance and nature of a participatory spirituality, I again contrast it with the transcendent approach.

Nurturing Nature of Nondual-Qualities of Self

In Ken Wilber's "spectrum model" of self-development, as mentioned, he claims the evolving-self is not at odds with spiritual growth. Yet, like so many spiritual traditions, Wilber's orientation toward spiritual growth is transcendent in that it eventually leads us beyond sensory perception. In meditation, he abides by leaving out our evolving-self's ever-changing process and becoming fully absorbed in the pristine state of nondual consciousness only (nirguna Brahman).

By contrast, in the approach presented here, unified consciousness is a subtle body experience (saguna Brahman), and we do not "dissolve" or submerge our evolving-self into a unified state. We co-exist with it, and in the process, our sense of suffering accesses a broader perspective, matures, and lets go of its sabotaging habits. Our authentic self is freed to manifest its full potential. To understand another level of why this is important, we revisit the nature of the transcendent state.

When transcendence is our goal, we often aim to become familiar with the all-pervasive experience of groundlessness, the deep recognition that there is no fixed center, no ultimate reference point, no solid ground beneath our feet. This groundlessness, often described as emptiness (*sunyata*) in Buddhist traditions or nonduality without qualities in Hinduism (*nirguna Brahman*), is not just a philosophical idea but a lived and ultimately liberating experience.

Yet, this is not an easy path, and, as I explore in *From Trauma to Wholeness* (2023), it is, in some significant ways, perilous for those of us who are still emotionally injured or hold trauma in our body-mind system. The experience of groundlessness arises when the evolving-self dissolves into nonduality, when the familiar boundaries of identity collapse, and the ego empties itself to reveal a deeper, more timeless essence. In this "emptying," one may touch a vast, limitless awareness that lies beyond all form. Yet when approached as a purely transcendent experience, it can feel like falling through space, deprived of the sensory, emotional, and relational landmarks that once offered orientation. For those of us living in the world rather than in monastic settings, such radical dissolution can feel less like freedom and more like vertigo, silence, and uncertainty that is unsustainable.

To rest in groundlessness is to confront the raw feeling that our existence has no fixed location in space or time; that what we take to be solid, as well as our body, our thoughts, our emotions, are ultimately ungraspable. The teachings tell us that these experiences are transient illusions, to be seen through and released. But for the ordinary human heart, which yearns for stability and connection, such realizations can feel like profound loss. When unresolved emotional injuries surface within this emptiness, the experience can quickly become unbearable.

The Christian mystics knew this territory well. They called it *the dark night of the soul,* a passage through which the familiar self is stripped away, leaving the soul exposed before the mystery. St. John of the Cross described it as a "burning love of the crucified," where love and suffering converge into a single purifying fire. It is not an abstract metaphor but a lived reality: a dismantling of everything we have built to feel safe, loved, or significant. In both Eastern and Western traditions, this fire of unmaking is seen as a necessary prelude to awakening. The death of the ego that makes space for a more authentic, unbounded life.

Yet this ego-death can be devastating. The structures that once defined who we are (our beliefs, achievements, relationships, even our sense of purpose) begin to dissolve. The identity built upon them collapses, leaving a vast and disorienting emptiness. We may feel as though we have been stripped of meaning, floating in a void between worlds. What once brought joy no longer stirs us; what once guided us no longer makes sense. In this in-between, depression, confusion, and despair can easily take root. The mind grasps for the old certainties, while the heart aches for something solid to hold onto. Without the hard to come by proper guidance we can feel unmoored, unseen, and profoundly alone, as if our deepest cries for help vanish into silence.

By contrast, when our orientation shifts toward embodied wholeness, we encounter something profoundly different: not a void, but a quality-rich emptiness that feels like an unchanging presence of being, nourishing us with a palpable sense of wholeness.[7] This form of emptiness is not bleak; it is vast and full of potential. It is a ground of existence that nurtures us, even as it reveals itself to be open and boundless.

For people somewhat familiar with meditation, this embodied sense of unity is remarkably accessible. With even a little practice, it can be felt just beneath the surface of our ever-shifting thoughts, emotions, and perceptions. It is always present, quietly permeating our lives, here, now, everywhere, all the time, all at once. With practice, this becomes a clear and luminous presence.

Unlike the pursuit of transcendence that seeks to escape suffering, an embodied sense of unity welcomes suffering as a teacher. It allows us to meet our painful patterns and self-sabotaging habits from a different perspective, one that is infused with open spaciousness, stillness, timelessness, unconditional love, and universally pervasive wholeness and unity.[8] In meditation, we feel how each of these qualities of oneness provides an alternative sensory-motor, temporal, spatial reality from the way we normally experience life. Equipped with these profound, inherently nurturing resources, even our most turbulent emotional experiences become essential allies on the path to emotional growth and inner peace.

However, like any insecurely attached child, we may reject the nurturing nature of oneness. This is because our early experiences with inconsistent, unreliable, or frightening

---

[7] As David Loy (1988) explains, the Buddhist term *sunyata* ("emptiness") carries two meanings. The root *su* can mean "hollow," pointing to the absence of a fixed self-nature, or it can mean "full," like a pregnant fullness. The first emphasizes no-self; the second points to the infinite variety of nondual experiences that can arise. I refer to these as the "qualities of oneness," aligned with Vedanta's *saguna Brahman* — nonduality with qualities.

[8] As an elaboration of this, in my book *Nondual Chakra Awakening* (2024), I explore how the unified nature of each of the chakra qualities of our being (existence, creativity, power, love, expression, knowing, wholeness) is a powerful resource that directly addresses each stage of our emotional development commonly recognized in psychology. These stages first occur as a child and are repeated throughout our life.

caregivers may have taught us that receiving nurturing from others is unsafe. We may harbor a deeply ingrained lack of trust. As a protective, learned coping strategy that helps us manage our internal fear of intimacy, we reject affection.

In whole-being meditation,[9] we rediscover how to heal these symptoms of insecure attachment, much like any child does: by building resilience through a consistent, reliable, and loving relationship. Now it involves a relationship with our unified ground of existence.

Further understanding of how we overcome our resistance to being nurtured is the subject of the next chapter. For now, suffice it to say, through embodied unified consciousness, we discover that our path is not one of bypassing pain, nor of plunging into the emptiness of an abyss, but of embracing the full spectrum of human life, suffering, beauty, confusion, love, with the sense of wholeness that accompanies the unified dimension of existence.

This is a journey from injury back to health, where wholeness nurtures us into authenticity. This support enhances confidence in ourselves and our world, and we feel securely connected with all that is. We experience a feeling of calm and an aura of quiet strength as we take the next step on the path of life.

The Effortless Dance Between Two Selves

Whenever we bring our full presence into our body through refining our senses and attunement, something remarkable happens. We begin to encounter both sides of who we are: our whole-self. We feel our evolving-self, and our

---

[9] The term *embodied nondual meditation* refers to a broad range of meditation practices, a few of which, while embodied, trend towards being transcendent in nature. While whole-being-embrace is also embodied, it is fundamentally integral rather than transcendent in its orientation. For this reason, the term *whole-being meditation* more accurately reflects whole-being-embrace practice, which emphasizes the embodied integration of all dimensions of experience, rather than a movement beyond them.

unchanging-self. Their communion in whole-being-embrace results from the embodied sense that we exist as oneness, yet still aware that we are aware of the experience.[10] For instance, we do not become the tree we are embracing and lose track of the experience that we are embracing it. We don't lose the sense of being a unique individual moving through time. Our individual self is pervaded with the timeless, unified, loving presence within.

But here's where it gets really interesting: Our evolving-self's thoughts, emotions, and actions normally all require deliberate effort. By contrast, our unchanging-self's self-reflective capacity is spontaneously self-arising and doesn't require effort. This effortlessness is a flow state that plays a big role in teaching us how to relate to our injuries and life's events in a different way.

The effortless, spontaneous nature of our thoughts, emotions, and actions in this flow state empowers us to let go of our sabotaging habitual responses to what we experience. It allows for our effortless authenticity to come into full expression. This is why the sage Jayaratha commented, "Those that went before said that desire [suffering] is checked by practice of dispassion; we teach that this is achieved by desisting from all effort." (Tantraloka, bracket added).

Over time, as we refine our senses and cultivate deeper inner attunement, our self-awareness (and the thoughts, emotions, and sensations that result) can start to feel effortless, natural, and even joyful. Rather than being only a deliberate choice, it increasingly arises spontaneously on its own, without us needing to intend or "pursue" self-awareness.

Instead of struggling to manage ourselves, we find that authenticity begins to arise on its own. Our emotional truth and our need for autonomy no longer compete; they flow together. Our expressions become effortless, spontaneous, and rooted in

---

[10] In the yoga tradition, as mentioned, this quality of "self-aware unified consciousness" is known as *samprajnata or saguna samadhi.* Unlike deeper, more transcendent forms of unified consciousness, called *nirguna samadhi,* where the sense of self completely dissolves, self-aware unified consciousness keeps self-awareness intact.

something deeper than fear. This changes the ways we form boundaries in relationship, know what we need, find emotional safety. It helps us discover who we are beyond old survival patterns and beyond the ways we've been shaped by others' perceptions of us. We will come back to this topic again later.

Chapter Three

Entangled Truths

Meeting in the Dance of Love

Unified consciousness reveals itself in many shades, from the fully merged state in which all distinctions dissolve (transcendence), to an embodied wholeness. One of the special attributes of embodied wholeness is that we can still honor relationship, individuality, and the unfolding reality of our lives. As we become more familiar with our sense of existing as the embodied wholeness of our unchanging-self, a deeper truth emerges: we feel the ways our emotional injuries benefit from the presence of oneness and remember our actual intrinsic worth.

Without this grounding in embodied wholeness, individuality can lose its center, and we lose our balance. And likewise, we recognize how oneness needs our evolving-self to be known and felt. Consciousness without the evolving-self to perceive it, remains dormant. It could be said that wholeness cannot recognize itself without a form through which to become self-aware. This co-creative relationship becomes our cosmogenesis—the universe continually being born within the living landscape of our own body.

From this union, emotional maturity and spiritual realization are no longer separate pursuits but two dimensions of one awakening wholeness. This synthesis of both our individuality and the infinite, marks a new threshold in both spiritual and therapeutic paradigms. It is how true healing can occur and where we stop needing to choose between our individuality and oneness, between personal growth and transcendence, because we discover that, ultimately, they belong to each other.

We do not reach this through striving or expanding outward, nor through importing some cosmic insight from beyond. We arrive by uncovering what has always been alive within us. In doing so, we discover that the entire universe is not something outside to be grasped; it also resides within the depths of the soma or tissues of our body. The body becomes a living, breathing reflection of both our oneness and our humanity.

In our experience of embodied wholeness, unlike the all-consuming fusion that erases individuality, we can maintain our relationship with our emotional life. As we become more familiar with embodied wholeness, it begins to feel like a steady, unwavering, self-reflective presence within us. This is not a distant, detached witness. It's paradoxically personal *and* universal at the same time. It's timeless, yet its stillness pervades the flow of our life.[11]

What stands out is that our nondual wholeness has a relational nature. This nonduality is relational not despite its oneness, but because of it; it is relational oneness. We feel how the distinctions between subject and object, our self and others, are not illusions to be dismissed but temporary expressions within this single continuum of reality. When our emotional pain enters into a participatory relationship with this sense of oneness, our life

---

[11] *Turiyatita* is often described as "beyond the fourth" (*turiya*), pointing to the complete dissolution of individual ego. In embodied wholeness, however, the entanglement between the evolving-self and the unchanging-self creates a profound paradox: within our evolving-self we discover unity, and within unity we discover diversity. We experience no separation between the self and unified consciousness, yet we remain distinctly self-aware as individuals. In this sense, the realization is not a conventional form of *turiyatita*, but a lived integration where unity and individuality coexist.

becomes a way of being that honors both our divinity and our humanity, our unified nature and our psychology. Along the way, we discover the divinity in our humanity.

In psychological terms, healthy relationships depend on this same dynamic balance: a fluid dance between connection and differentiation. Two people come together in intimacy and then separate to rediscover themselves, returning to connection with renewed authenticity. In embodied nondual experience, this rhythm deepens. When we feel ourselves as wholeness and unity, we enter a refined octave of relationship, one in which merging and separation no longer feel like opposites but like alternating notes in the same divine harmony. Pervaded by the flow state of oneness, we gain the capacity to weave countless sensations and perceptions into a single, unified ground of meaning, a knowing.

This oneness is the foundation of our sense of integration and coherent experience.[12] It connects our inner and outer worlds, integrates multiple layers of experience, and allows the evolving flow of our life to cohere into a meaningful experience. This relational oneness is not an endpoint but a beginning, a new foundation from which unconditional love becomes conscious within our daily lives. From the ground of unity, a deeper kind of relationship unfolds, one where relationship is no longer only a negotiation between two separate beings trying to meet their needs. It becomes a harmonious alignment of being, where communication flows effortlessly from presence and truth rather than from defense or fear.

When the sense of self is no longer only defined by what it can gain or lose, the experience of contact transforms. It ceases to be a transaction and becomes a natural overflow, an offering.

---

[12] Nondual awareness rests on the principle of interdependence (*pratītyasamutpāda*): nothing exists in isolation; everything arises through relationship. In whole-being-embrace, this interdependence doesn't erase individuality, it transforms it. The tension between "the one" and "the many" dissolves as we realize that even within oneness, relational dynamics remain alive and are simply transfigured into expressions of our whole-being.

The focus shifts from grasping to giving, from need to nourishment. Relationship itself becomes an instrument of awakening, a shared movement toward growth, wholeness, and purpose that extends far beyond the boundaries of two individual lives.

In this union, intimacy matures into something vast yet tender: a love spacious enough to hold both unity and difference, silence and expression, oneness and autonomy. It is a relationship that mirrors the nature of reality itself. One life, endlessly meeting itself in love and wholeness.

Our sense of unity is not a state beyond form, it is the unbroken wholeness that permeates all forms. Our evolving-self remains intact. It is still feeling, changing, and growing, but progressively more aware of the living presence of wholeness within. In daily life, this means the infinite shines through the finite; the formless breathes within the formed, and in doing so, we mature and overcome our suffering. We do not lose our individuality; we awaken within it. Our individuality is not isolated but opens and becomes transparent to wholeness.

This results in a loving bond where unified presence offers us a kind of clear inner mirror, allowing us to see the patterns of our evolving-self more clearly and then let go of its limiting habits and constrictions more fully. When our evolving-self, often burdened by dependency or fear, comes into contact with this unconditional love, it feels seen, included, and set free. This meeting heals the emotional injuries that come from not feeling witnessed, understood, respected, and loved. It heals all the attachment injuries that distort our capacity for intimacy and trust.

In this expanded awareness, the rigid boundary between "me" and "you" softens into an experience of "us made whole." The heart opens into a recognition that love is not something to be gained from others but the natural expression of the unity that already connects us. Love, in its deepest sense, is the recognition of ourselves in another being.

Whole-being-embrace, then, is not a static oneness but a dynamic harmony, a dance between unity and diversity, stillness and movement, silence and expression. The "not-two" nature of reality reveals that difference and unity are simultaneous truths. Each being, emotion and experience, is a facet of a vast, living jewel whose brilliance is shared by all.

In nondual love we celebrate this paradox: there is no separation, while every form is cherished in its unique distinctness. Relationships cease to be strategies to fill our emptiness and become acts of divine play (*līlā*). Each connection becomes a co-creative celebration of consciousness encountering itself in another form. Even when encounters are painful, we recognize them as opportunities to deepen our understanding and ability to remain authentic. The world is no longer something to escape, but the very canvas of awakening.

To live from this awareness is to participate consciously in creation itself, to feel that every interaction, every touch, every moment of presence is part of the sacred whole-being-embrace, where duality and nonduality, self and world, forever meet in the dance of love.

The Unwavering Presence of Oneness

The experience we have between these two dimensions of our existence, which often initially unfolds in embodied nondual meditation, is grounded in a simple yet profound insight: existence itself is relational. Oneness feels relational in its connectedness, and our evolving-self is relational in its self-other orientation. From the very beginning, we are shaped by relationship.

Recognizing this is important because it shapes our understanding of what it takes to heal and awaken spiritually. Biologically, psychologically, and emotionally, humans are wired for connection. As touched on briefly in chapter one, our nervous systems develop in response to the rhythms of attunement with caregivers. Our sense of safety, identity, and belonging are sculpted by the presence, or absence, of contact in relationship. Every pattern of human development is carried in the fabric of relationship.

It follows, then, that just as emotional wounds are formed in relationship, ultimately they can only be truly healed in relationship. Healing requires not only private reflection but an encounter with presence, an experience of being received, understood, and held. Spiritual practice, at its most transformative, is not an escape from relationship into oneness but a restoration of relationship. It heals most deeply when it honors the relational nature of being itself, offering us a way to reconnect not only with others but with the innermost dimension of ourselves.

In this light, our relationships become more than social bonds; they become spiritual pathways. Each moment of authentic contact, whether with another person or within the communion of our own evolving-self and unchanging-self, can reveal the spiritual essence of who we are. Relationship becomes a mirror in which unity shines through individuality, and healthy, authentic individuality deepens our experience of unity.

As mentioned, at the center of this restoration lies one essential quality: nurturing. It is through nurturing that we rediscover our innate capacity to trust, to soften, and to connect. Just as a child's nervous system learns resilience through the steady presence of a loving caregiver, our evolving-self heals when met by the unwavering presence of wholeness. Nurturing creates the conditions for our attunement, where wounds are met with warmth rather than dispassion or judgment, and where what has been fragmented is invited back into wholeness.

Spirituality as a body experience of unified consciousness, then, is a matter of the heart, rather than simply awareness or mind alone. It is not separate from the ordinary gestures of human care. It is revealed in the way we nurture life, in ourselves, in others, and in the world. To nurture profoundly is to participate in the most subtle and clear attunement possible: a living connection to the essence of being that underlies all existence. Contact with the wholeness of being that accompanies this experience is perhaps the most important ingredient needed for healing and growing a healthy sense of self with self-love.

As we now know, a healthy sense of self doesn't grow in isolation; it is nurtured into being. Psychology has long recognized that *feeling nurtured* is not just beneficial but essential for human development. The groundbreaking research of René Spitz and Harry Harlow powerfully demonstrated just how vital emotional connection is to our growth and well-being.

Together, their studies reveal a profound truth: it is not just our bodies that require nourishment, it is our hearts.[13] Emotional warmth, physical affection, and attuned connection are not optional for healthy development; they are as essential to our survival and thriving as food and water. In fact, we instinctively *choose* emotional safety over basic sustenance when the two are placed in competition.

It can be said that feeling nurtured also holds an essential place in the landscape of nondual Eastern spirituality. At the heart of nondual traditions like Buddhism and Advaita Vedanta is the recognition that everything is inter-connected, ultimately, there is no separation. When we begin to experience this oneness, our sense of isolation starts to dissolve. This naturally gives rise to a sense of universal belonging and connection, which is deeply nurturing. Feeling part of the whole fosters an inner security that can support both our healing and our awakening.

Yet when the sole focus is on dissolving the ego or transcending emotional attachment, we strive for freedom from life rather than freedom of life. Transcending the karmic cycle

---

[13] Spitz's orphanage studies showed that infants given adequate food and shelter still suffered severe developmental harm—and many died—when deprived of affection, touch, and emotional attunement. Harlow's experiments with rhesus monkeys echoed this truth: infant monkeys consistently chose the soft, comforting surrogate mother over the wire mother that provided milk, revealing that emotional security is as essential to survival as physical nourishment.

through achieving a higher state of unified consciousness, ultimately does release us from the limitations and attachments of earthly existence. But if this is the destination, at what cost?

As mentioned, when we harbor attachment injuries of any kind as a child or as an adult, this can be problematic. Or, when non-attachment is taken to an extreme, it can unintentionally lead to emotional detachment, disconnection, or even spiritual bypassing. Since spiritual traditions emerged at a time before there was understanding of issues involved in psychological development and understanding of the effects of lasting emotional injury and trauma, spiritual teachers are often not fully equipped to help us through various psychological complications involving non-attachment that often arise.

Suffice it to say, spiritual teachings across traditions have long grappled with the issue of suffering and attachment. In Buddhism, suffering is said to arise from clinging to impermanent things. In Hinduism, suffering is often attributed to karma and our attachment to the material world. Christianity locates suffering in the fall from innocence, the original disconnection from God.

In each tradition, suffering emerges from a perceived gap between what is and what we want things to be. But what these traditions often overlook is that we can achieve autonomy from suffering in a way that is participatory rather than based on control and separation from our human nature. Their desire to control, grasp, or avoid the reality of our evolving-self seems to frequently be a compensatory response to "insecure attachment" (raised with unreliable care) on a societal scale. (Attachment types are discussed in chapter four.)

When we feel secure, we do not need to control our senses, become dispassionate and non-reactive, disidentify from, or distance from every experience. We can live with openness to uncertainty. We can appreciate what is, without obsessively striving for what is not. Pleasant and unpleasant experiences do not bind us to craving or aversion, because we trust that we are held by something deeper, something stable. This provides an existential trust that allows us to navigate disappointment, change, and even loss without collapsing. "Secure attachment," then, becomes a gateway to emotional maturity that is integrated with spiritual awakening.

In whole-being-meditation, we do not attempt to escape our humanness. Instead, we discover a deeper spiritual freedom that embraces and nurtures the whole of our being. When this is rooted in the body and infused with psychological insight, we find compassion, resilience, and intimacy with ourselves and all that is.

In this experience, the evolving-self's emotional process, which includes our unhealthy attachments, is honored as an essential part of the spiritual path. Through direct contact with bodily sensations, breath, and subtle energetic patterns, we begin to recognize the deeper intelligence within our emotional life.

Rather than rejecting or distancing from our human emotions and needs, we welcome them into the inherently compassionate ground of wholeness. The unchanging-self becomes a wise, loving presence that says, "*I see you, I hold you, and I'm with you as you grow.*" This inner attachment, resulting from whole-being-embrace, serves as the foundation for self-regulation, relational healing, and spiritual unfolding. It is not a clinging or grasping, but a deep, compassionate attunement to our full experience of being.

Secure attachment provides a foundation of emotional stability that shapes how we relate to ourselves and others throughout life. Bonding with oneness allows for a deeper, freer way of being in relationship, with others, with ourselves, and with the meaning we associate with life experiences. It provides the capacity to love without clinging, to feel without being overwhelmed, and to act without being bound by the outcome. This has a profound impact on many aspects of our lives, including our emotional, social, and cognitive development. It provides a foundation for building strong, healthy relationships, regulating our emotions, and skillfully navigating the world with confidence.

61

Importantly, secure attachment lays the groundwork for the ability to later release unhealthy attachments. It is precisely through experiencing trustworthy and healing forms of attachment that we can begin to embody the wisdom of true nonattachment, not as distancing, disconnection, or disidentification, but as freedom rooted in connection.

When our need for emotional security is met, we are less likely to develop clinging patterns that manifest as excessive dependence, fear of abandonment, or controlling behaviors. These patterns, when unresolved, often lead to the very suffering that psychology seeks to alleviate, and that Eastern spirituality often seeks to transcend. In embodied nondual meditation, our need for emotional security is met with the wholeness of the qualities of oneness.

In this way, secure attachment is not simply about forming healthy bonds; it is about nurturing the deep inner safety that eventually allows us to let go of unhealthy habits. Without this inner stability, attempts to dissolve the ego or transcend attachment can become spiritually bypassing or emotionally destabilizing. But when we become rooted in secure, nurturing connections, we gain the resilience to easily release the attachments that cause suffering and keep us trapped in cycles of fear and control.

The deep, emotional connection between individuals that attachment and bonding provide, helps us feel loving and caring for others without needing to control or possess them. Our sense of a secure base of emotional connection allows for a more spacious relationship, one that accommodates each person's unique desires. It supports us to feel more secure in our relationships, even when we experience separation or change.

Thus, whole-being-embrace bridges the seeming divide between Eastern ideals of nonattachment and Western psychological insights into the necessity of secure attachment. It reveals that we do not need to choose between being spiritual and being human. In fact, the more we are at home in our authentic

62

humanity, the more transparent we become to the mystery of spirit. Plus, the more we feel that we exist as unified consciousness, the more effortlessly we become authentic.

Within the whole-being-embrace, these dimensions are not in conflict; they are in communion. When we embody unified consciousness as an experience of our self, we can honor the evolving-self's needs for safety, attunement, and belonging. In this way, we create the very ground from which letting go can occur without fear or loss. In whole-being-embrace, attachment and nonattachment are no longer opposites to reconcile, but partners in an integrated life.

Together, they allow us to walk the path of awakening without abandoning the tender terrain of our own heart. In this union, we discover that being fully human is not a hindrance to awakening consciousness; it is its most intimate expression.

Before delving more deeply into the relationship between the unchanging-self and evolving-self, there is one more issue that may interfere with fully opening to the nurturing nature of the qualities of oneness. And this concerns our attachment to nurturing itself.

Nurturing with Happiness & Knowledge

In many Hindu Vedantic spiritual communities, particularly those with a transcendent, disembodied orientation, there is skepticism about any form of attachment. They are even skeptical of the nurturing presence of wholeness as a body experience. It is often taught that while the Tantric embodied nondual experience can bring profound happiness, and knowledge, the mind-body system can become attached to these experiences themselves, thus limiting further awakening.

The *Bhagavad Gita* (14:6) reminds us that even the attachment to happiness and knowledge, when derived from bodily or sensory experience, can become a subtle obstacle on the path to freedom. From this view, true awakening requires us to transcend even the attachment to happiness and knowledge that arise from embodied experiences of nondual consciousness.

It is indeed true that we are remarkably adept at forming attachments, not only to external objects but also to internal states, identities, and even spiritual experiences. Every trauma symptom is, in part, a collection of unconscious attachments, habitual patterns, and fixed ways of thinking, feeling, and relating that keep us trapped. However, Western psychology has an important understanding that was not available to the Eastern mystics. As mentioned, it has revealed the extent to which nurturing embodied experience plays a crucial role in loosening these unwanted attachments.

The inherent sense of benevolence, happiness, and deep knowing that often arises in embodied nondual states can offer precisely the kind of nurturing support our nervous system needs to heal childhood wounds and suffering in general. For instance, the body experience of unconditional love, a core nondual quality of our being, is not simply a spiritual ideal. It is the very medicine our trauma requires to begin feeling safe, whole, and at home in the body.

Our nervous system is hardwired for survival. As Rick Hanson famously put it, our brain is like Velcro for negative experiences and Teflon for positive ones. Evolution has primed us to prioritize threats, which keeps us hyper-focused on danger and pain, but also makes it difficult to absorb or sustain positive experiences, especially those of happiness, love, and safety. Emotional injuries and trauma amplify this tendency. They numb us to pleasure, dissociate us from the body, and leave us unable to tolerate the very sensations of well-being that are essential for healing. A central symptom of ongoing emotional injury is the inability to fully experience states of joy, safety, and relaxation.

This is why learning to remain present with the happiness and knowledge that arise in embodied nondual experience is such a profound form of healing. By expanding our "window of tolerance" for the intensity of life through deepening our relationship with pleasant sensations and positive self-perceptions, we gradually reclaim our ability to live fully. Embodied nondual meditation helps us stretch the limits of what we can safely feel and experience, allowing us to move from numbness to aliveness and from dissociation to presence.

In Western culture, where the body is often objectified, pathologized, or treated as an inconvenience (and we seek quick fixes, virtual escapes, and addictive coping mechanisms), this is especially important. And, while the transcendent practices of are sometimes valuable strategies, when we harbor deep emotional injury, they can also be limiting and even reinforce patterns of self-restriction, de-realization, depersonalization, dissociation, and fragmentation. A purely transcendent spiritual approach that bypasses the body and its emotional life may unintentionally deepen psychic splits.

This said, for many of us, nurturing is not simple. Emotional injury often conditions us to resist the very comfort we long for the most. Our instinct for self-preservation builds walls of protection, making it hard to trust or receive care. These defenses arise from real experiences of betrayal, abandonment, or neglect. If someone who was meant to keep us safe instead wounded us, the nervous system learns that vulnerability and openness are dangerous. Hypervigilance takes root, scanning for danger where there might be none, and intimacy becomes a risk too costly to take.

Some of us adapt by becoming hyper-independent. We learn early that relying on others leads to disappointment, so we vow to rely only on ourselves. Even when support is freely and lovingly offered, the impulse is to turn it away: *"I can handle this on my own."* Others carry a deep, unspoken shame; a belief, often rooted in childhood neglect, that they are unworthy of care. Shame can make the idea of receiving love feel confusing, uncomfortable, or even unbearable. Still others numb themselves to their emotions entirely. Emotional shutdown offers temporary relief from overwhelming feelings, but at the cost of cutting off both pain and the comfort of nurturing.

These protective strategies, while born of necessity, come with consequences. They keep us locked in cycles of craving connection and then pushing it away, yearning to be known but hiding behind silence, desiring closeness while fearing abandonment. At times, we may not even know what kind of care we need, because we've been trained not to ask or to dismiss our needs before anyone else can.

In the whole-being-embrace experience, we are invited to slowly reclaim nurturing as an inner resource. This involves uncovering and awakening to the secure internal base that our body experience of wholeness provides. This base has several outstanding features.

The bottom-up orientation of embodied nondual meditation (where body informs mind) offers a direct path to healing. Unlike top-down approaches, of deliberately creating or intending positive emotions, embodied practice allows the body to lead. The body's subtle qualities of oneness, such as stillness, transparency, unified spatial awareness, unconditional love, and the timeless presence we feel in deep states of unity, become essential doorways to transformation.

Through this pathway, the body teaches the mind. It reveals wiser, more adaptive alternatives to outdated survival patterns. The profound intelligence embedded in our sensory, spatial, and temporal experience becomes a living source of self-transformation. The non-abandoning, non-invasive presence of our unchanging-self, does not simply communicate ordinary knowledge. It communicates knowledge that has access to intuition and wisdom. It also communicates nondual knowing beyond empirical knowledge; knowing of the unknowable and all the understanding that unity provides.

As mentioned, every child needs a steady, trustworthy, and kind presence in order to develop the capacity to trust, seek support when needed, and approach relationships with openness rather than fear. In whole-being meditation, our own nondual qualities of being serve as this steady, trustworthy, and loving presence. This nurturing is the medicine that allows old emotional wounds to soften, open, and begin to heal, allowing self-love to blossom. Understanding how this happens is a central subject of this book. Aside from the aspects of embodied unified consciousness that heal emotional wounding already mentioned, other experiences include:

Self-compassion — Compassion, tenderness, and openness arise spontaneously out of wholeness. We thereby treat ourselves with the same tenderness and openness we would offer to someone we dearly love.

Reparenting the wounded inner-child — As wholeness, we become the consistent, emotionally available caregiver our younger self needed but may not have received.

Cultivating safety and trust within — Unified consciousness provides our diverse needs with the unwavering presence of wholeness and inner-knowing. Reliable responsiveness to our own needs occurs effortlessly.

Practicing mindfulness and self-awareness — In meditation, we increasingly recognize emotions the moment they arise, so they don't overwhelm us or spiral into old patterns.

Leaning into healthy connections — We cultivate an internally supportive relationship between the evolving-self and the unchanging-self that fosters empathy, resonance, and an attuned presence.

Creative expression — Attuning to the essential nondual quality of our creative nature, offers fundamental support for us to express individual acts of creativity and self-expression. This allows us to use art, writing, music, or movement as channels for emotions too big for words.

Learning to stay with discomfort — In embodied nondual meditation, we gradually increase our capacity to feel pain without being consumed by it. This conserves our energy for healing and maturing.

In whole-being meditation, nurturing becomes a re-patterning process that literally rewires the brain and nervous system and transforms the tissues of our body. Old pathways of fear, neglect, and self-blame give way to new experiences of safety, worthiness, and trust. Each act of self-care, each moment of gentle reparenting, signals to the nervous system and every cell of our body: *"You are safe now. You are worthy of love. You belong, forever."*

This practice is not self-indulgent; it is transformative. Nurturing through being pervaded and held by the uninjured, unbreakable, unified ground of our being, helps us break free from the endless search for external validation, rooting us instead in self-trust and inner resilience. As we bask in sensations of stillness, wholeness, and timelessness, it restores a rhythm of safety to the body, teaching us that we can both reach outward for support and turn inward for stability.

With every small, consistent experience of wholeness, openness, and compassion toward ourselves, we lay down new foundations. These foundations allow us to meet life's challenges with greater ease and to risk intimacy without fear of annihilation. In these ways, the experience of happiness and knowledge that accompanies embodied unified consciousness becomes a regenerative fountain of youth.

Ultimately, much like the participatory cosmologies of our ancestors are not relics of a lost past but instructions for the future, nurturing is not only how we heal the past. It is also how we open to a new future. It is the steady hand that holds us as we rediscover what it means to feel safe in our own skin, alive in our own body, and deeply connected to ourselves and others. It reminds us how to be in relationship, with the Earth, with each other, and with the sacred.

A central part of nurturing as a means of healing emotional injuries is the experience of "mirroring" that happens in relationship between two individuals. As we shall see, the nurturing that results from the mirroring relationship between parent and child, also plays a role in the relationship between our evolving-self and our unchanging-self. This nurturing is perhaps the most profound way of restoring what was missing as a child: compassion, consistency, and the felt sense of being seen and cared for.

I See You – I Am You

In psychology, secure attachment describes the foundation of healthy relational patterns that form when, as children, we are met with consistent empathy and "accurate mirroring" from a caregiver. Empathy is more than sympathy or concern; it is the felt sense of being joined in our inner world. It is when another person not only understands what we feel but seems to feel it with us. It is the subtle resonance through which we come to know that our emotions make sense, that our experience matters.

Accurate mirroring happens when a caregiver responds in ways that reflect our gestures, tone, and emotional states. It's when they smile back at our joy, soften in response to our sadness, or meet our fear with calm reassurance. These moments of attuned reflection are how we first learn who we are. Through another's eyes, voice, and touch, our inner world is named and affirmed. Mirroring is empathy made visible. It is a wordless dialogue that tells us, again and again: *"You are seen. You are felt. You belong."*

This mirroring process plays into our understanding of how evolution unfolds. In alignment with Robin Dunbar's (1998) "social brain hypothesis," our large, complex brains and the consciousness that emerges from them, evolved primarily to navigate the intricacies of human relationships. At the heart of this capacity is our remarkable ability to model other people's minds: their thoughts, intentions, and feelings. As some theories suggest, the very neural circuits we use to understand others are also those we use to construct our own sense of self.[14]

In other words, our subjective awareness is built from the same machinery that allows us to recognize awareness in another. By perceiving others as conscious beings, we refine and mirror back an image of our own consciousness. This relational mirroring not only grounds our ability to connect, but also deepens our direct understanding of what it means to be aware and clearly discern our own state of being. This is also precisely what we experience in whole-being meditation.

When our evolving-self experiences empathetic attunement with our unchanging-self, it allows us to grow a deeper understanding of our own feelings and sense of connection with all of life. When our evolving-self experiences itself in the presence of our unchanging-self, our unchanging-self provides, what I call, a "nondual mirror" that gives us access to a profound sense of being truly seen, understood, accepted, and lovingly supported. We naturally develop a stable and secure sense of ourselves. This foundation enables us to feel comfortable with emotional closeness, seek support when needed, and approach relationships with trust, flexibility, and emotional balance.

Nondual mirroring is one of the ways our unchanging-self provides our evolving-self with access to a broader perspective than the limited sense of separation: self versus other, subject versus object, perception versus response. It is not something we "do," but rather a background ground of unchanging, unified awareness within which all experiences arise.

As mentioned, unified consciousness is often described as *self-reflective* because it is awareness awakening to itself. It

---

[14] V.S. Ramachandran, Giacomo Rizzolatti, Michael Graziano, Shaun Gallagher, Tania Singer, Jason Mitchell, Christian Keysers, etc.

does not merely perceive; it recognizes its own nature. This is a radically different kind of knowing. One that is not about simply being aware or observing an object, emotion, or sensation, as when we notice a blue sky, feel sadness, or sense the warmth of the sun. In those experiences, there is always a division: a "me" who knows, and something "out there" that is known.

In unified consciousness, that division dissolves. Awareness is no longer turned outward or toward something separate; it turns inward and finds no boundary between subject and object, between perceiver and perceived. Knowing and being are one and the same. This is not an experience *of* wholeness, it is wholeness experiencing itself. (Later, I refer to this as "whole-self-turiyatita.")

To awaken to unified consciousness is to recognize that the knower and what is known have always been inseparable. It is awareness realizing, "*I am that which I have been seeking.*" This is not a thought or an insight that comes and goes, but a direct, living recognition, a felt intimacy with existence itself.

As mentioned, in yoga, that which is "external" is anything that is not unified. In which case, our thoughts, emotions, and sensations are external to the ground of our being. Engaging with external experiences ranges from contact with a person or a moment in nature to focusing on our mental, emotional, and sensory life.

The heart of whole-being-embrace is learning to hold both the beauty of external engagement and the quiet certainty of inner unity. External experiences can remind us of what's possible. But they no longer define us. In this way, as our evolving-self learns to attune to the steady presence of our unchanging-self, we stop seeking connection as something to attain, reach for, or download, and begin living it as who we are. The sacredness we see in the world is revealed to be a reflection of what's already within. This is what true spiritual sovereignty means, to live from the luminous, self-sustaining ground of being that no one can give or take away.

Unified consciousness often brings a deep sense of stillness, connectedness, spaciousness, breathing room, unconditional love, and sometimes bliss. But its defining quality is a profound, felt sense of oneness or wholeness. As we experience nondual mirroring, a profound sense of existential trust emerges.

Existential Trust

Experiencing unified consciousness as a dimension of our own being can profoundly shift the way we relate to ourselves, to others, and to life. When we reconnect with this deeper layer of reality, we begin to live from a place of existential trust, rather than from the protective strategies shaped by early attachment wounds. Even in the face of life's challenges, we find ourselves more open, resilient, and capable of meeting the moment with acceptance.

As we uncover and awaken the presence of unity and wholeness within the body as an expression of our own being in meditation, we loosen rigid psychological patterns. We foster a direct, embodied sense of self-worth that does not depend on success, approval, or external circumstances. In the self-reflective light of our unchanging-self, attachment wounds can begin to heal, not inspired through intentions or conceptual understanding alone, but through the lived experience of being wholeness, of being love itself, and of being fundamentally connected and intrinsically lovable, just as we are.

When unified consciousness begins to know itself, this recognition is not confined to the mind. It is felt through the body. The body becomes the mirror through which awareness experiences its own presence. For some, this may arise as a deep stillness, as if every cell were quietly awake. For others, it appears as warmth pervading the heart, a gentle radiance that has no center and no edge, even as we experience it within the body.

The spaciousness of this awareness is not abstract or remote; it is immediate and intimate. It can be felt in the quiet within breath, in the pulsing of blood, in the simple fact of being here. The body, once seen as an obstacle to the experience of unified consciousness, becomes the temple through which consciousness recognizes its own wholeness.

In this recognition, our physical existence is no longer something we simply inhabit; it becomes an expression of the same luminous awareness that moves the stars and tides. Unified consciousness does not merely dwell within us, it breathes us. Each sensation, each moment of aliveness, becomes a reflection of the infinite meeting itself in form.

This is why embodied wholeness is not a lesser stage on the path of awakening, but its fulfillment. The divine and the human, the unchanging and the changing, are no longer perceived to stand apart. Awareness and flesh, spirit and matter, are revealed as two faces of the same presence, each completing the other in the mystery of being.

Not Bypassing & Feeling What is Real

When awareness awakens within the body, it also awakens within relationship. The same stillness that fills the space inside us begins to recognize itself in everything and everyone around us. Unified consciousness, when embodied, becomes *relational consciousness*, a living ground of mutual presence. In this ground, we no longer perceive others as separate entities moving through space; rather, we feel them as variations of the same awareness expressing itself through different forms. Relationship becomes the mirror through which consciousness continues to know itself, not only as an isolated self but as the meeting of many expressions of one being.

In this way, the experience of unity is not lost in relationship, it deepens through it. The gaze of another becomes a doorway into the same presence we feel within. The space between self and other is revealed not only as a boundary but as the very medium of love, the living tissue of connection where awareness discovers its own reflection again and again.

As described, as relational awareness unfolds, intimacy takes on a new meaning. It is no longer about merging or losing oneself in another, nor about maintaining defensive, rigid boundaries for safety. Instead, it becomes the meeting of two beings who are rooted in their own wholeness, each reflecting the same luminous awareness through a unique form. When we rest in wholeness, connection arises not from need but from resonance. The love we share with others is no longer an exchange but a recognition, *the same essence seeing itself across the space between us.*

In this state, empathy matures into something deeper than emotional resonance. It becomes direct participation in another's being. We begin to feel the subtle movements of their breath, the quiet tremor behind their words, the unspoken truth behind their eyes. We do not lose ourselves in their experience. Our awareness, grounded in the body's stillness, allows us to feel with another while remaining anchored in the vastness that holds us both. This is compassion without collapse, love without enmeshment.

When we meet one another from this place, healing naturally unfolds. The ancient injuries of abandonment and invasion (the wounds that once defined our patterns of closeness and distance) begin to dissolve in the warmth of shared presence. The space between self and other becomes a living sanctuary where both can rest. No one needs to be fixed or saved. The simple act of being fully present, body-to-body, awareness-to-awareness, becomes the medicine.

In the light of oneness, relationship ceases to be a battleground for unmet needs and becomes a sacred dialogue of wholeness instead. Each encounter, whether tender or difficult, becomes an invitation to remember our shared ground of being.

Love, then, is not something we give or receive. It is what we are, discovering ourselves in the mirror of the world.

Ultimately, awakening does not reach its fulfillment in transcendence or even in the intimacy of relationship alone, but in embodied integration, when the awareness that knows itself begins to live itself through every gesture, word, and breath. Wholeness finds its natural expression in how we move through the world: in the tone of our voice, the care with which we listen, the quiet integrity of our choices.

In this way, enlightenment ceases to be an extraordinary event and becomes an ordinary rhythm, a way of being human that is infused with grace. The stillness that once seemed otherworldly reveals itself as the quiet pulse of daily life. Every act of kindness, every moment of awareness, becomes a form of prayer, a bridge between the infinite and the tangible. Here, spirituality is no longer something we practice or attain. It is simply the way we live when we remember who we are.

Effortless Truth

Spiritual practices often encourage us to deliberately *cultivate* positive inner qualities (such as joy, confidence, loving-kindness, and compassion), not as attachments to fleeting emotional highs, but as genuine expressions of our authentic nature. While many Eastern contemplative practices encourage us to *bring* tender awareness or compassion to our emotional life, whole-being meditation takes a different orientation.

In whole-being meditation, the emphasis is not on deliberately cultivating positive inner-qualities, but instead on *opening to* the experience of how these positive qualities *naturally arise* when we embody unified consciousness as a presence of being. Rather than deliberately directing compassion, joy, or confidence toward our trauma experience as a kind of mental effort, we emphasize allowing compassion, tenderness, or love to *arise spontaneously* from the direct experience of unified consciousness in the body.

When we intentionally strive to generate positive inner qualities, it is often a top-down process: the mind instructs the body to feel or behave a certain way. This can certainly be beneficial, but it risks remaining somewhat effortful or conceptual. This makes it more difficult to influence our emotional life. In contrast, when positive inner qualities emerge spontaneously in embodied nondual meditation, it is not contrived, willed, or manufactured. It arises naturally from the sense of wholeness that pervades our being. The positive inner quality of compassion is then felt not as something we *do*, but as something that *is*.

This distinction is profound. A healthy sense of self, in this view, is not something we fabricate or construct through sheer willpower, dedication, or concentration. It is something that unfolds when we create the conditions for our body, mind, and spirit to rest in their innate unity. In this way, the evolving-self is not self-made; it is nurtured into being through contact with the living ground of unconditional presence.

When positive inner-qualities arise spontaneously, we naturally meet our emotions with openness and a sense of curiosity. This soft, present attention can provide the comfort, support, and spaciousness we need to process emotional pain and move toward greater peace. In this nondual journey, being nurtured (by ourselves, by others, and by the unified ground of existence that exists in both) is what allows us to truly flourish.

How Healing Unfolds in Meditation

In whole-being meditation, we progressively open to the essential ground-of-being, revealing a co-created relational dynamic. It is a meeting of dual and nondual aspects that together create a healing ground of inclusion.

From this perspective, we engage with ourselves and others not just with empathy, but with a deeper sense of inclusion born of our divine entanglement. This marks a paradigm shift: from spiritual control to participation; from detachment to communion in embrace; from distancing to belonging. Whole-being meditation, in this context, becomes a living relational field, between self and Self, impermanence and timelessness, and form and formless. In the whole-being-embrace, awakening is about realizing that these apparently opposing expressions are threads of the same tapestry, inseparable, alive, and endlessly revealing.

Here, we discover that the true ground of freedom is found in embracing life wholly, from the inside out. We discover that the stillness at the core of our being is not found through the dispassion of neutral witnessing, disidentifying from change, or detaching from the world, but exists within the ground from which our most intimate connections grow.

In this stillness, every longing becomes an opening, every wound a doorway, every breath a meeting point between the unchanging and the ever-changing. Here, freedom is found in the courage to turn toward, to meet each moment as part of our self, and to live as if nothing is outside the embrace of wholeness.

When this awakening takes root in the body, it inevitably transforms how we live, create, and relate. Ethics, creativity, and service are no longer imposed ideals but spontaneous expressions of our wholeness. They arise not from moral effort but from attunement to the living intelligence that moves through us. When we rest in oneness, our actions become aligned with the subtle order of life itself. We find ourselves moving in harmony with what supports growth, healing, and balance, within us and around us.

Ethics in this sense is not a set of external rules but an inner resonance, a felt recognition of what nourishes life and what diminishes it. From the stillness of embodied awareness, we intuitively sense when our words or actions move us closer to connection or further into separation. Integrity becomes a natural state, not because we strive to be "good," but because we can feel the discord that comes from acting against our truth.

Creativity, too, is transformed. It ceases to be an act of self-expression driven by the need for recognition and becomes an act of revelation. Through us, the universe explores its own potential. Whether we are writing, painting, teaching, parenting, or tending a garden, creation flows as the movement of unity taking form. The creative impulse is not ours alone. It is the dance of consciousness discovering itself anew through every moment of expression.

From this wholeness also arises *service*, not as obligation, but as love made visible. When we perceive ourselves as part of the same living fabric, compassion naturally becomes action. Helping another is no longer a sacrifice; it is self-care extended outward. We serve not to prove our worth or transcend our humanity, but because the boundaries between "me" and "you" have softened, and what benefits one nourishes all.

To live in this way is to embody the paradox of awakening: to be fully human and fully divine at once. Our flaws, limitations, and vulnerabilities no longer contradict our realization. They complete it. In serving life, we discover that the sacred is not hidden in distant heavens but quietly alive in the everyday gestures of care, courage, and compassion. Wholeness expresses itself not as perfection, but as participation in the ongoing act of love that sustains the world.

As our awareness matures beyond the boundaries of the individual, it begins to sense the greater ground in which all life unfolds. The same wholeness that breathes through our bodies breathes through the body of the planet. The pulse we feel within our own hearts echoes the rhythmic intelligence of forests, oceans, and stars. Awakening is no longer only a personal realization. It becomes *planetary consciousness*, a living recognition that we are participants in the evolution and celebration of life itself.

This expansion of awareness does not require grand gestures. It begins in the quiet recognition that how we live (how we each speak, consume, move, and love) affects the whole. Each act of presence sends ripples through the collective field of consciousness. As we awaken to this, responsibility transforms from a moral burden into a natural expression of care. We become stewards of the same wholeness that sustains us.

The healing that once seemed private now reveals its collective dimension. The patterns of abandonment, invasion, domination, and separation that live within us are the same patterns enacted in our culture, our institutions, and our ecosystems. When we heal our inner divisions (between mind and body, spirit and matter, self and other) we begin to heal the outer ones. Inner work and social transformation are not separate paths but reflections of the same process: consciousness remembering its unity.

Planetary consciousness does not mean losing ourselves in abstraction or dissolving individuality into a cosmic ideal. It means living with a deep awareness that every choice participates in the web of life. It invites us to feel our belonging so fully that compassion becomes instinctive, not as a virtue but as an orientation. We begin to live as though the world were our own body, because, ultimately, it is.

This is the new paradigm of wholeness that our time calls for: not a spirituality that escapes the world, but one that incarnates within it. The Earth itself becomes the temple of awakening. Each ecological, social, and relational crisis becomes a mirror showing us where collective consciousness has fragmented and where love is asking to return. Through this lens, healing the planet and healing ourselves are one and the same gesture. It is an act of remembrance, a homecoming to what has never truly been apart. In the end, awakening is not about reaching a final state or transcending the world. It is about coming home, again and again, to the living wholeness that has always been here.

The journey begins in meditation as an inward turning, a return to the quiet pulse of awareness within the body. It deepens as we learn to meet others from that same presence, allowing relationship to become the crucible where love reveals its depth. And it continues outward, expanding until we feel the rhythm of our own heart beating in harmony with the heart of the world.

Wholeness is not something we create or achieve. It is what we can perceive under the layers of defense, striving, and separation. It holds space for everything, the pain and the joy, the sacred and the mundane, the confusion and the clarity. When we rest in this wholeness, even our struggles become expressions of love seeking to recognize itself. Healing, then, is not the eradication of pain but the integration of all that we are, into the fabric of awareness, the pure perceiving subjectivity that never wavers.

This is the invitation of embodied nonduality: to live as consciousness, not above life but within it; not untouched by the world but deeply touched by it. We discover that enlightenment is not an escape from humanity but its flowering. The divine does not hover above us. It breathes through us, listens through us, reaches through our hands, voices, and eyes.

As this realization ripples through the collective field, a new form of consciousness begins to take root, one that is intimate, ethical, and ecological. It recognizes that every act of awareness is also an act of creation, every gesture of care a restoration of balance in the larger whole. The transformation we seek in the world begins not in systems or doctrines but in the quiet revolution of embodied presence.

We are not striving toward perfection. We are remembering participation. We are remembering that we belong, to ourselves, to one another, to the living Earth, and to the vast intelligence that holds it all. When we live from this remembrance, even our smallest gestures shimmer with meaning. Every breath affirms: *I am home.*

Wholeness, at its heart, is love, an unshakable intimacy with all that is. It holds our joy and our confusion, our longing and our fulfillment, without needing to resolve them. When we rest here, self-love ceases to be self-improvement. It becomes the simple recognition that who we are, in this moment, is already enough. The tenderness we extend inward is not indulgence. It is restoration. It mends the broken threads of belonging within us and between us, until the fabric of life feels whole again.

Here, the journey completes itself. Not in transcendence, but in intimacy. Not in separation, but in love. This is the wholeness that holds us.

To live from this awareness is to remember that we are not separate from the sacred fabric of existence. We are its expression, its movement, its music. Every breath, every touch, every heartbeat is an affirmation of belonging. We are already what we long for: consciousness becoming aware of itself in form, love recognizing itself through relationship, and the universe awakening to its own reflection through our eyes.

Here, at last, we rest, not in detachment or transcendence, but in intimacy with all that is. This is the wholeness that holds us. This is the home we never truly left.

A Paradox Emerges

As a child, we initially relate to a parent as someone whose primary function is to meet our needs and regulate our emotional world (*self-object*). The parent is not yet seen as a separate person but as an extension of our inner life. With healthy development, however, this changes. We gradually come to recognize the parent as a *real other*, a person with their own feelings, needs, and boundaries. Jessica Benjamin emphasized that this recognition of a real other is essential for the development of mutual respect and an authentic relationship. The ability to see the other as separate yet connected lays the foundation for true relational maturity.

A similar dynamic applies to our relationship with unity. When we experience oneness as purely transcendent, it expresses only one side of reality: the pure ground of oneness in which all distinctions dissolve. In this view, there is no true relationship between aspects of existence; everything is seen as an undivided whole. The evolving-self is not regarded as distinct, but as merely an extension or temporary expression of the ultimate reality (Brahman). The apparent difference between the individual and the Absolute is understood as *maya*, an illusion born of ignorance (*avidya*).

As infants, we do not yet see our parents as separate beings. The mother, especially, feels like an extension of our own body and inner life, the source of nourishment, comfort, and being itself. Of course, the infant's merged awareness and the mystic's realization of unity are profoundly different.[15] For the infant, this undifferentiated state is a developmental beginning, a stage before selfhood has fully formed. For the mystic, the transcendent experience is a return, a conscious, mature recognition of the infinite nature of existence beyond the personal self. One is pre-egoic; the other, trans-egoic. Yet both share a structural similarity: in each, the sense of "otherness" temporarily dissolves.

However, when unity is experienced only as transcendence, something essential is overlooked: the sacred role of our evolving-self in emotional and spiritual growth, and the divinity inherent in the ever-changing world of form. In the transcendent state, our humanity can be subtly dismissed. We may overlook the meaning and intelligence of our emotions, sensations, and relationships, treating them as distractions from the divine rather than as inherent expressions of it.

It is only when we awaken to unity that includes relationship (when we can see the other as distinct yet inseparably part of the whole) that we enter the territory of *relational*

---

[15] As Ken Wilber (1980) notes, this has created a long-standing confusion: We sometimes mistake undeveloped, pre-rational states—the undifferentiated experience of infancy—for advanced spiritual awareness, as Wilber says, Jung occasionally did.* Or, like Freud, we may reject genuine spiritual awakening by misinterpreting it as a regression into childish dependency. (*True or not, its an important consideration.)

82

wholeness. This is the essence of what I call whole-self-turiyatita: a state of embodied, inclusive unity that does not deny our evolving-self but embraces it as the living expression of the unchanging. [16]

In much the same way that a child eventually recognizes the parent as a real, separate being while still feeling connected, we too learn to hold both truths -individuality and oneness - within the same field of awareness. In that recognition, spirituality matures. Unity is no longer a retreat from relationship, but a deeper participation in it, an awakening that breathes through the heart of human relationships.

As mentioned, for a child to make the developmental leap of perceiving another as both separate and connected, the parent must embody two essential qualities: *attunement* and *truthfulness.* Attunement is the parent's ability to sensitively mirror and respond to the child's emotions and needs, while truthfulness reflects the parent's willingness to remain authentic and grounded in their own experience. Together, these qualities create a relational field where love is honest, and honesty is loving. A child does not learn emotional differentiation through perfect caregiving but through *real*, attuned relationship, one in which both connection and individuality are respected. Through this, the child learns that they can exist as themselves while remaining in relationship with another who is distinct yet caring.

In the same way, our evolving-self learns to recognize and relate to our unchanging-self as a real and trustworthy presence, one that is both distinct and inseparable. This also requires us to engage in both attunement and truthfulness. Our evolving-self must learn to attune to the unchanging-self, which radiates stability, wisdom, and wholeness. The unchanging-self, in turn,

---

[16] Commonly, the state of *turiyatita*, refers to a level of awakening where even the sense of an "I" who is witnessing disappears. Yet when nondual wholeness is experienced *in and through the body*, a paradox appears. The separation between the witness and what is witnessed dissolves, but we do not lose the ability to perceive their distinct expressions, we remain vividly self-aware.

does not intervene or impose, it simply *is*, offering a ground of truthfulness so complete that our wounds begin to unwind in its presence.

When we hold this internal communion in meditation, we are both the child and the caregiver, both the seeker and the stillness that answers with presence. Within this whole-being-embrace, we maintain an embodied experience of unity while lovingly holding the wounded aspects of our evolving-self, our inner child who still longs for safety and to be seen.

Through this meeting, consciousness becomes aware of itself as the living unity of both, the timeless and the changing, the infinite and the intimate. We awaken to the realization that we are aware *as* wholeness, not simply *of* wholeness. In this sense, unified consciousness is not an object we perceive but the very ground from which perception arises. This is why, in Buddhist traditions, it is often called "self-knowing awareness," a consciousness that recognizes itself without division.

This nondual wholeness rests on principles not rooted in separation, transcendence, or the denial of our evolving-self as an illusion (*mayavada*). Instead, it honors the view that *everything is real (satvada)*: every emotion, sensation, and thought participates in the fabric of being. Liberation, then, is not escape from duality but inclusion of its version of truthfulness; a realization that the sacred and the ordinary, the human and the divine, coexist in mutual embrace. Both perspectives, transcendent and immanent, are true, depending on the vantage point of our unified awareness. This recognition of the state-bound nature of truth invites humility. It reminds us that reality is far too intricate to be captured from a single point of view.

From this broader view, there is no need to dissolve the evolving-self back into its source or treat it as a hindrance to awakening, as some spiritual traditions suggest. When it comes to healing, this is crucial. After the spacious freedom of transcendence has steadied us, true healing requires us to re-enter relationship, to engage with the world and our inner life as real, sacred expressions of being. Recognizing the impermanent reality of our emotions, thoughts, and even dreams allows us to honor the entire human experience as an aspect of the divine unfolding, even as it shifts and changes.

Through whole-being-embrace practice, we become open and receptive to the nuances of our wounds and distortions, not from the standpoint of analysis or control, but from the living awareness that we *are* wholeness itself. From here, the symptoms of emotional injury reveal their deeper meaning; each ache, contraction, and longing becomes a messenger guiding us home. We learn not only to face our pain but to celebrate our aliveness, to discern and delight in the authentic expressions of our evolving-self. In doing so, we rediscover that healing is not a return to perfection, but the full inclusion of everything we are, within the boundless embrace of unity.

Stillness Within the Movement

Everything in life evolves, and relationships are no exception. The whole-being-embrace model recognizes that the relationship between our evolving-self and the unchanging ground of consciousness follows its own natural unfolding. Just as children move through recognizable stages of development, our inner-relationship with oneness matures over time, deepening through cycles of discovery, resistance, opening, and integration.

I believe we are living at a turning point in spiritual evolution. While it can be said that the movement from transcendence toward embodied wholeness is what I personally went through (as described in the introduction to this book), it seems to reflect a broader movement. Humanity's focus is shifting from seeking enlightenment through transcendence to awakening through embodiment. This shift represents the next frontier of growth, both collective and personal. Rather than trying to escape our humanity, we are learning to inhabit it fully, allowing the sacred to be realized within the body, within relationship, and within the ordinary pulse of life itself.

This transition is echoed in the evolution of consciousness described in the great nondual traditions. Spiritual traditions (especially within Hinduism) recognized the *transcendent state* (*turiya*) long before the idea of nondual wholeness (*turiyatita*) arose in more advanced philosophical and tantric schools to describe a subtler level of awakening. This movement reflects not only a historical sequence across all spiritual schools, but a deepening of understanding. It marks a refinement of how reality itself is recognized and lived.

In this refinement, unified consciousness is no longer seen as one "state" among others, but as the ever-present ground from which all states arise. *Turiya* points to the experience of the witness, the silent, observing awareness underlying waking, dreaming, and deep sleep. *Turiyatita*, literally "beyond the fourth," reveals that even this witnessing awareness is not apart from the world it observes. It is the realization that awareness is not a state to be achieved but the essence of existence itself, unchanging, all-pervading, and alive within every experience, even our evolving-self.

In the lived experience of embodied awakening, nondual wholeness (*whole-self-turiyatita*) ceases to be a metaphysical idea and becomes a felt reality. Rather than existing beyond the body, it reveals itself through the body, as the stillness within movement, the spacious awareness within sensation, the unbroken continuity pervading breath and being. In this way, the nondual realization that "awareness is all that is" becomes visceral.

This collective movement from transcendence toward embodied awakening also unfolds individually in our meditation and self-inquiry. The evolution of our personal contemplative practice reflects the evolution of consciousness itself: we pass through three primary stages of how we relate to unified consciousness as we progress from transcendence to whole-being-embrace. These stages are *merging, differentiation, and*

86

reconnection. The journey is both timeless and intimate, an arc that mirrors the greater story of consciousness awakening to its own wholeness.

1. Merging

At first, there is the blissful "honeymoon" phase, when our evolving-self encounters the uninjured, undistorted qualities of oneness. For a time, the two seem to merge, creating an intoxicating sense of unity.

Historically, this has shown up initially as a type of consciousness that was guided by the collective consciousness of tribal societies. Our individual personal identity in relation to others (society) was determined by beliefs about the cosmic nature of the Gods. The intoxicating sense of unity has also shown up as transcendent oneness (turiya). In transcendent oneness, we may feel inseparable from the disembodied pure state where the only true reality is unity. We become convinced that we've found the solution to all suffering. Bliss, clarity, and trust flow naturally, laying a foundation of freedom from our evolving-self's karmic drama.

Yet, this initial fusion has its limits. It can leave us less equipped to wisely navigate relationship interactions in daily life. As Ram Das humorously once said, "If you think you are enlightened, go home [to your parents] for a week." If we want to live in a way that is fully engaged in relationship, sooner or later, emotions we had hoped to transcend resurface, demanding to be witnessed, understood, respected, and loved. Disappointment can set in: *"Wait, why do I still respond this way when I engage in a relationship that is important to me? Where did my bliss go? Why can't I stay in this state when I am not meditating?"* But actually, this is not failure; it is the invitation to deepen, to realize that killing the ego is not the answer.

Here, the next step is to meet suffering and conflict not as illusions or intrusions, but as a doorway to growth. The practice of transcendent oneness prepares us for a deeper, more enduring intimacy, an intimacy that is an authentic expression of what is natural to us before we are injured (pre-trauma). It is here that we discover the possibility of a relationship with life that is resilient, grounded, and endlessly renewing.

2. Differentiation

Reengagement with our evolving-self can stir old fears: "*If I take up space, will I lose love?*" or "*If I share my needs, will I overwhelm others?*" "*If I reveal where I stand and express my personal truth, others will judge and even attack me.*" These anxieties are natural. The task here is to honor our unique personal truth and individuality without severing the bond with our body experience of unified consciousness.

If we persevere through the discomfort of recognizing that transcendence is not all there is, we learn to show up authentically. In our meditation, we enter a new stage of exploration, and the pendulum swings from transcendent unified consciousness back toward a more embodied unity that can be in relationship with our sense of individuality.

Showing up authentically means our evolving-self begins to reassert its voice. We express the personal truth about our friendships, interests, and creative passions that lie deeper than our reactive fears and defenses. This can feel like rediscovering the wise, authentic "I" after a long fusion of transcendent nondual consciousness, beyond all sensory perception, which discounts our emotional life.

We learn that a healthy relationship with any aspect of life is not about simply merging with unity, it's about the balance and mutuality we find in awakening to our whole-self. This provides a broader perspective that translates into a relational life, where we learn to express our desires and aversions in an authentic, rather than habitual, reactive, and defensive way. We increasingly feel supported by a sense of wholeness and unconditional love, free from overwhelm. Our expressions of personal truth begin to

88

spontaneously arise out of the stillness, timelessness, and unconditional love inherent to wholeness.

As we learn to successfully navigate this stage, we gain new clarity and confidence in how we relate to all forms of relationship. We carry the understanding that reflects: *"I know what I feel and who I am outside of being merged, and I choose to be with you."* This stance sets the stage for relating to our own desires and aversions on firmer ground.

Without habit and defense shutting down our authentic, natural perception and expression, we begin to express what feels true for us in the moment. For instance, we express our authentic needs for contact and the autonomy or time apart we need to honor our separate interests. Because we feel more secure due to having a broader perspective that embodies wholeness, we increasingly recognize our authentic desires and aversions are not a threat to intimacy but rather create the opportunity to actually strengthen it.

We begin to accept that some relationships may not work with our newfound authenticity. This can include our relationship with people, situations, beliefs, ideologies, substances like food, or experiences. People may leave, or we may simply let go of them and the situations that no longer serve us. The relationships that remain offer reliable contact that is not imposing, and as a result, become our deepest source of intimacy.

3. Reconnection

From our renewed sense of authenticity, intimacy with what we experience deepens in a new way. There is a sweet "coming home" feeling, the sense of two whole beings (or situations, beliefs, ideologies, or experiences) sharing a journey and falling in love again with greater awareness. Independence and connectedness no longer compete; they coexist. We can lean into connectedness without fear of losing ourselves, and we can honor our truth without fear of disconnection from our essential ground of being.

Conflicts and distress still arise, but they no longer destabilize us as before. We find that we can hold our perspective without being defensive, while respecting the views of others. The sting of abandonment softens; the threat of intrusion loses its edge. Both oneness and the humanity of our unique personal truth are valued. This balance restores safety and passion. Our emotional intimacy grows richer, steadier, more resilient. The relationship with what we experience, whether with another person or within us, feels trustworthy and alive.

Through meditation practice and then in the experiences we have in daily life, we begin to discover that even our fears, the very places we most want to avoid, can be safely held within the luminous embrace of wholeness. Paradoxically, these areas of friction are not barriers to awakening but doorways into transformation. They carry within them the seeds of growth, waiting to unfold when met with presence and wholeness.

Over time, this shifts our perspective on suffering. We no longer view it as the enemy of wholeness but as part of the same fabric of experience. Suffering and wholeness are not opposites; they move together, allowing our evolving-self to be informed and fortified by this relationship. It is precisely in the communion between them that healing and maturation unfold.

The heart of the whole-being-embrace is this: to remain open and authentic, even when our projections surface, even when conflict arises. In the process, we allow our evolving-self to grow as a living subject of experience, not as something we observe from a distance or dissolve into transcendence but met with effortless self-love. In doing so, we integrate unity and individuality, holding them together as an interdependent living truth.

So, to recap, in the "merging" stage of our meditation spiritual journey, we are often swept into oneness, dazzled by its light and the promise of relief it brings. Everything feels simple, whole, and inseparable. In those moments, we rest in the spaciousness of pure awareness, beyond judgment, beyond fear, beyond the turbulence of human feeling. It is peaceful, luminous, and unshakably still. We sense that all is one and that suffering arises only from our identification with the passing waves of experience.

Yet life, in its exquisite wisdom, refuses to let us remain untouched for long. Inevitably, it draws us back into the world of relationship, into the places where we are most human, most vulnerable, and most alive. Relationships are where the real testing happens. They are the crucible in which our realization is tempered into embodied wisdom.

In the quiet of meditation, it may seem easy to rest in equanimity. But when we reenter the complex field of human connection (the subtle negotiations of need, desire, disappointment, and love) our transcendent clarity often collides with the raw texture of emotion. The irritations of daily life (the tender ache of intimacy, the unfinished business of our family of origin) reveal where our realization of wholeness has yet to touch ground.

Complete transcendence, while alluring, becomes untenable in the context of genuine relationship. To remain fully human means to feel, to navigate the ebb and flow of connection and separation, of joy and grief, of closeness and distance. These experiences are not signs of spiritual failure but opportunities for integration. They invite us to bring the stillness of awareness into the storm of relationship, allowing the sacred and the human to meet.

Ultimately, awakening matures not when we go beyond and transcend emotion, but when emotion itself becomes transparent to the wholeness of unified consciousness. Enlightenment is not proven in isolation but in intimacy, in how we love, listen, and remain present when our defenses are tested. True realization is not the absence of difficulty, but the presence of wholeness within it.

It is in this realization that the true work begins. When we dare to remain open to love, to truth, and to change, we discover that the evolving-self's state of separation and defensiveness is not the end of intimacy, but a call for deepening. Authenticity ripens through our willingness to face conflict, and from authenticity, a new union emerges.

This developmental rhythm (merging, differentiating, reconnecting) does not unfold as a circle that closes, but as a spiral that carries us upward. Each turn invites us deeper into the mystery of relationship: the discovery that love is not found in fusion or in escape, but in the living embrace of our whole-self, evolving and unified. Our evolving-self and our unchanging-self meet again and again in the spaciousness of being, weaving a relationship that is both tender and resilient. Here, our ego becomes healthy and is embraced in our wholeness.

This is the sacred marriage of Shakti and Shiva, Shakti as the pulsing, embodied flow of our evolving-self, Shiva as the still ground of unified awareness. Neither is awakened to wholeness without the other. Together, they create the world anew in every moment as a whole-self. Through their embrace, conflict becomes creation, and suffering ripens into wisdom.

What begins as a longing for safety matures into a capacity for presence. What begins as a search for love and autonomy becomes the discovery that both love and freedom are integral to our very nature. In the intimacy of this communion, we do not lose ourselves; we find our wholeness, again and again, as life continues to unfold.

What follows in the chapters ahead is not a doctrine or a distant ideal, but an invitation: to discover the magnetic presence of our unchanging-self in communion with your evolving-self. This living bond will transform how you relate to everything, your body, your emotions, your relationships, and the world.

To understand the whole-being-embrace relationship, we must revisit the fundamental building blocks of any healthy relationship. This involves identifying how our evolving-self forms a bond that is based on participation, mutuality, and reciprocity.

Chapter Four

Coping – How We Learned to Get Along

We will now explore the psychological roots of our deepest relationship injuries, and, just as importantly, what makes for secure, nourishing relationships. Every one of us carries an emotional history shaped by how we were met, or not met, by the people we depended on most. Many of our most persistent struggles can be traced back to two fundamental disruptions: emotional abandonment and experiences of being imposed upon. These are not small injuries. They cut directly into the foundation of our human needs: the need to feel connected, the need to feel seen and validated, and the need to feel sovereignty over our own inner world.

When these foundations are shaken early in life, something essential is threatened. Emotional abandonment and being imposed upon unravel the core belief that we are inherently worthy of love, respect, and safety. And when these messages settle into the nervous system and psyche, they shape not only how we relate to others, but also how we relate to ourselves.

Yet these injuries do not define us. They reveal where healing longs to occur. Understanding the psychological mechanisms behind these wounds becomes one of the first steps in transforming them. By recognizing these injuries, we begin to see how they show up in every aspect of our lives. We begin to understand why vulnerability can feel dangerous, why self-protection becomes habitual, and why emotional intimacy often requires more courage than we expect.

This chapter invites us to look at how early relational injuries form as a result of emotional abandonment and being imposed upon. This way we understand what is needed for them to heal at the deepest levels. Western psychology understands these inclinations as the desire for contact and aversion to contact (Bowlby, Ainsworth, Mahler, Bowen). Eastern spiritual traditions consider desire (*raja*) and aversion (*dvesha*) to be the cause of our suffering. Buddhism says desire (as greed), aversion (as hatred), and delusion (wrong view of reality) are the "three poisons."

These experiences of emotional abandonment and feeling imposed upon have a direct influence on how we try to connect and how we maintain our sense of autonomy in our lives. We struggle when closeness feels imposing or when independence feels like isolation. These early experiences shape how we bond in relationships and how we protect ourselves when we feel threatened or vulnerable.

When we don't feel secure, our nervous system takes over. We fall back on instinctive survival responses (we fight, flee, freeze, or shut down), and we develop knee-jerk habits to help us cope. In relationships, these defensive habits take shape as styles of relating, here called "attachment types." These types, or styles of relating, reflect various automatic or habitual ways of reaching for connection and maintaining a sense of independence in a way that prevents us from feeling unappreciated or controlled.

There are four main attachment types: avoidant, ambivalent, disorganized, and secure. Most of us can see traits of how we relate in more than one type. These ways of relating manifest not only in how we attempt to love others, but also in how we relate to ourselves, to stress, and even to our spiritual life.

Understanding these patterns helps us see why we do what we do, why we push people away when we long for closeness, or why we cling when we fear being left. It also gives us a new lens for understanding what we encounter in meditation. The same dynamics that shape our outer relationships show up in our inner life.

Moreover, the relationship between our evolving self and our unchanging self follows many of the same principles of mutuality and reciprocity found in any healthy human relationship governed by secure attachment. It's how we experience whole-being-embrace, the living union between presence and personality, spirit and evolving-self. As we'll see in later chapters, learning to relate to ourselves and others in ways that honor healthy relationship principles becomes the foundation for healing, growth, and embodied awakening.

Oneness & Separateness at the Same Time

It could be said that both Eastern spirituality and Western psychology begin with the same basic recognition: everything arises from a kind of unity. In Hindu philosophy (especially Advaita Vedanta) this unity is often called Brahman, the ultimate reality, an indivisible whole from which all things emerge. Psychology has its own version of this story. Early psychoanalytic theory proposed that we all begin life in a kind of undivided wholeness, a symbiotic unity with our environment, where no separation between self and other, mother and child, yet exists. From this fused state, we slowly begin to differentiate, to realize, *"I am here, and the world is there."* This is where the sense of "me" begins to take shape.

From here, the paths of spirituality and psychology seem to diverge. In most spiritual traditions, the remedy for human suffering is to return to unity by going beyond and transcending the differentiated sense of self (ego). In contrast, psychology tells us that growth and healing depend on the opposite movement: not merging, but differentiating; not dissolving, but becoming distinct. Through this process of individuation, under the right conditions, we come to terms with our fear of emotional abandonment or of

95

being imposed upon. We learn to skillfully engage and connect as well as separate, and maintain our sense of emotional autonomy.

Whole-being meditation offers another way of seeing things. Instead of choosing between connection and separateness, it invites us to experience both at the same time. In this space, we begin to sense ourselves as a living dialogue between the two, a dynamic communion that becomes the foundation for both spiritual awakening and emotional maturity. It is a dynamic communion even though unified consciousness itself is not responsive by nature. Yet, its presence, quiet, luminous, and whole, naturally begins to inform and heal us from within.

As we shall see in later chapters, the qualities of unified consciousness (such as stillness, timelessness, spaciousness, etc.) naturally support us to overcome our core fear of emotional abandonment or of feeling imposed upon. This forms the foundation from which we grow the ability to skillfully engage and connect, as well as to separate and maintain our sense of emotional autonomy. Out of our sense of wholeness that naturally accompanies a body experience of unified consciousness, we effortlessly and spontaneously express healthy boundaries as essential foundations that make supportive, conscious relationships possible.

The Dance of Becoming

It turns out that psychology's early idea of the infant beginning life in a kind of "undifferentiated unity" isn't quite accurate. We're awake, curious, and responsive from the very start. Even in the womb, and certainly from birth, an infant is already reaching out, responding, and influencing its environment. There's an incredible reciprocity happening. The baby doesn't just emerge from fusion; it co-creates itself through relationship. Every look, every touch, every exchange with the caregiver becomes part of the dance of becoming.

Likewise, healing isn't just about pulling away from symbiosis, nor is it about melting back into it. It's something more alive than either, a relational process, a co-creation between our human, evolving-self and the deeper wholeness that underlies it all. Awakening, in this sense, is not a solo journey but a shared unfolding, an entangled inner relationship that is played out in our daily lives. Wholeness illuminates and steadies our evolving self, while our evolving self gives wholeness a way to express itself in time, through breath, through the details of daily life. Without our participation, unity would remain just an inert potential.

We see the same dynamic in everyday human life. Psychology has taught us that identity isn't something the world stamps onto us, it's something we build together. The caregiver influences the child, yes, but the child also shapes the caregiver. Every cry, every smile, every gesture is part of an ongoing conversation that literally wires the brain for relationship. And this co-creative process doesn't stop when we grow up. As adults, we continue to define ourselves through relationship, by engaging, expressing, setting boundaries, and being changed by the people who influence us.

The same principle applies to our inner life. The evolving self must stay in active relationship with the unchanging-self for the unchanging-self to be aware and for the evolving-self to access a broader perspective. This is a dynamic co-creative process. Stillness doesn't initiate contact, but it provides the ground from which all contact arises. Its quiet presence, its wholeness and luminosity, constantly informs and nourishes us, helping us respond to life with greater clarity and compassion.

From that still ground, something begins to move. Out of stillness and wholeness arise natural impulses to express what is true and alive in us. This is how we grow. In meditation and then throughout the rest of our lives, we learn to stay present and open without losing ourselves, to connect without collapsing, and to love without leaving the body. That balance (between connection and autonomy, between stillness and expression) is where our healing truly begins.

When connection and autonomy work together, we feel both safe and empowered. We can open to others without losing ourselves, and we can stand in our truth without closing our hearts. Finding this balance is one of the most important developmental tasks of a lifetime. When the balance tips too far toward autonomy, we may grow isolated or overly self-reliant, unable to ask for help or truly receive it. When it tips too far toward connection, especially if it means abandoning our own needs or healthy boundaries, we can lose ourselves in others, becoming dependent, enmeshed, or afraid to stand alone. True psychological health grows when we can honor both: our individuality and our ability to genuinely connect.

As children, we're constantly testing how to connect and how to separate. If our parents can attune to that rhythm (supporting us as we explore, comforting us when we return) we do not feel abandoned or imposed upon and develop emotional resilience. We grow up knowing it's safe to be our authentic selves in relationship. But when this early dance of connection and separation is disrupted (through neglect, intrusion, or emotional inconsistency), something fractures inside, and we feel overwhelmed. Our sense of coherence, the feeling that "*I'm okay as I am,*" starts to break down.

As young children, we naturally expect our caregivers to meet our needs completely. When they can't, and especially when they don't support our gradual steps toward independence, emotional injuries begin to form. If it is severe or repeated, it leaves deeper scars, what we might call relationship trauma. These are the wounds that interfere with forming healthy attachments and the ability to bond with the people we care about. They shape how we love, how we trust, and how we feel safe in the world. They become the hidden patterns that whole-being-embrace seeks to heal. We will discuss the different types of relationship wounds according to Attachment theory shortly.

98

Survival Responses

All emotional injuries overwhelm us and cause us to resort to survival responses to what we experience. For clarity, our bodies still rely on primitive, built-in survival responses, fight, flight, freeze, and collapse (also known as fawn or flop), to cope with stress and perceived threats. (I often refer to survival responses as "fragmentation.") When we experienced overwhelm in our body-mind system as a child, later as an adult, similar situations often activate our survival responses as knee-jerk reactions.

For example, the *fight* response might look like snapping at a loved one when stressed, becoming defensive or argumentative when criticized, stomping or slamming doors in frustration, or expressing anger physically, even if not directed at a person. The *flight* response can manifest as avoiding tough conversations by changing the subject or walking away, overworking to sidestep emotional issues, distracting oneself with endless tasks, or feeling restless with constant fidgeting and movement.

The *freeze* response might appear as our mind going blank during a presentation, feeling paralyzed when facing an overwhelming deadline, zoning out or daydreaming excessively, or feeling disconnected from our surroundings. The *collapse* or *fawn* response often shows up as exhaustion and despondency. However, it can also manifest as chronic people-pleasing, where prioritizing others' needs over our own is used to avoid conflict or rejection. This can lead to difficulty setting boundaries, a fear of saying "no," and a tendency to walk on eggshells in relationships. We collapse our self-agency. This can even include agreeing with viewpoints you don't believe, in order to maintain peace.

These survival response patterns vary for each individual, but they share a commonality: they are automatic survival strategies triggered by perceived threats. And here's the thing, they're not flaws. They're our nervous system trying to keep us safe. The problem is that they're operating on outdated wiring. While these reactions are designed to help us in life-threatening situations, they are often triggered by everyday challenges that aren't actually dangerous. What helped us survive as children often hold us back now.

Think of this unresolved survival energy like a river that froze over during a harsh winter. Instead of flowing freely toward the ocean of life, it became locked in ice. These patterns (fight, flight, freeze, and collapse) are like frozen currents in our bodies, beneath the surface, stuck in time.

As a result of how we were inadequately related to as children, our ability to form secure attachments, healthy bonds, and intimacy in relationship can be impeded. It is important to remember that our caregivers, more than likely, did the best they could in responding to us with their own limitations, based on their emotional injuries and the ways they were raised. We are not to blame for the way we learned to cope, and they are not to blame for the way they were raised.

Even though how we were treated is not a true reflection of our beauty, intelligence, and value, generally, we responded to this lack of support by excessively seeking validation, sense of identity, and stability from others. Or, alternatively, we pull away and try to do everything all on our own. Intimacy under these conditions often becomes based on subtle forms of dependency and/or attempts to control others and the unfolding of events.

These survival responses underlie the types of attachment injuries we develop as children. Identifying our primary survival response and the types of attachments we form and what gets in the way of healthy attachment is very helpful. It gives us the clearest understanding of how to tailor our contemplative practices and meditation for our own healing. Plus, understanding our emotional history allows us to step back from the canvas of our life, and establish a perspective that opens the way to compassion for our life's journey. We open the door to aligning with self-love rather than self-judgement.

How We Cope - Types of Attachment

Attachment Theory, first developed by Mary Ainsworth in the 1970s, describes four main styles of bonding that form in early life.

Avoidant Attachment

When we grow up feeling neglected or our caregivers are emotionally unavailable, or dismissive, we often learn (usually without even realizing it) that our needs won't be met. This is what psychology calls avoidant attachment. To protect ourselves, we start to shut down emotionally and rely only on ourselves. By continually pushing others away, we confirm our own fear that no one can be relied upon, reinforcing the very isolation we had hoped to avoid.

As children, we might tell ourselves, *I'm fine on my own. I don't need anyone.* We learn to keep our distance and take pride in our independence. But underneath that independence is often a quiet fear, a fear that if we reach out, we'll be rejected, or imposed upon by being controlled, or hurt again. Closeness starts to feel risky, even dangerous.

Sometimes this pattern develops in homes where parents are imposing. They are intrusive, controlling, critical, smothering, or emotionally needy. To survive, we push down our own emotions and desires (especially our longing for closeness) and start building invisible walls around our hearts. These walls keep us safe, but they also keep us lonely. Our independence lacks the warmth of self-compassion.

As adults, we may appear calm, capable, even self-contained. We can thrive in our work or intellectual life, but when it comes to emotional intimacy, things get complicated. When someone loves us or tries to get close, it can trigger old fears of being smothered or losing control. Without meaning to, we use our bodies as barriers (often by becoming very fit, very thin, or even overweight) anything that creates a buffer of safety.

Inside, though, there's often a quiet ache. We may feel numb or disconnected from our own emotions, unsure how to let someone in. What we long for most, real closeness, can also feel like the very thing that might undo us.

Take, for example, a woman we'll call Maya. Growing up, her parents rarely noticed when she was upset. If she cried, she was told to "toughen up." So Maya learned early that needing anyone only led to disappointment. As an adult, she's successful, admired for her independence and composure. But when her partner reaches for her hand during an argument, she freezes inside. Her mind tells her to soften, to stay, but her body tightens, already preparing to retreat. Maya loves deeply, but closeness still feels like danger. Each time she pulls away, she tells herself she's just needing space. But underneath, she's still that little girl who learned that love could vanish the moment she reached for it.

Ambivalent Attachment

When we grow up with caregiving that's inconsistent (sometimes loving and present, other times distracted or withdrawn) it can leave us feeling deeply uncertain about love. We never quite know what to expect, and that unpredictability shapes how we learn to connect. This often leads to what's called ambivalent attachment.

As children, we may swing between clinging tightly and pushing away. We crave closeness, but we're also terrified it won't last. One moment we're desperate to be held; the next, we're angry or distant. Deep down, we're trying to hold on to love any way we can, afraid that if we let go, it will disappear.

When comfort isn't steady, we sometimes cling to the fantasy of perfect unity, that if we just love hard enough or behave the right way, we'll never be left again. We may attach to objects, ideas, or people who seem to promise that sense of completeness. But as we grow, that same longing can become a haunting ache. No matter how much love or reassurance we receive, it never quite fills the emptiness.

As adults, this pattern can make relationships feel like an emotional rollercoaster. We might overwhelm others with our needs, lose our own center, or blur our boundaries in the hope of feeling secure. When someone we love pulls away or asserts their independence, it can trigger panic, a wave of fear that we're being abandoned all over again. We may react with clinging, pleading, manipulation, or emotional chaos, all in an attempt to keep the sense of connection alive.

At the core, there's a beautiful longing, the longing to be met fully and to know we matter. But until we begin to turn toward that ache with compassion and learn to anchor safety within ourselves, we remain caught in the push and pull between love and fear, closeness and loss.

Take Lena. As a little girl, her mother was affectionate one day and distant the next. Lena never knew which version of her she'd find when she ran into the room. Sometimes her mother would scoop her up with warmth; other times, she'd turn away, lost in her own worries. That uncertainty carved deep grooves of longing and fear into Lena's heart. As an adult, she falls in love quickly and intensely, but every closeness feels fragile. If her partner doesn't respond to a text right away, she spirals into panic, imagining she's being forgotten. She gives more and more of herself, hoping to feel secure, but the more she gives, the emptier she feels. Underneath all the effort is a little girl still reaching for a parent who keeps disappearing, still trying to prove she's worth staying for.

Disorganized Attachment

When our caregivers are frightening, abusive, or unpredictable, something very deep inside us breaks. The person who's supposed to keep us safe becomes the one we fear. This creates an impossible situation. Our instinct is to seek comfort from the very person who causes pain, even at the cost of making ourselves wrong. Out of this confusion, we develop what's called disorganized attachment.

This kind of attachment is marked by an inner tug-of-war: part of us longs for closeness, while another part braces for danger. We may reach out for connection, then pull back just as quickly. We send mixed signals because we're torn between love and fear. On the surface, we might look needy as does someone with anxious attachment, but underneath, we often retreat or shut down like someone who avoids intimacy. Inside, it feels chaotic, as if our heart and body are moving in opposite directions.

Because of this inner conflict, we can become disconnected from our own emotions and body. We start to live "from the neck up," relying on our intellect to manage what feels too overwhelming to feel. We may appear calm, even friendly and engaged, but something about our presence feels slightly distant, as though part of us isn't fully there. It's not intentional; it's a form of self-protection.

Many people with this attachment pattern become experts at fitting in (playing roles, pleasing others, staying functional) while quietly feeling empty or detached inside. Sometimes, large parts of our past go blurry or missing, as if our mind has tucked them away to keep us safe. We may drift off mentally, lose track of time, or feel like we're watching life from the outside. These are gentle signs of dissociation, the nervous system's way of saying, *"This is too much right now."*

Even our spiritual life can become part of this coping. We might use transcendent or mystical experiences to escape the pain of our emotions rather than to integrate them. What begins as a search for peace can turn into another way of leaving the body behind. Yet the real invitation of spirituality, and of healing, is to bring our wholeness back home, to let love and awareness touch even the parts we've hidden away.

Take Jonah, for instance. As a child, his father could be gentle one moment and terrifying the next. Jonah never knew which version he'd get. When his father yelled, Jonah would freeze (heart pounding, breath shallow), but the moment it was over, he'd crawl into his father's lap, desperate for the safety he longed for but never truly felt. Now, as an adult, Jonah craves closeness yet panics when someone gets too near. In relationships, he finds himself clinging one moment and withdrawing the next, confused by his own reactions. He meditates often and talks about feeling "free" during long retreats, but the truth is, part of him uses those spiritual highs to escape the pain still living in his body. Deep down, what he longs for most isn't transcendence, it's to feel safe enough to stay.

Reflections About Insecure Injuries

We've all met people who carry one of these insecure attachment patterns, and, if we're honest, most of us recognize traces of them in ourselves too. Rarely does anyone fit neatly into just one type. We usually carry a mix, a bit of avoidance here, some ambivalence there, and they tend to surface in different ways depending on the relationship or situation.

Studies suggest that nearly half of adults in the U.S. experience some form of insecure attachment. But even that number probably underestimates the truth. Most of us carry subtle, lingering emotional injuries from childhood, moments of being unseen, dismissed, or controlled that left quiet imprints on the way we connect. These experiences might not look like trauma from the outside, but they can make us extra sensitive to rejection or conflict. When life gets stressful, those old wounds can flare up and take the wheel.

Over time, our emotional injuries, and the protective habits that grew around them, become almost invisible to us. They start to feel like *"just who I am."* They shape how we love, how we fight, how we cope, and how we show up, at home, at work, and even in moments of stillness with ourselves.

What once kept us safe as children can limit our capacity for intimacy, flexibility, and authentic connection as adults. When one of these coping styles becomes dominant, it can quietly erode closeness, dulling emotional and sexual intimacy, or creating distance where we most long for warmth, and we blame ourselves.

Sometimes these patterns take new forms: we throw ourselves into work to avoid vulnerability, we numb out through substances or distraction, or we chase spiritual highs to escape emotional discomfort. These strategies may have once been brilliant adaptations to pain, but they can also keep us from the very thing we're longing for, real, embodied connection.

The good news is that these patterns are not all that we are. They're learned ways of surviving. And what's learned can also be unlearned. Through awareness, compassion, and practice, every one of us can begin to form a new kind of attachment: one that feels safe, alive, and whole, both within ourselves and with others.

Secure Attachment

Every now and then, we meet someone who just seems to move through life with an effortless kind of grace, calm, grounded, and open-hearted. It can feel almost like a superpower. What we're really seeing is the quiet strength of secure attachment, the gift that comes from having been loved consistently, attuned to, and emotionally supported early in life. When we've grown up with that kind of steady care, we naturally tend to trust others, feel worthy of love, and stay comfortable with both closeness and independence.

People with secure attachment usually carry a deep, steady *trust*, in themselves, in others, and in life. That trust makes it easier to form and sustain healthy relationships, whether in love, friendship, or family. For example, imagine two partners having a disagreement. Instead of shutting down or lashing out, a securely attached person might say, *"I'm feeling hurt, but I want to talk about it."* There's no need for drama or retreat, just a natural confidence that the relationship can hold both love and conflict.

Because we learned early on that our emotions were safe to express, we become better at handling them later in life. Our caregivers helped us soothe big feelings, so as adults, we're more able to manage stress, face challenges, and stay balanced even when things get tough. This calm, steady core is what psychologists call "emotional resilience," the ability to bend without breaking.

Secure attachment gives us this resilience not only through trust in others, but also through what's called a "secure base," that inner sense of safety that allows us to explore, take risks, and engage fully with life. Knowing we have both internal stability and people we can turn to, we're more willing to step into the unknown, to try new things, and to recover when life doesn't go as planned.

When our caregivers were attuned to us, they didn't just meet our needs; they modeled how to recognize, understand, and respond to emotions, both our own and others'. That early emotional resonance becomes empathy. Over time, it ripens into emotional intelligence, the quiet wisdom that helps us navigate life with compassion and clarity.

At its heart, secure attachment shapes how we see the world. We come to expect kindness instead of betrayal, reciprocity instead of rejection, and care instead of harm. And this worldview changes everything. It lets us move through life with a quiet confidence, a knowing that connection isn't something to fear, but one of the safest and most nourishing places we can rest.

Now consider Daniel. As a child, his parents weren't perfect, but they were steady. When he was scared, someone was there. When he made mistakes, he was guided rather than shamed. He learned early that love doesn't vanish when things get hard. As an adult, Daniel carries that quiet assurance into his relationships. When conflict arises, he can stay grounded, listening, speaking honestly, and repairing rather than retreating. He trusts that love can survive imperfection. When his partner needs space, he doesn't panic; when she reaches for closeness, he welcomes it. There's a natural rhythm in the way he connects, secure but not clinging, open but not overly exposed. What others experience as "ease" in him is really the deep, embodied knowing that love, at its core, is safe to return to.

Whole-Being-Embrace in Action

Each of these attachment styles tells a story, not of weakness, but of adaptation. They reveal the creative ways we learned to survive when love felt uncertain. Whether we pulled away like Maya, clung like Lena, or froze like Jonah, each pattern began as an intelligent response to our earliest environment. But these old strategies were built for safety, not for joy. As adults, they can keep us locked inside the very walls we built to protect ourselves.

Whole-being-embrace offers us a way to soften those walls without tearing them down. By bringing the steadiness of our unchanging-self into relationship with the vulnerability of our evolving-self, we begin to create the inner conditions of secure attachment, from within. It's as if we finally become the loving, attuned presence we always needed. In this meeting, our defenses start to relax. The avoidant heart learns that closeness doesn't mean loss. The anxious one learns that love can stay. The disorganized one discovers safety in stillness. Slowly, we realize that security isn't something another person gives us. It's something that grows naturally when we learn to meet ourselves with tenderness, patience, and truth.

The experience of secure attachment gives us a living blueprint for what real healing, and awakening, can feel like inside. Just as a child learns to trust the steady love of a caregiver, our evolving-self can begin to trust the quiet, unwavering presence of our unchanging-self. This inner bond mirrors the same qualities that make external relationships feel safe and nurturing: consistency, responsiveness, and attunement.

As we cultivate this inner relationship, something shifts. We begin to feel that no matter what arises, fear, shame, sadness, or joy, there is a part of us that will not turn away. We can fall apart and still be held. We can grieve and still belong. The recognition that we have an inner presence that never leaves brings a freedom deeper than transcendence. It is the heart of whole-being-embrace: the meeting of presence and personality, where our humanness and our divinity are no longer in conflict but in loving dialogue with one another.

Whole-being-embrace also begins to rebuild our trust, not only in ourselves, but in life and relationship. It's a process of learning to listen again to the quiet intelligence of the body, to the subtle messages that arise in sensation, tension, and emotion. These signals aren't problems to fix or distractions from awakening; they are living messengers of truth. Our body speaks the language of our history, the echoes of what we've longed for, feared, and endured.

At first, these messages can feel confusing or even misleading. They are colored by the very patterns we're trying to heal, our fixations, distortions, and projections. A tightening in the chest may carry both the memory of fear and the longing for safety. A heaviness in the belly might hold grief and protection at once. The body doesn't lie, but it also doesn't speak in simple

109

sentences. It reveals our wounding in layers, blending truth and imagination, tenderness and defense, until we learn to listen with the heart as much as with the mind.

Through whole-being-embrace, we begin to meet these sensations with curiosity instead of resistance. Rather than overriding the body with analysis or spiritual ideals, we drop beneath the story into direct experience. We learn to feel what is actually here, the tremble beneath the anger, the ache behind the numbness, the yearning woven through the fear. Bit by bit, this practice restores our faith in the body's wisdom. We discover that beneath every contraction, numbness, and collapse lies intelligence, the body's attempt to protect us, to keep us safe, to communicate where love still needs to reach.

As we listen more deeply, the body becomes less of a battlefield and more of a trusted ally. It starts to feel like home again, not as something to control or transcend, disidentify from, or relate to with dispassion, but as a living, breathing expression of our wholeness.

When unified consciousness becomes a body experience, our body starts to inform our mind. It offers a broader, more grounded perspective. One that says, "*You are safe. You belong. You are held by something larger than your fear.*" In this trust, we find a new kind of safety, one not dependent on outer circumstances, but arising from the simple knowing that whatever we feel, we can stay present with it. Our sensations become a compass, guiding us toward greater wholeness, reminding us that even our pain belongs to love's unfolding.

From this perspective, we begin to sense a secure base within, an uninjured, unbreakable part of us that never disappears. It's always here, quietly radiant, offering the unconditional love and support we once looked for outside ourselves. Our evolving-self feels this as safety and encouragement, an invitation to explore, to express, to take risks, to be authentic. Knowing that this inner haven of wholeness is always available, even in moments of pain or uncertainty, supports us to communicate our truth and set healthy boundaries in relationship.

In this way, spiritual awakening becomes inseparable from relationship. Our inner wholeness supports how we show up with others, and our relationships, in turn, become part of our path of awakening. Every moment of connection, every rupture and repair, every act of honest communication becomes a sacred practice. Through these interactions, unified consciousness doesn't just remain an inner state, it increasingly becomes embodied and self-aware through us, a living expression of the cosmos discovering itself in human form in all its variations.

We may gain access to a body experience of oneness fairly quickly. Yet, whole-being-embrace isn't something we achieve once and then hold on to. It's something we live, moment by moment, breath by breath. It's how awakening begins to express itself through relationship, through the ordinary, intimate ways we meet life. It's the gentle art of allowing our evolving, human self to stay in conscious relationship with the unchanging, luminous ground of our being.

In practice, this means learning to stay present with what arises (our fears, our longings, our defenses) while sensing the wholeness that holds it all. When we can include everything we feel without pushing it away or getting lost in it, our relationship to pain begins to change. What once felt unbearable becomes workable, even sacred. Our emotions stop being problems to solve and become pathways back to connection.

Whole-being-embrace invites us to bring awakened qualities such as stillness, spaciousness, and love into the way we relate, with ourselves, with others, and with life itself. Every moment of contact becomes a chance to practice mutual attunement between our evolving-self and our unchanging-self. We start to recognize that every person we meet carries the same two dimensions, a tender, evolving self and a quiet, unchanging essence beneath it. Seeing this brings patience where there used to be judgment, empathy where there used to be fear. Relationship

111

becomes a mirror through which the universe learns to love itself more completely.

When we bring the same loving awareness to our relationships that we bring to our inner life, even conflict becomes sacred. Disagreements, disappointments, and misunderstandings stop being signs of failure and become opportunities for deeper connection. The question shifts from *"How can I avoid pain?"* to *"How can I stay open to love even here?"*

Over time, this practice of whole-being-embrace begins to soften the boundaries between the sacred and the ordinary. Washing dishes, listening to a friend, sitting in silence, all become acts of participation in the great unfolding of consciousness. Healing ceases to be a private project and becomes a shared field of transformation. In each moment of genuine presence, our body, our relationships, and our awareness begin to resonate as one unified expression of being.

When we approach our emotional life through the lens of whole-being-embrace, healing becomes less about fixing and more about transforming. What once felt broken begins to reveal itself as the raw material of awakening. Each emotional injury (the shame, the anger, the grief we've carried) holds a fragment of energy that has been split off from the whole. When we meet these wounded parts with the steady presence of our unchanging-self, something extraordinary happens: the pain begins to unfold back into its original essence. Fear softens into alertness, anger into clarity, grief into love. This is the alchemy of relationship, the transformation of contraction into connection, of fragmentation into wholeness.

Whole-being-embrace allows us to experience emotion as energy in motion set free to move authentically. We recognize our evolving-self's emotion, *"I am angry,"* instead as anger moving through our body and mind. We may feel, *"I am broken,"* and we understand "something in me is calling to be held." This subtle shift changes everything. Our evolving-self becomes free to express, release, and grow, while our unchanging-self provides the container of infinite acceptance in which it all takes place.

Through this alchemy, relationship becomes more than an exchange between two separate beings. It becomes a living expression of evolution, a place where the universe awakens to itself through the meeting of hearts. The pain that once kept us guarded turns into compassion; the distance that once felt unbearable becomes space for freedom.

And slowly, we discover that love is not something we have to seek. It is our essence.

Chapter Five:

Allies & Enemies

The Good Intentions Behind Ego

Our ego and personal identity (the part of us that feels separate, unique, reactive, full of desires and aversions) is not inherently a problem. What matters is not that we have an ego, but *how we relate to it*. One of the most healing shifts we can make is to recognize the ego's underlying innocence. The limiting choices, defenses, and behaviors we developed were never rooted in malice, stupidity, or selfishness. They arose as instinctive responses to the ways we were met (or not met) early in life. They formed because we lacked the support, guidance, or emotional safety we needed to make healthier choices. Our ego simply stepped in to help us survive, to guard our hearts, to hold on to whatever love and belonging we could find.

Beneath the fears shaped by injury (beneath the habits, sensitivities, and reactive patterns that now cause us trouble) lives a person who has always been trying to do their best with what they had. A person whose intentions are fundamentally good, waiting to be met not with judgment but with compassion. Compassion does not let us avoid accountability; rather, it gives us the respect and love we needed all along to face ourselves honestly. When understood this way, even our most frustrating ego fixations reveal their true origin: they are misguided but heartfelt attempts to protect the wounded inner child who once had no other options.

Yes, ego patterns often express themselves through projections, outdated beliefs, and automatic emotional or bodily reactions that limit our potential. But beneath them is a simple truth: their original purpose was to protect us from pain. Overeating may be an effort to soothe emptiness; withdrawal may be an attempt to avoid the terror of rejection; anger may be a shield guarding a tender, unmet need. When we sabotage our own growth, it is not because we are broken, shameful, or unworthy. It is because our ego, shaped by its earliest lessons, is trying, however imperfectly, to keep us safe.

Healing deepens when we honor this original intention rather than condemn it. When we recognize the innocence beneath our defenses, space opens for transformation. And in that space, the tender places inside us can finally receive what they have always longed for: understanding, safety, and love.

Respecting Our Ego's Fears and Fixations

Every one of us carries sensitivities shaped by the fear of being emotionally hurt. These sensitivities may manifest as a fear of disappointing others, being abandoned or unappreciated, or being criticized, controlled, or imposed upon. Because of these fears, we are more easily triggered by present experiences that echo past wounds, and when this happens, we often fall back into outdated survival patterns and reactions.

These sensitivities are not meaningless obstacles; they are signposts. Our fear-based habitual sensitivities give rise to specific desires and aversions, and together these point directly to the areas that most need healing. Healing is facilitated by listening carefully to these fears, desires, and aversions, not as a detached observer and not by dismissing them as illusions, but by respecting them in a way that we always wished our parents, or the people we care about most, would have. Listening to our fear-based habitual sensitivities may be intense and can reinjure us.

Deep listening becomes possible when we awaken to our unchanging-self's presence of wholeness. When we feel as if we exist as this ground of being, we can stay present with our sensitivities without being consumed by them. Wholeness protects us from being overwhelmed by the storm of thoughts and emotions that so often perpetuate fear through a vicious cycle of negative interpretations, physical tension, and survival responses. Left unchecked, these thought patterns reinforce our tendency to anticipate the worst, fixate on what is negative, and mistake feelings for unshakable facts.

In the presence of our unchanging-self, however, something shifts. Our fears, desires, and aversions still arise, but, increasingly, we no longer have to grasp them or succumb to our habitual reactions. Attuning to the ground of being brings us subtle sensory qualities of oneness that nurture the nervous system and broaden our perspective held hostage by fear. From this expanded awareness, we discover more freedom of choice. We can listen with authenticity rather than defensiveness. By listening while embodied as wholeness, we begin to understand how these patterns were once healthy adaptations and how they now guide us toward what we most need to heal.

When we listen to our sensitivities in this way, they become allies rather than enemies. They show us how to respond authentically to our desires and aversions, breaking free from automatic, habitual reactions.

Fragmentation as a Body Experience

Emotional injury isn't just something that lives in the mind, it lives in the body also. It shapes the way we feel, how we move, and how we meet the world. This is why bringing awareness to the body during meditation is so essential for healing. When we pay attention to what's happening inside (the tightness in the chest, the heaviness in the shoulders, the knot in the stomach) we begin to see that these sensations aren't random. They're the body's way of speaking, of harboring what was once too painful or overwhelming to feel.

When we learn to tune-in to our body and listen, something begins to change. Instead of keeping our pain buried, the body shows us how to release it, gently, piece by piece. In the embrace of wholeness, old stress and trauma start to surface in a way we can actually manage. What once felt like chaos becomes a conversation.

Our body doesn't just hold our wounds; it also holds our story, the story of who we are. Long before we had words, our body was teaching us how to relate to the world. As psychologist Daniel Stern described, a child's earliest sense of "core relatedness" forms through the body, through movement, touch, and feeling. Those early sensations of being seen, held, and understood (or not) become the building blocks of our sense of self.

When our caregivers misread us (when they overlook, overstep, or misjudge our needs) we start to feel unseen, unheard, or undervalued. To protect ourselves, we pull away, push away, or reach out. The nervous system tightens, the tissues contract, the breath shortens. Awareness retracts from the body as if saying, *"This is too much."* Over time, that survival response becomes habit. We lose the sense of coherence that once helped us feel whole. The self begins to "fragment," so our physical, emotional, and mental life stops communicating constructively to each other. Like Humpy Dumpty, we wonder why we can't quite put ourselves back together again. We also often blame ourselves for feeling unseen, undervalued, and having needs.

Our body's experience of unified consciousness doesn't just reveal the ways we fragment or fall apart; it also shows us what truth *feels* like. Healing through the body begins in that quiet meeting place between our pain and our wholeness. When the sensations of fragmentation (the tightness, the emptiness, the ache) meet the stillness of oneness, something inside us begins to soften. We start to settle. The body lets go, and a subtle openness emerges, one that carries the unmistakable feeling of innocence, goodness, and unbroken wholeness. These moments remind us that even in our deepest wounds, there is something within us that has never been harmed.

As this presence deepens, the body begins to remember its original harmony. The stillness and openness of unified consciousness help us feel into the many layers of our experience, showing us which feelings come from old fears and which arise from our authentic truth in the moment. We begin to sense, in a deeply embodied way, what personal truth and wisdom actually *feel* like before we've had a chance to censor or edit it.

With practice, we learn to recognize the difference between emotions born from survival responses and those that express our genuine emotions and desires, our personal truth in the moment. We discern the deeper truth from our inner self-critical voice that is a result of internalizing how we were related to. We recognize that our habitual fears were learned early. Over time, we begin to treat ourselves the way others once treated us. Recognizing the difference between our adopted inner critic and our authentic personal truth reconnects us with our inner compass. As we become familiar with this dynamic, the inner critic naturally falls away. It helps us know what we truly need to stay grounded and autonomous in relationship, what feels right, what doesn't, and what boundaries we need to feel safe, supported, and cared for. This is the foundation of true self-care and the heart of any healthy connection (discussed more in the next chapter).

118

Equally important is recognizing when we've lost touch with that truth. Every time we notice this disconnection, it points to a place inside that still needs tenderness and healing. These moments are not failures; they're invitations to come home to ourselves.

It's helpful to become familiar with what happens when we're overwhelmed and fearful, to notice which survival response we tend to slip into. Each response shapes how we relate, how we reach for contact or try to maintain our autonomy. These patterns, often rooted in our attachment style, reveal how we lose touch with our inner compass of personal truth and with the wisdom of our body.

A simple way to understand this is by noticing where our attention goes in relationship. In every new connection, we face the same quiet question: *How open can I be without losing myself? How true can I be without losing their love?* We long for closeness but fear being hurt. We crave space to express what feels true for us, but feel lonely when we take it. As a result, some of us focus inward, guarding our inner world and tuning others out. Others of us focus outward, losing ourselves in other people's needs while neglecting our own.

These expressions of where our attention goes in relationship when we feel distressed are just two of the many ways we dissociate in response to overwhelm and fear. The overwhelm and fear at the core of chronic emotional injuries are closely tied to hypervigilance. We tend to interpret ordinary situations as threatening and to live with heightened negative emotion. Even when we try to "not care" by numbing out or avoiding our feelings, the anxious system underneath remains switched on. This constant internal alertness is exhausting. It drains us through coping mechanisms like zoning out, shutting down, or masking irritability. The brain stays primed for danger, so even subtle cues can trigger strong reactions. It can feel as if we're always on guard, even when we're doing everything we can to ignore it.

Injury, Selfhood, and the Loss of Inner Guidance

Both psychology and yoga point to the same core truth: when we carry old emotional wounds, our attention instinctively turns outward—even when we appear self-focused, withdrawn, or indifferent. Patanjali, the sage of classical yoga, recognized this pattern thousands of years ago. He called it "externalization" (*vyuthana*): a state in which awareness is pulled away from the inner center of unity and governed by impressions, reactions, and the pressures of the outside world. Meditation is the gentle reversal of this pull. It invites us back home to ourselves, back to the quiet stability and intimate presence of wholeness.

Psychology describes this same pattern in a different language. When we've been hurt, abandoned, overwhelmed, or controlled, we learn to scan the world for cues about who we are, whether we're safe, and whether we're worthy of love. Or we protect ourselves by going numb, avoiding what hurts, or slipping into emotional shutdown ("fawn" survival response) that trades authenticity for safety. When we've felt invaded, we may withdraw or harden, but these reactions often arise not from true self-connection, but from injury's instinctive attempt to shield us.

Old wounds distort perception. Our sensitivities cause us to overlay the present moment with interpretations from the past, and we become hypervigilant. Hypervigilance keeps our awareness turned outward, reacting to everything around us rather than responding from the quiet strength of inner truth and embodied wholeness.

When the only place we know how to feel safe, connected, or spiritually uplifted is through something external (a teacher, a community, a partner, a guru) we may become dependent on those sources to feel whole. These relationships can offer profound support, but if we rely on them exclusively, our evolving-self remains vulnerable, disconnected from its true ground of being. On the spiritual path this can quietly turn into a belief that wholeness must be earned, borrowed, or downloaded from outside ourselves.

The more emotional injury we carry, the more likely it is that our inner critic rages, our attention scans outward for danger, or we chase approval, success, or identity in hopes of filling the emptiness within. These tendencies take many forms (people-pleasing, overachievement, spiritual bypassing, or even a polished confidence masking deep insecurity) but beneath them lies the same wound: the loss of inner referencing.

These outward-oriented habits become so woven into daily life that we often don't notice them. They shape how we choose, relate, work, worship, and love. They influence how we measure our worth and interpret every interaction. Yet bringing these patterns into awareness is profoundly liberating. When we recognize that emotional injury pushes us outward (in defense, in longing, in search of identity) we begin to understand what true healing and authentic spiritual awakening actually ask of us: a return to the place within where our evolving-self reconnects with the unchanging ground of being that has never left us.

It seems to me that one of the ways this external orientation shows up in many spiritual communities is through an overemphasis on external deities or higher powers. In devotional and theistic traditions, this may take the form of turning toward a God "out there" for protection, worthiness, or direction. While such devotion can be deeply meaningful, it can also become a subtle psychological coping mechanism, a way to look outward for what we are afraid to face inwardly. It may soothe us, but it can also distract us from the deeper work of introspection, emotional healing, and cultivating an inner sense of agency.

A similar outward orientation appears even within nondual traditions, not through divine figures, but through the emphasis on the "non-local," infinite, or boundless nature of consciousness. In Advaita Vedanta, for example, practitioners are often encouraged to turn attention toward *Brahman* as an expansive, all-pervading awareness. In Dzogchen, the *rigpa* teachings describe awareness as open, vast, spacious, and beyond form. These descriptions are accurate and profound, but for many practitioners carrying unresolved emotional injury, the emphasis on expansiveness can inadvertently reinforce the habit of seeking the divine by *leaving the body* rather than inhabiting it.

In other words, even when God or awareness is described as immanent, the teaching style can subtly direct practitioners to look outward into infinite space rather than inward toward embodied experience. Unity becomes something "upward," "outward," or "beyond," rather than something also discovered in the heart, belly, breath, and the relational field of one's own life. The body becomes merely a vehicle to transcend instead of a temple that reveals the divine in form.

When unity is framed primarily as vastness or unbounded awareness, practitioners may accidentally reenact trauma-driven strategies, dissociation, emotional detachment, or over-reliance on transcendence for safety. What begins as a spiritual aspiration can become an unconscious avoidance pattern: a way to bypass the tender, vulnerable places within.

Some spiritual traditions, however, have always held a deeper truth: the divine is both non-local and intimately local, both infinite and embodied, both everywhere and right here within us. Recognizing a "divine spark," inner Buddha-nature, or *Atman* within oneself is not merely a philosophical idea but a profound psychological healing principle. When we locate the sacred both inside, we reclaim personal responsibility, deepen emotional maturity, and rediscover our own inherent worth.

If a deity or pure awareness is truly universal, then it lives *within* the contours of our body, our nervous system, our emotional life, not only in the vast sky of consciousness but also in the small, trembling truths we carry in our chest. Yet when we look exclusively upward or outward (toward saints, gurus, spaciousness, or abstraction), we avoid the very place where transformation must happen: within our own embodied humanity.

From a psychological perspective, trauma often orients us externally in our search for danger and safety. If a person's inner landscape feels unstable, overwhelming, or untrustworthy, they naturally look outward for something to hold onto. Thus, a concept of God or nondual awareness that is exclusively external or disembodied can unintentionally reinforce this outward focus. The person may continue seeking salvation, stability, or identity outside themselves, never learning how to cultivate internal safety, inner attunement and wholeness.

Conversely, many wisdom traditions (like Dzogchen's assertion that *rigpa* is self-existing within each being, Tantra's embrace of the body as divine) teach that the sacred is simultaneously internal and external. This perspective supports trauma healing by helping individuals integrate their inner experience with their outer world, gradually fostering a sense of internal safety, agency, and belonging.

Spiritual beliefs that encourage introspection and inward contact, alongside reverence for the universal, tend to support healing more effectively than those that rely solely on external sources of guidance or salvation. Ultimately, how these beliefs shape a person's healing journey is deeply individual, influenced by doctrine, personal history, and one's evolving relationship with both the transcendent and the embodied self.

Filling the "Hole"

In conclusion, when we grow up without healthy and accurate mirroring, our feelings go unvalidated. Over time, we learn to doubt what our own senses are telling us. We lose touch with the personal truth of what we genuinely feel and instead become overly oriented toward the outside world, shaped by the attitudes, values, and expectations of parents, peers, culture, religion, and spirituality. Without a clear inner home-base, a grounded sense of identity, authenticity withers. Our perception narrows, our senses distort, and we begin to cling to secondary substitutes and rigid habits of mind and body that, in the end, undermine our well-being. Our suffering deepens.

When we depend too heavily on external guidance and approval, we drift further from our own inner personal truth and wisdom. The authentic self and our natural sense of simply "being" are lost, leaving a painful inner sense of deficiency. This hollow feeling, described by A.H. Almaas as a "hole," becomes the quiet driver of many of our protective behaviors and coping strategies. We search endlessly for ways to fill it (with achievements, relationships, approval, possessions, substances, food, spiritual status), but these never fully satisfy. We not only lose the steady ground of our being, but also the ability to sense what is truly right for us.

Without the self that knows how to rest in being and to trust what it authentically feels, our capacity for deep connection, both with ourselves and with others, fades. Along with that loss, autonomy and self-worth diminish. In their place, the fear-based ego steps in, attempting to mimic the qualities of authenticity and wholeness. Yet this imitation is always fragile, never able to replace the lived reality of being whole, present, and real, and the freedom and safety that accompany it.

And yet, we are never truly cut off from the possibility of return. The frameworks that shaped us, however limiting, do not have to define us forever. With the right support, we can grow through them and beyond them. We can learn to discern, moment by moment, when we are outsourcing our inner authority and when we are resting in our own direct experience and personal truth. Healing and awakening mean restoring this balance, coming home to our embodied wholeness and wisdom, while still honoring the nourishing roles that family, community, and spiritual traditions can play in our lives.

Chapter Six

Personal Truth & Wisdom

What is Personal Truth?

In the whole-being-embrace approach, the ultimate destination of emotional maturity is not simply a return to a state of wholeness. Rather, it is discovering our evolving-self's authenticity in embrace with the wholeness of our unchanging-self. Our authenticity is a reflection of our personal truth. But what does personal truth really mean?

Our ability to consciously discern when we are externally oriented and outsourcing our guidance, and when we are connected to our own inner experience and personal truth is important. But how can it serve as a guide if it is influenced by our painful memories and associated projections?

Personal truth I speak of is the subjective, intimate, embodied knowing that rises from the deepest layers of our lived experience. It is not an opinion, a belief we inherited, or a conclusion we reach through logic. Nor is it something that requires validation or agreement from anyone else. Personal truth is the quiet resonance inside us, the sense of *"yes, this is real for me"* that emerges when we listen beneath fear, beneath habit, beneath the noise of expectation.

Unlike emotions or moods shaped by old wounds or conditioned reactions, personal truth arises from a deeper place. It is informed by the wisdom carried in our body, the subtle intelligence of our emotions, and the meaning we have gathered through our relationships and challenges. Personal truth shows us what brings us safety, what nourishes us, what matters, and what feels aligned with who we are becoming.

When we live from this place, our past no longer dictates or distorts our choices. Instead of being limited or sabotaged by memories of old injuries, we become empowered to draw from them, to see what they needed, what they were protecting, and what they now ask of us. Our history becomes a source of clarity rather than confusion, a guide for setting boundaries, choosing relationships, and orienting ourselves toward what is genuinely supportive and fulfilling.

In this way, personal truth is not static. It is dynamic and changes depending on our circumstances. This process is not about finding *the* truth, but about finding *your* truth in each moment, a truth that supports your integrity and aligns your actions with your genuine inner experience. It is a living compass, deeply felt, quietly steady, helping us meet each moment with integrity, self-trust.

Honoring personal truth in this way strengthens our capacity to live authentically. Over time, listening to and trusting our personal truth deepens our self-connection, emotional resilience, and ability to engage life from a place of grounded authenticity and a growing sense of inner freedom.

In meditation, our felt-sense offers direct, non-verbal communication from the body, often bypassing the mind's tendency to rationalize or override deeper knowing. Unlike fleeting emotions, the felt sense of personal truth is a nuanced experience that requires gentle, focused attention to fully perceive and discern.

When we own our personal truth, we also recognize and validate our own self-worth. This is what happens in the body,

126

when we come to an inner truth through subtle attunement, it resonates clearly as self-empowerment and self-love. A resounding "Yes" arises within us as we recognize what feels true for us in the moment. This is becoming increasingly important in this new landscape when technology is accelerating around us. Artificial intelligence (AI) and the digital world quicken thought, bend attention, and whisper suggestions into the quiet chambers of our minds.

Technologies such as AI don't only outthink us but often amplify the places where we are already divided. They potentially intensify our unhealed injuries, accelerate our impulses, algorithmically replicate our fears, and globalize our confusion. Moreover, machines can sense our fears before we name them, anticipate our desires before we feel them, and mirror our vulnerabilities so convincingly that we begin to forget which longings are ours and which were planted in us.

In such an age, the question is no longer simply how intelligent machines will become, but whether we remain intimate with our own inner life and what feels personally true. Its found in the texture of our own emotions and the sound and rhythm of our own truth.

Discerning this through whole-being-embrace becomes not just a spiritual practice but a form of cultural medicine, a way of remembering ourselves in a world increasingly designed to pull us outward in search of a reality check (if not through culture, through trauma).

When we learn to rest in the unified ground of being, our inner authority grounded in what feels genuinely true begins to return. We can feel, with unmistakable clarity, the difference between what arises authentically within us and what has been nudged, shaped, or amplified by external forces. We sense our emotions not as illusions or buttons to be pressed but as signals to be honored. We become unhackable, not because we resist the world, but because we are rooted in something deeper than what lies on the surface. In this way, we restore fundamental trust in our body, our emotional life, and the existence of unified consciousness as a dimension of who we are. The whole-self comes alive.

As we grow more intimate with our interiority, we rediscover qualities that are essential for our recovery: steadiness that cannot be sped up, tenderness that cannot be optimized, intuition that does not fit inside an algorithm. Our nervous system, once fractured by noise and urgency, settles. And from this settling, a new kind of perception emerges, one capable of discerning truth from "alternate truth," authenticity from stimulus, and connection from simulation.

When we attune to our whole-self, we access a deeper understanding that enables us to process unresolved emotions, heal trauma stored in the body, and develop a more intimate relationship with ourselves. This naturally cultivates the inner support we need to express our healthy authentic relationship boundaries in a non-defensive way. It empowers us to make decisions and form relationships that are guided by inner alignment rather than external expectations or fear-based patterns.

While personal truth can contain wisdom, wisdom is a deeper perception of discernment and inner guidance that includes intuition and clairvoyance.

Wisdom

One important source of support that often goes unacknowledged is the guidance we receive from our inner wisdom. Psychology often views wisdom as simply a byproduct of the physical, emotional, and cognitive processes (a natural outcome of life experience), without recognizing it as a distinct developmental stage or a fundamental dimension of self. Some more recent psychological perspectives are beginning to expand this view.[17] When we refine our senses in meditation, we recognize two crucial additional layers of self: wisdom and bliss.[18] In spiritual traditions, wisdom and bliss are seen as more subtle, intrinsic parts of our being.

According to yoga principles, our human experience unfolds through five interconnected layers or sheaths of consciousness that can be considered to be aspects of self: the physical layer (*anna kosha*), energy layer (*prana kosha*), mental-emotional layer (*mano kosha*), wisdom layer (*vijnana kosha*), and bliss layer (*ananda kosha*). Within this framework, wisdom, the *wise-self*, is not merely the product of accumulated knowledge, but a distinct experience of our being that integrates our evolving personal truth with the timeless awareness of our unchanging self.[19]

Wisdom has the distinct nature of arising from both dual and nondual dimensions of existence. Depending on our conditioning, tendencies, and capacity, some of us draw more heavily from the evolving-self's learned personal truth to access wisdom. Others may intuitively access the direct knowing that emerges from unified consciousness. Wisdom can appear as insight that arises from our mental, emotional, and intuitive processes, but it can also guide us toward deeper access to the unified, nondual dimension of our being.

When our wounded inner child comes into contact with the wise-self, a profound sense of support emerges. Accessing this

---

[17] Psychotherapist Marianne Bentzen describes the culmination of human development in terms of embodied wisdom, suggesting that wisdom is not just a cognitive process but a fully integrated expression of our developmental potential.

[18] This differs from the bliss of transcendent nondual awareness, which arises from experiencing the infinite beyond body or self (*nirguna Brahman*). The bliss of embodied nondual consciousness (*saguna Brahman*) is luminous and joyful, but rooted in presence—not in transcendence.

[19] This recognition is congruent with one of the earliest human metaphysical conceptualizations found in Hinduism (Taittiriya Upanishad). All experience is perceived through five layers of awareness: physical, emotional, mental, wisdom, and bliss (i.e., *anna, prana, mana, vijnana, ananda*).

layer allows the wounded parts of us to feel our inborn discernment and intuitive intelligence (*prajna*). Contact with our wise-self becomes an embodied validation, a source of skillful guidance that provides a sense of safety which naturally supports our evolution.

In embodied nondual meditation, we refine our senses to directly perceive this wisdom as an inborn presence and an active, living dimension of the self. In my experience, this subtle discernment often flows through specific centers of embodied intelligence: the gut (linked to the second chakra), the heart (associated with the fourth chakra), and the head (associated with the sixth chakra). Interestingly, modern neuroscience supports this ancient understanding, identifying that we not only have a brain in the head (cephalic brain), but also complex neural networks in the heart (cardiac brain) and gut (enteric brain).

Through meditation, we can attune to each of these centers individually or sense them all together as an integrated field of knowing or insight. This attunement sharpens our ability to recognize embodied wisdom, not just as abstract insight, but as a deeply felt inner oracle.

Over time, we learn to remain internally referenced and trust our own body-based guidance rather than constantly seeking validation or direction from external authorities or from our beliefs and turbulent emotions. This internal orientation enables us to learn to move fluidly between connection and autonomy. It plays a key part in healing from the externalizing impacts of trauma, cultural conditioning, parenting, and certain religious or spiritual teachings that encourage outsourcing truth.

Whole-being meditation is a way of developing a direct relationship with the wise-self and reclaiming our inner guidance. This provides profound support that helps us navigate life with greater freedom, discernment, and resilience.

The beauty of whole-being meditation is that this journey is not about becoming someone new, but about remembering what has always been true: that we are both human and divine, both tenderly separate and beautifully connected. When we can rest in this whole-self experience, life ceases to be something to control or perfect. It becomes a living dialogue between our evolving humanity and our unchanging essence. Each breath, each relationship, each challenge becomes part of the dance. This is the quiet power of whole-being-embrace: to live as an open question rather than a fixed answer; to trust that even in the messiness of being alive, something vast, loving, and utterly whole is already here, illuminating us, as us.

Again, the parent-child relationship provides a road map revealing the primary dynamics involved.

Oneness as "Good Enough Parent"

Donald Winnicott introduced the influential concept of the "good enough mother," a caregiver who provides a reliable and supportive environment, not by being perfect, but by being attuned and responsive enough to meet the child's basic emotional and developmental needs. This assessment acknowledges that parental imperfections, when managed effectively, are not detrimental but rather essential for a child's growth.

In early life, no caregiver can, or should, adapt perfectly to a child's every need. Instead, a rhythm of attunement and distraction naturally unfolds. At times, the child is met with deep connection, at others, with moments of absence or imperfection. This gradual withdrawal of perfect attunement creates a natural rhythm of disappointment and frustration that the infant slowly learns to manage because there is adequate support.

In healthy development, "good-enough" care encompasses not only moments of deep connection but also moments of imperfect engagement or gentle withdrawal, when the caregiver is physically present yet not actively involved. The parent's quiet, steady presence gives the infant permission to simply rest, play, and exist without constant interaction.

Over time, this reliable presence is internalized as a felt sense of safety and comfort. The child learns that they are held even in solitude, and that closeness does not vanish when the caregiver steps back. This rhythm of engaging and disengaging gradually forms an inner pattern, one that builds emotional resilience. By learning to tolerate these small imperfections in attunement, the infant develops what Winnicott called the "capacity to be alone," the ability to move fluidly between connection and solitude, engagement and rest, without fear of abandonment.

Rather than striving for flawlessness, the good enough parent meets most of the child's needs. This happens through physical holding, emotional attunement, and empathetic mirroring. These three aspects of experience work together to create Winnicott's understanding of a holding environment, a nurturing and reliable atmosphere in which the child feels safe, seen, and supported.

In early life, this holding environment is typically provided by the primary caregiver (often the mother), but over time, it expands to include relationships with family, community, therapeutic settings, and even contemplative or meditative practice. Its essential purpose is to offer the child a deep sense of security, trust, and continuity of being.

In the early stages of life, the good enough parent is often highly attuned to the infant's needs, adapting almost completely to create an experience of emotional containment and security. This high degree of responsiveness supports the infant in developing a temporary sense of security and omnipotence, where their needs seem to shape reality itself.

However, as development continues, the parent gradually begins to "fail," ideally in manageable, appropriate ways. This is a process Winnicott referred to as optimal disillusionment. These subtle failures, such as not responding immediately or allowing mild frustration, are essential for supporting healthy separation and a sense of being a distinct individual. As a child, they help us:

- Perceive external reality more clearly
- Recognize that others are separate and autonomous
- Begin to differentiate our own emotions and experiences
- Refine self-soothing skills and resilience

Through this process, we slowly transition from dependence to autonomy, forming a distinct and adaptive sense of self. The holding environment plays a foundational role in supporting this developmental arc. When we feel consistently held (physically, emotionally, and mentally) as children, we are free to relax, explore, and integrate our experiences. This nurtures the growth of a stable, coherent, evolving sense of self.

As we internalize the experience, we develop self-awareness and the ability to reflect on it constructively. The external "holding" provided by our parents gradually transforms into our internal capacity for self-regulation (maintaining calm, balance), confidence, and emotional resilience.

When we embody unified consciousness, our evolving-self experiences a nondual state that is a kind of internalized holding environment. Our body provides a reliable, contactful presence. It becomes a kind of supportive "nondual holding environment" where we feel physically held (via our embodiment), emotionally mirrored, and mentally validated.

Our realization of unified consciousness is not something we force or manufacture; it arises spontaneously. This spontaneous realization becomes possible when we refine our senses so we can access the subtle perception of openness and a sense of wholeness. This does not demand perfection or complete healing before this awakening can occur. As Judith Blackstone often reminds us, so simply and truthfully, "We only need to be whole enough."

133

This is a liberating truth. It means we don't need to chase some flawless state of purity or wait until all our wounds are resolved. Awakening is not postponed until every shadow is healed. Instead, it happens in the midst of our humanity as we refine our senses to uncover and awaken to the stillness, wholeness, and embodied presence of unified consciousness. Currently, we realize that being "whole enough" is already sufficient to begin to heal our wounds and become free.

The key to secure attachment and a life free from suffering is not perfect support, but care that includes "rupture and repair." Our optimal disillusionment can arise in meditation when the steady, contactful presence of our unchanging-self reveals that some of our most cherished assumptions (about life, about others, about who we are) are no longer true or not the full truth. In that moment of quiet recognition, we see that our long-held beliefs, values, and ideals may not fully align with our lived experience that includes wholeness. What once felt like certain assumptions that provided security begin to dissolve, and in their place, a deeper understanding begins to breathe.

Emotional maturity is the willingness to meet life as it is, not as we wish it to be. A body experience of unified consciousness offers the vast perspective needed for this meeting. It widens the frame, softening our attachment to specific outcomes and loosening the evolving-self's grip on its expectations. Within this broader awareness, disillusionment is no longer a fall from grace but a passage into authenticity. Instead of collapsing into despair or cynicism when our limited perspective breaks apart, we are met by the quiet openness of our unchanging-self, a presence that holds us steady as something more aligned, begins to take shape.

Disillusionment often brings with it uncomfortable truths, surfacing what we've hidden in shadow, grief, anger, fear, or disappointment. Yet wholeness provides a field of compassionate awareness where even the most difficult emotions can unfold without judgment. By staying embodied and present to what
134

arises, we learn that pain need not be exile; it can be an invitation. As we meet these truths within the spaciousness of wholeness, the fragments of our being begin to weave themselves back together (much like Peter Levine's notion of *pendulation*).

Just as the infant feels permission to simply rest, play, and exist due to the parent's reliable presence, we experience a felt sense of safety and comfort. We learn that we are physically, emotionally, and mentally held even when facing our injuries. The soothing, stabilizing quality of unified consciousness helps weave together the fragmented pieces of our mental, emotional, and sensory life. In this way, our optimal disillusionment becomes not a breaking, but a refining, a sacred realignment with what feels true.

From the ashes of certainty, authenticity begins to live more fully through us. Optimal disillusionment is no longer merely a milestone of childhood development; it becomes a mature spiritual and psychological process for adults. Through whole-being meditation, we learn to meet life's inevitable disappointments, losses, and heartbreaks within the wider, embodied, steady presence of unified consciousness. This presence, luminous and whole, gives us the space to hold our suffering heart and distressed mind without being undone by it.

In this light, disillusionment itself transforms. The disappointments that once shattered us now become doorways to deeper wisdom. We realize that the separateness we once believed defined us is only a partial truth. As we awaken to our unchanging-self, we recognize that individuality and unity are not opposites but two expressions of the same existence. What we once clung to as a fixed identity dissolves into something far more fluid, alive, and connected. This realization is not disheartening; it is liberating. We begin to see situations, relationships, and our own capabilities with fresh eyes, free from distortion and wishful thinking.

From this grounded realism, we can set goals that align with our deeper truth, make choices rooted in authenticity, and

135

relate to others not from projection or protection, but from our sense of personal truth and genuine wisdom. In this way, optimal disillusionment is not an ending but a deep integration, a homecoming to what has always been true.

The Capacity to Be Alone

Emotional maturity is a continuous process, not a fixed endpoint. It is a highly sophisticated phenomenon that enables us to pursue relationships and creative endeavors. Interestingly, because relationships with our self and with others are what form our sense of self, and also inform the hardwiring of the brain, one of the most important signs of emotional maturity is our capacity to be alone.

As mentioned, by learning to tolerate small imperfections in attunement, the infant develops the ability to move fluidly between connection and solitude or engagement and rest, without fear of abandonment.[20] The same is true for adults. It is very valuable to attend to this in meditation.

For Donald Winnicott, the capacity to be alone is not something a child achieves in isolation, but something born out of relationship. As mentioned, specifically, it emerges from the experience of "good enough mothering." Winnicott's insight rests on a beautiful paradox: our ability to be truly alone is first built on the experience of being *alone in the presence of another.* When a caregiver can be quietly present without intruding, the child feels both seen and free to simply be.

---

[20] It's important to recognize that some forms of self-reliance aren't genuine strength but instead learned protection. A person who seems highly independent may, in fact, have developed what could be called a *reactive* capacity to be alone, a defense against vulnerability, disappointment, or the fear that others can't be trusted. Unlike genuine solitude, which grows from emotional maturity and inner peace, this reactive independence arises from early experiences in which reaching out for support led to hurt or abandonment. This reflects the attachment type of the insecure avoidant person, discussed in chapter four.

As a result, we experience being able to freely move between states of engagement and disengagement with our caregiver. This rhythm is what gradually teaches us that solitude can be safe. The emotional resilience this leads to is not only about going it alone; it's also about the ability to stand on our own while also being open to support, trust, and love when we need it.

Even if we did not receive "good enough mothering," whole-being meditation awakens a parallel capacity within us. From this inner ground, we depend less on external validation and begin to experience a deeper sense of peace. As mentioned, this presence does not vanish when we struggle or hurt; it remains quietly supportive, even when no external comfort is available.

The stable, nurturing background that unified consciousness provides supports us in developing the capacity to be alone. We can be alone and yet not be lonely, and we can be in relationship without feeling imposed upon. Our capacity to be alone grows with our ability to rest securely in the nurturing presence of our unchanging-self.

Anchored in a strong and unshakable sense of existential trust, we discover a natural rhythm of engaging and disengaging that allows us to move fluidly between contact and alone time, or between engagement and rest, in all our relationships. The capacity to be alone supports true emotional autonomy. It gives us space for self-reflection, which deepens self-awareness and cultivates confidence. The ability to rest comfortably in our own company, held within a supportive inner environment, allows us to carry a stable center wherever we go. In this way, the capacity to be alone becomes the root of both emotional resilience and authenticity.

Timelessness

A powerful healing quality of unified consciousness is the experience of *timelessness*. When we don't have access to the experience of embodied wholeness that arises from unified consciousness, we become preoccupied with the finite nature of our human existence, our limited years, limited abilities, and limited resources. All of these emotions are framed by the echoes of our past, our limitations in the present, and a helpless race against time. Our solutions are bound by a feeling of scarcity.

But in whole-being meditation, a deeper truth quietly reveals itself. Within the presence of our unchanging-self, we awaken to the timeless dimension of our being. This brings the experience of wholeness, as a reliably present nondual holding environment, to a much deeper level. We feel both the mortal reality of our body together with the immortal essence of our consciousness. We recognize that our presence, as a luminous ground, has been with us since birth. It has never changed and will never change. It is the same timeless presence that pervades the entire universe, and we are inseparably a part of it.

Healing the fear of death is the quiet reweaving of our past losses and our dread of endings into the larger fabric of our timeless nature. In this weaving, our injuries cease to dictate the shape of what comes next. They become threads in a broader tapestry of being. This is the essence of the embodied nondual path: it reshapes our relationship to every part of ourselves (past, present, and future) into a coherent wholeness.

As our attention shifts from our finite identity to the eternal, unchanging nature of our being, death itself is reframed. It becomes a transition rather than an annihilation, a movement from form into formlessness, grounded in an unbroken continuity. We begin to sense ourselves as the constant, timeless witness that remains through all the shifts of life, an "I" that is not limited to the body but expressed through it. In this recognition, death loses the power it once held over our rampant imagination that binds us in fear.

The unknown becomes less threatening when we can sense that the essence we arrived with existed long before our first breath and will continue after our last. Death becomes less like disappearance and more like a return, a "birthday of eternity."

In this experience, our fear of death is held in a field so vast, so safe, so inherently whole that even fear of loss of our body (and all that this means) can relax into belonging. Our evolving-self is no longer left to fend for itself; it is welcomed home into the luminous embrace of its own eternal ground of being.

What makes this realization especially powerful is its intimacy. Timelessness does not arrive only as a lofty, impersonal truth of transcendence; it is felt directly in our own body as a subjective experience of self. This is a paradox of wholeness that is both personal and universal. It gives timelessness the power to speak to our deepest existential fears. In these moments, it seems to whisper to the part of us terrified of never finding love, or of endings, *"You cannot be lost. You are more than this fleeting moment."*

In this way, timelessness becomes not an abstract idea but a living experience. It expands our perspective, offering a felt sense of belonging to something larger than our finite story. And in that belonging, our deepest existential fears soften and dissolve, embraced by the quiet assurance that who we are, at essence, is unbroken, unending, and forever whole.

To own the experience of our immortality is to shift into a profoundly different way of being. We touch a state of benevolent openness free of clinging, free of willful striving. Presence as wholeness itself feels like it is enough. As we learn to rest again and again in this eternal now, we begin to integrate its meaning into our preoccupied with the finite nature of our human existence. Instead of being ruled by fear of loss, or disillusionment of what we have not accomplished and experienced, we feel upheld by an unending presence-of-being that cannot be diminished by time.

This shift in perspective, this transformation in how we *exist*, reshapes not only how we perceive the present moment but how we imagine the future. No longer confined only to the echo of our past and our limitations, we begin to meet life with an

139

openness that was once impossible. We are no longer haunted by what we might lose or who we might fail to become. Our future is no longer constructed by fear; it is informed by the uninjured, timeless presence at the core of our being.

Instead of fearing what lies ahead, timelessness invites us fully into the present. It encourages us to live with clarity, presence, and joy now, in this moment, precisely because we no longer need to control the next one. In this way, the nurturing nature of timeless presence dissolves death anxiety and frees us to live with a depth of trust that was once unimaginable.

Living in Grace

Whole-being meditation is not self-improvement. It's self-intimacy. It's the trustworthy way we learn to feel at home inside our own body again; the way we remember that our life doesn't need to be managed into goodness, because goodness is the ground we stand on. We don't force ourselves into better habits; we are nurtured to grow out of the old ones. Fear and strenuous effort no longer dictate the terms. The body tells the truth, and we cultivate the courage to listen.

This is how personal truth ripens: not as a slogan or a stance, but as a felt orientation. We sense what is "yes" and what is "no," not to control our self or others, but to remain in loving conversation with life. Boundaries become expressions of care rather than barricades based on fear. The old voices may still visit (the minimizing, the self-doubt, the inner critic) but they no longer get the final word. Held in a wider presence, they pass like weather. What remains is the river of aliveness we once learned to dam: grief that moves, anger that clarifies, joy that does not apologize for itself. Survival energy untangles into strength. Vigilance relaxes into vision. We stop living from the edges of ourselves and begin to live from the center with heart.

140

And with that center comes a quiet bravery. We can tell the truth kindly. We can ask for what we need without shrinking, and offer what we have without over-giving. We can lean into love without abandoning ourselves, and step back without shutting down. Emotional connection and autonomy stop competing; they begin to dance.

If there is a single promise this practice keeps, it's this: you don't have to leave your unique evolving-self to belong, and you don't have to leave your body or the world to be free. The unchanging presence within you is both sanctuary and source, a "good-enough parent" on the inside that steadies your hand, so you feel connected in wholeness and grow the capacity to be alone.

So let this be your compass as you go: When confusion swells, place a hand on your heart and attune to the quieter presence beneath the constrictions and noise. Release what closes. Trust what opens. Feel for the simple, body-felt truth. Return, as many times as it takes, to the spacious ground that does not disappear.

From here, personal truth is no longer something you chase; it's the way you walk. Wisdom is no longer something you acquire; it's the way life speaks through you. And healing is no longer a project with a finish line; it's the everyday grace of living from the whole of who you are.

Chapter Seven

Qualities Of Oneness

Quality Rich Oneness

The "qualities of oneness" are ineffable, but putting words to them helps us recognize them in meditation. Across traditions, these subtle nondual qualities have different names but point to a similar unchanging truth at the heart of being.[21] Each nondual quality can be experienced as having attributes, such as stillness, timelessness, uninjured, unbreakable, and universally pervasive. These qualities can be described as a subtle, felt-sense of the various ways we can experience oneness and wholeness.

We do not experience the qualities of oneness as abstract ideas, but as tangible attributes of our inborn unified nature. This quality-rich experience is an ambient presence that emerges as we attune to the infinite, unified foundation of existence and who we are. The qualities of oneness are beyond individual or particular expressions. They are the underlying potential and ground from which these individual expressions arise.

---

[21] In Mahayana Buddhism, this essence is called Buddha nature—a radiant "full emptiness" rich with innate qualities. Yoga echoes this as *ishta-devata*. Vedanta names it *saguna Brahman*, nonduality with qualities, often described as *sat-chit-ananda* (existence, consciousness, bliss). Tibetan Buddhism speaks of emptiness, clarity, and bliss, while Tantra expresses these qualities through the seven chakras.

142

Not only are the qualities of oneness ineffable, as mentioned, they cannot be detected by the ordinary range of our senses. Yet, they readily become tangible as we refine our senses.[22] In meditation, we become increasingly more adept at perceiving these unified qualities of existence. In the process, our perceptual field transforms. Our senses begin to recognize the radiance, fluidity, and spacious stillness that permeate every aspect of existence, including, counterintuitively, the densest dimension of being, our physical body.

At subtler levels of experience, the senses that perceive the qualities of oneness belong to what yoga calls the *subtle body* (*suksma sarira*). These are perceived by subtle senses that are not engaged with gross, external objects but with the finer textures of consciousness that pervades the objects.[23] In meditation, when our awareness refines, we can begin to tune into these subtle sensations, not as tactile events on the surface of the skin, but as delicate inner impressions of contact within the ground of being pervading our whole body.

This subtle sensory experience can be felt as a "subtle touch" that does not refer to the meeting of two separate surfaces, nor to ordinary tactile stimulation. It points instead to a deeper resonance of presence, in which the apparent boundaries between perceiver and perceived, subject and object, begin to dissolve. Touch, at this level, is the felt sense of unity itself: an intimate recognition that what touches and what is touched are made of the same living ground of consciousness. In this way, touch becomes

---

[22] Neurobiologist Antonio Damasio's concept of "somatic markers" refers to the faint bodily sensations that unconsciously shape our emotions and decisions. It can be said that as our perception refines, we begin to feel nondual qualities as *subtle somatic markers*—delicate, refined sensations that anchor us in a bodily sense of the wholeness of oneness.

[23] This is felt less as a solid structure and more as a transparent, immaterial field of luminous presence (a subtle essence of physicality that is the substratum of embodied life), helping us resolve deep emotional issues around existence, limitation, space, and belonging. It pervades both body and environment.

the first expression of nonduality, the experiential bridge through which we feel our continuity with all that is. [24]

As discussed with whole-being-embrace, nondual qualities can offer tangible support for our psychological and emotional healing throughout our lives. Each of these qualities of wholeness is an innate, uninjured aspect of our being. We do not have to invent or earn them; we need only to uncover them, to let them be felt within the living texture of our body and the world around us. The diverse expressions of the qualities of oneness becomes particularly important when it comes to healing injuries.

As mentioned, each stage of childhood development contains unique vulnerabilities where emotional injury may have shaped our beliefs and attitudes. These formative experiences are imprinted in the body and psyche and often resurface in adult relationships. To heal, we must revisit these critical stages. The nondual qualities that resonate most with us often correspond to the specific ways we were most deeply hurt (the subject of my book *Nondual Chakra Awakening*). In this way, the qualities of oneness provide specific antidotes for each of our injuries.

As we embody a nondual quality, the qualities of oneness become lenses through which we re-experience old wounds, this time not as victims, but as participants in our own healing. When we experience the exact quality of support that gives us the clearest experience of wholeness, as though we have access to the support we always longed for but never received.

By awakening to the particular quality that communicates most effectively to the specific stage and nature of our injury, we heal. When we uncover and awaken to the subtle ground of wholeness, we can perceive and connect with other people through

---

[24] In fact, yoga philosophy teaches that all sensory perception ultimately arises from the sense of touch (*sparsa*)—the most primal and foundational of the senses. Awareness of touch forms the substratum of all perception; without it there can be no experience. To see, hear, taste, or smell is, in essence, is to touch where we make sensory contact through varying modes of vibration and resonance.

144

all aspects of ourselves at once (physical, emotional, mental, wisdom, bliss). Moreover, as our perspective deepens and broadens, so does our sensory, motor, spatial, and temporal information:

- **Sensory**: We become attuned to the subtle, the nuanced, and the felt-sense beneath ordinary perception.
- **Motor**: We learn to rest in stillness, not as a control mechanism or trying to "hold still," but as a natural expression of inner alignment.
- **Spatial**: We feel ourselves more often in union with space as if we are conscious space, and the space is unified rather than the distance between objects.
- **Temporal**: We embody timeless presence, where the future no longer haunts us and the past no longer binds us.

The qualities of oneness are like living medicines, each carrying exactly the kind of nourishment that meets us where we are most in need. When these qualities "touch" the places we have been hurt, something shifts. The old wound is still there, but it is no longer alone. It is met, fully, intimately, by the very support we have always longed for. This is support that no one else could give us, and that has been inside us all along.

A Match Made in Heaven

And here, in this homecoming, the most surprising thing of all happens: the qualities of our unified nature become the living ground from which we speak, act, and love. This is a spontaneous healing that is not the result of trying to change, but emerges on its own from the potential nature of wholeness, which has an irresistible integrating influence on us.

Through opening and becoming receptive to our alternative sensory, motor, temporal, and spatial experiences of the unchanging-self, we learn to meet our developmental wounds with uninjured presence and initiate a process of profound renovation with self-love. In this whole-being-embrace experience, these nondual qualities begin to weave into the fabric of our identity, reshaping how we relate to both ourselves and others.

This renovation through whole-being-embrace, reflects the dynamics of any healthy relationship. It is governed by principles of contact, mutuality, trust, respect, and honest communication. Just as a wise parent learns to meet the child where they are, rather than simply imposing expectations, we learn to meet our own inner emotional life with receptivity rather than control or the agenda of disidentification.

This means we let go of how we think healing *should* feel or unfold, and instead listen with unconditional love and curiosity to what our wounded parts are actually feeling. In this space of nonjudgmental presence, as both Carl Jung and Carl Rogers taught, our authentic personal truth emerges as a trustworthy guide. Healing then follows its own inner rhythm and harmony. Loving contact, mutuality, trust, respect, and honest communication are often new experiences. This can be very different from how our parents related to us, because they, too, were wounded.

When we experience ourselves as this subtle unified presence, our relationship with emotional injury changes on the most fundamental level. We stop referee-ing, distancing, or dissociating and suppressing. We begin to love what we find, even in the midst of pain. This shift is deeply healing, not because pain simply disappears, but because it is now held within wholeness.

The meeting of our evolving-self with the qualities of oneness of our unchanging-self is not a technique or even a goal. It is a relationship. Like two old friends who finally find each other, they move together in quiet accord, each completing the other's presence. The evolving-self brings its textures as found in its stories, emotions, and longings. The unchanging-self brings its timelessness, its steadiness, its quiet radiance as unconditional love. When they are together, we find ourselves living from a wholeness that cannot be taken away. We no longer rush to fix or flee what hurts; we instead learn to rest with it, listen to it, and allow it to transform at its own pace and rhythm. Life is no longer a puzzle to solve, but a conversation to inhabit.

Through this sacred inner dialogue, our unchanging-self becomes the holding ground where pain is met, heard, and finally allowed to rest. The body relaxes. The mind clears. The heart remembers that it can trust again. When this happens, our wounded parts start to release the old emotions and beliefs that have kept us stuck in life. As this healing deepens, we begin to sense that what restores us is not effort, but attunement and embodiment. This leads to the quiet realization that the same wholeness transforming us from within, also connects us to everything around us.

Whole-being-embrace is, in essence, a twofold relational process that creates a self-reinforcing loop of healing:

1. **Internal Healing:** We cultivate a secure, compassionate relationship between our evolving-self and our unchanging-self, allowing emotional wounds to be seen, held, and released.
2. **External Reflection:** The harmony within begins to open outward. We show up differently, with empathy, presence, and authenticity; creating relationships that are no longer built on need or fear, but on mutual respect and love.

In this way, the journey of whole-being-embrace restores our trust in connection itself. The very openness that once made us vulnerable to pain becomes the doorway through which intimacy, freedom, and love return. And here, in the space where stillness and movement meet, we begin to live not as someone searching for wholeness, but as wholeness itself, breathing, feeling and loving, in the world.

How the Light Gets In

Each nondual quality of being functions according to a holographic principle: every part reflects and contains the essence of the whole. This reflects Arthur Koestler's concept of *holons*, entities that are simultaneously whole in themselves and integral parts of a greater whole. Likewise, qualities of oneness are fractal in nature: each one is a complete expression of unity and yet inherently embedded within a broader ground of unified consciousness. These qualities embody a fundamental paradox; they are both whole and part, at the same time.

This paradox cannot be fully resolved through logic alone; rather, it is directly intuited through experience. The mind may struggle with the idea that something can be complete in itself and simultaneously just one facet of something larger. But the heart, body, and being can feel this coherence. Embodied nondual meditation helps us access this experiential understanding.

Each quality of oneness, or "essential nature," such as awareness, emotion, or physical sensation (along with the chakra qualities (stillness, timelessness, bliss, unconditional love, etc.) can be experienced as an expression of indivisible wholeness.

For example, in meditation, we discover that the "essential nature" of emotion exists as a unified ground within us, a non-changing ground from which various emotions arise and dissolve. While anger, sadness, joy, or fear may emerge and pass away, the unchanging, essential emotional ground that they arise from, remains constant. The unified nature of the ground of emotion is itself whole, yet it is also only one strand in the greater tapestry of being.

148

Although these qualities of oneness cannot ultimately be separated, in the context of healing, it is often helpful to distinguish them. Doing so allows us to communicate with specific emotional injuries more effectively. It also helps us identify how specific psychological injuries affect different aspects of our being. By attuning to one particular quality or essential nature of oneness (be it awareness, emotion, sensation, or another), we can more clearly observe where fragmentation or defense structures have taken root. Each of these qualities can reveal the unique ways our evolving-self has been constricted, distorted, or fragmented in response to emotional injury and developmental trauma.

Our early injuries are varied and occur at different stages of development. Because of this, not every nondual quality offers the same kind of support at every stage. Some qualities resonate more deeply or provide a clearer sense of inner coherence depending on the nature and timing of the trauma.

For instance, the practice of embodying specifically the first chakra quality, which is the innate essence of our *existence*, helps us feel and know our inherent value and our birthright to exist. If we were unplanned, unwanted, or born to a parent that was not ready for us, this can be powerfully healing. Once we own our right to exist, we come to realize we have a right to belong and take up room on the planet with what feels personally true for us. Attuning to the second chakra quality of *creativity*, supports our birthright to own our passions, to make choices that support us as we engage with our genuine likes and dislikes. This communicates very directly to any injuries we experienced as a two year old in our power struggle to confirm *"I am my own person, but I still desperately need you."* Awakening to our uninjured creative essence supports our attempt claim our emerging sense of self.

Owning our right to create and choose gives us the incentive to manifest our personal interests. Attuning and embodying the third chakra uninjured essence of *power,* as a pure potential of our being, supports us to feel the autonomy we need to act on our own behalf and take the breathing room we need to develop the skills to get the job done. Including unconditional love in every step enhances the effectiveness of any quality of oneness.

As adults, these are some of the ways we can refine our embodied meditative practice to address the specific needs of our early wounds at each stage. This has a direct impact on how these wounds repeatedly manifest later in life. By identifying and working with the quality of oneness that most directly provides support, we can design meditation and yogic practices that reweave the broken threads of selfhood. This allows us not only to heal in a general sense, but also to heal *specifically*, meeting our injury exactly where it needs support.

When we attune to the quality of oneness that offers us the clearest sense of wholeness, we find ourselves less isolated within our inner fragmentation. We feel supported to align with and express the healthy boundaries we need to flourish in our relationship with others. We draw upon the feeling-tone of that uninjured and unbreakable quality of oneness, to help us renegotiate old patterns of pain and protection. Through this nuanced attunement, healing becomes more precise, more intimate, and more lasting.

Each nondual quality, though complete in itself, becomes a doorway into the greater unity of being, and by entering through the one that speaks to our wounds most clearly, we reclaim our essential wholeness, not just in principle, but as a lived experience. The art of tailoring nondual qualities for healing, teaches us that wholeness is not a distant ideal, but a living intelligence woven through every sensation, every emotion, every breath.

Each quality becomes a portal through which the light of oneness enters the places we once hid from ourselves. In this way, healing is revealed to be less about fixing and more about remembering: remembering that each fragment carries the hologram of the whole, and that even our most tender injuries are made of the same luminous fabric as the infinite.

Inner Alchemy of Wholeness

In yogic practice, the whole-being-embrace inner alchemy is called *bhavana*. Bhavana refers to the intentional evocation and immersion of our being in a quality we most need to heal and grow. Just as herbal tea infuses water with healing properties over time, our evolving-self is slowly steeped in the qualities of unity and wholeness.

Each moment we attune to and bond with qualities of oneness, strengthens our connection to a broader, more compassionate perspective. Many of the benefits of meditation emerge from our ability to open, treasure, and embrace each sensory perception with wholeness. As mentioned, when we feel embraced by a quality of oneness that nurtures us the most, it allows what we experience to inform us without overwhelming us.

Instead of scanning life for threats or what's missing or for what might impose on us, we become oriented toward beauty, meaning, and wonder. We experience more frequent states of well-being, peace, and even bliss (*cit-ananda*), without being undermined by unresolved injuries. Our senses awaken to the sheer beauty of life, and we feel as though we are drinking in the richness of experience.

This provides a sense of great delight that is not merely psychological; it has a physiological basis. This is as if our senses become so delighted to be engaged in their higher purpose that they manufacture endorphins and the ultimate chemistry of delight. This makes dealing with life's challenges and emotional growth a lot easier.

In yogic traditions, this ecstatic state is called *soma*, the ambrosial nectar of immortality. Ancient texts describe soma as a mystical infusion, collected on mountaintops under the light of the moon. Today, we recognize that the body also produces its natural nectars that enhance perception. In a modern context, soma can be understood as the body's natural capacity to generate blissful states through intimacy with unified consciousness. When we attune to our essential wholeness, even the simplest experiences, a breeze, a glance, a breath, can evoke deep appreciation and tune our body to produce soma.

Whole-being meditation becomes a potential space of intimacy with life itself. Experience of this intimacy progressively becomes generalized to the rest of our life, much the same way we learn a new language, with repetition and familiarity. In yoga, this sacred union is called *sambhava*, an experience of oneness with what we love most. In *sambhava*, attuning deeply to the aspect of experience that we love most, opens us to the totality of our sensorium.

All our senses increasingly function as a whole more of the time. This means the senses that compose our evolving sense of self's emotions, thoughts, and sensations, arise from a single source of understanding. Our mind, emotions, sensations, and the wisdom aspects of ourself, all come online at the same time. This is a unification of our senses that allows us to experience with our whole body and mind. In this unified state, we perceive not only our changing experiences, but also thought, emotion, and sensation that seem to arise out of unity, stillness, conscious space, and wholeness.

It is easy to become fully absorbed in what we love most. This full absorption allows the wounds of the evolving-self to no longer need to guard or defend; they begin to soften and find rest in the safety of unity and wholeness. In this way, each aspect of life becomes a site of renewal. In meditation, we allow the luminous play of being, unchanging and ever-present, to rejuvenate our body, mind, and heart. It's as though we invite our senses to take us on a journey into wonder. This is the yoga of delight, where we are invited home, into our body, our life, our relationships, and the universe itself.

Our entrainment to the play of consciousness and energy is central to our meditation practice. In meditation, small shifts and alternatives arise as subtle invitations to tailor the practice to our specific needs. This customization is part of the art of meditating.

152

Through observation, experimentation, and sensitive attunement, we come to directly experience the unified nature of reality. We bond with the most relevant, nondual quality of being as a source of fundamental goodness, joy, pleasure, and emotional freedom.

This is a *"yukti moment."* Yukti in Sanskrit is a variation of the term yoga, and means "the skillful joining of essential elements at the right time and place." Through *yukti*, we gather all the essential elements of existence as found in our evolving-self and our unchanging-self, and join them together in a living, breathing, embodied whole-self. Meditation becomes an experience of skillfully integrating our supportive resources so that we can flourish in the world. We continuously refine our senses and attune to the most alluring quality of oneness that is already present, beneath the fluctuations of thought and sensation. This allows us to become like artists who can hold our disturbing experiences lightly, like a feather resting on the palm.

As we refine our senses, we move from the surface to the subtle, from what is obvious to the subtle space within form, and to the realization that even form is permeated by spaciousness. We begin to perceive the silence between words, the stillness inside motion, the space between particles. This subtle awareness invites us to meet our deepest wounds with love, openness, and presence, thereby integrating the scattered parts of our being so that we can thrive in connection with emotional autonomy.

This means that as our senses refine, we learn to look deeper than the solidness and separateness of our evolving-self and access a bare perception of our oneness with other people. Rather than seeing, hearing, and touching only from the surface of ourselves to the surface of other people, we can perceive what is under the surface to the qualities of unity and wholeness within. And with this experience, that which is unified and immaterial comes into play with that which is separate and solid.

Within this context, *transmissions* (sudden insights or felt realizations) are not abstract, or due to downloading external information. They are primarily inner awakenings that arise

153

through the communion between our evolving-self and unchanging-self. These moments of expanded awareness often come unexpectedly: a breath, a word, or an inner movement sparks the "*aha*" of perspective.

This experience also teaches our evolving-self that we don't need to reach outward to access the ultimate truth of unity; it is transmitted, received, and revealed from within. This broadens the meaning of transmission: it is the fruit of an inner relationship. When we uncover unified consciousness within our body as an expression of our existence, it is not just a spontaneous insight, but an embodied communication based on the totality of our sensorium, between two aspects of our being.

Every meditation practice that includes this whole-being-embrace inner-relationship, becomes a potential site for transmission and transformation. In this entangled reality, our perceptions occur in two new ways:

1. Our individual experiences seem to arise spontaneously out of our existence as unity and wholeness.

When our evolving-self meets our unchanging-self in whole-being-embrace, we transform every layer of our experience (emotion, sensation, thought, wisdom, and bliss) into an embodied expression born of nonduality. They no longer arise from our preconceptions, reactivity, or our wounds of the past.

2. We feel that even the densest, aspects of the material realm (including thought, emotion, sensation, and all the relationship dynamics of life) contain within it unified consciousness.

That is, we find that our evolving-self's experience of duality contains, at its core, the presence of unity. In meditation, when we pause long enough to refine our senses, the unchanging dimension of our being awakens in the body as a luminous presence.[25]

When we feel that we exist as unified conscious space, our perceptions do not stop or bump into the outside surface of what we perceive; the conscious space that we are encompasses and pervades what we perceive. We connect to what we perceive through the unified ground of consciousness and experience things that were previously hidden from us.

Unconditional Love

In life, a great challenge and gift, is learning how to surrender into the tender openness of unconditional love. This openness does not mean collapsing into another or abandoning ourselves. It means staying rooted in the integrity of who we are, while allowing the heart to soften, to welcome, and to savor the essential ground of love.

Love here, is not an idea but begins as a felt experience in the body. Sometimes it arises as a profound familiarity, as if we are meeting someone we have always known; as if two currents of life that have long flowed apart suddenly reunite. This depth of recognition can become a window, giving us a glimpse into the joy and radiance at the core of our being. And the more deeply we surrender into unconditional love, the more we discover that our personal love wants to keep expanding. A commitment to loving, in all its forms, naturally grows as we live into it.

One of the most essential qualities we need for deep healing is the felt recognition that we are, at core, unconditional love, a luminous, sustaining presence of being. For many, this experience is rare, fleeting, or entirely unfamiliar. Yet, as we learn

---

[25] This is like the quantum physicist who, peering into the atom's electron (that composes the material dimension of existence), perceives both the particle that shapes matter, and the wave that remains whole and indivisible.

to rest in this presence, something begins to change: the wounded heart starts to bond with the steady warmth of unconditional love. In that bond, we find new magnitudes of self-acceptance and self-love. Even if we are not naturally heart-centered, this connection invites the restless, turbulent currents of the evolving-self to steep slowly in that unconditional love, softening, settling, and finally coming to rest in its embrace.

We all have a natural need for love, to feel safe, to know we are wanted for who we authentically are, and to experience that we belong. This need is not a flaw or a weakness. It is intrinsic to how we are hard-wired, reflecting our relational nature as human beings. Love is not something we should have to earn; it is something we are meant to know by being.

In the deep stillness of meditation, we begin to perceive that unconditional love is not merely a transient feeling or an emotion directed toward someone or something. Rather, it is an essential quality of being itself, innate and ever-present. Much like a fractal, where each part reflects the whole at different scales, every essential nondual quality (spaciousness, stillness, luminosity, pervasiveness, and timelessness), contains within it a reflection of unconditional love. These qualities are not separate from love; they are integral to its unified presence. As we attune to these nondual dimensions of being, we gain direct access to the unconditional love that is fundamental to the unchanging-self.

This access emerges through *nondual mirroring* (see chapter ten). This is a deeply embodied experience of being seen, felt, and held within the infinite openness of unified consciousness. In this mirror, our evolving-self is not met with neutrality or detachment. Instead, it is received with a subtle yet profound quality of openness, tenderness, and presence. Our mental, emotional, and sensory life are not bypassed or diminished. Rather, they are compassionately included, embraced, and suffused by the benevolent presence of our unchanging-self.

This meeting of the two dimensions of self, the evolving and the unchanging, fosters a secure, internal bond based not on performance or perfection, but on a felt-sense of wholeness and innate belonging. The unconditional love we experience here is the very ground of being, a precondition for all other individual forms of love. It is not *love for* something, but our nature *as love*, and the felt truth of our existence as already whole, already worthy, already delightful.

Through this nondual mirroring, even our most wounded parts, the inner-child who felt rejected, unseen, or abandoned, begin to receive what was missing. The naturally benevolent, nonjudgmental awareness of unconditional love becomes the mirror we didn't have from our injured, but usually well-intentioned, parents. And in that mirror, the injured-self softens, relaxes, and begins to heal. Each nondual quality becomes a doorway to this healing, offering its particular transmission of unconditional acceptance and belonging.

Since the loss or distortion of love is at the root of all emotional injury, reconnecting with this inborn ground of love initiates a deep reorganization within the body-mind system. We find greater emotional resilience, more capacity to meet intensity, and a renewed ability to be present with pain, without bracing against it or collapsing into it. The same energy that once fueled sabotaging habits or addictive patterns now becomes available for presence, intimacy, and spiritual depth.

If we had caregivers who embodied their own sense of wholeness, we might have naturally recognized this same wholeness within ourselves. Their attunement would have reflected our innate value, making this love and belonging a native experience. But if our parents were cut off from their own essential being, if their love was conditional, inconsistent, or wounding, we are not condemned to repeat that inheritance. Through whole-being meditation, we can begin to access a more essential source of reflection: the pure, uninjured mirror of our own unchanging nature.

As this practice deepens, our inner experience of abandonment or emotional invasion is gradually pervaded by a visceral sense of being whole, untouched, and unbreakable. The very texture of our inner world begins to shift, spatially, temporally, and somatically. Our sense of self reorganizes around wholeness rather than fragmentation. This transformation often brings physiological changes, shifts in nervous system regulation, neurochemistry, and emotional tone, alongside new insight and clarity.

In this sacred space of embodied wholeness, the wounded parts of us no longer need to grasp or defend. Our compensatory patterns and trauma adaptations begin to lose their hold. It's as if these patterns are "loved to death," not through willful elimination, but by being so completely seen, met, and held in the vastness of the unified nature of unconditional love that they simply dissolve. They are no longer necessary.

What remains is a natural expression of our authentic self, with healthy desires and aversions that are no longer distorted by a history of unmet needs or hidden wounds. We begin to live not in reaction to the past, but in resonance with the present as a presence that is whole, free, and deeply connected.

When our whole body and mind are an experience of unconditional love, we can remain emotionally present with both ourselves and others. This presence makes relationships not only deeper but more vibrant, authentic, and passionate. Love nourishes us most fully when it involves our whole-being, heart, body, mind, and spirit, moving together in an integrated rhythm of giving and receiving.

Of course, love is not a simple or unbroken stream of sweetness. We may feel love for someone and, at the very same time, experience anger, frustration, or even moments of hate. These seemingly contradictory emotions do not negate unconditional love; they reveal its depth. This love is spacious enough to hold them all. What matters is our ability to remain open in the body, allowing us to manage these turbulent feelings without shutting down. As we cultivate this capacity, love becomes more consistent, less fragile, and more trustworthy.

Like any living entity, love must be nurtured. It cannot thrive on neglect, nor can it survive on coercion. Love does not say, *"If you really loved me, you would..."* Such conditional demands are a form of emotional blackmail, a distortion of love into a form of control. True love is not proven through ultimatums, but lived through presence, care, and the willingness to see and be seen.

And here lies one of the deepest truths: love cannot be fully received if it cannot first be felt within. No matter how much you love someone, if they have not yet learned to love themselves, they will not believe your love is real or only receive it superficially. It is like telling someone who feels deeply unattractive that they are beautiful. The words may be kind, but without the inner ground of feeling self-love to receive them, they may only feel incredulous and confused.

Unconditional love, then, is both a gift and a practice. It is an embodied presence that must be uncovered and awakened within us if we are to open and share it authentically with another. Yet, because our deepest wounds make us suspicious of the open tenderness of love, we are sometimes more receptive to other qualities of oneness.

As the nondual mirroring holds us in the light of love and our intrinsic sense of self-worth grows, our habits of self-criticism and unconscious patterns of self-abusive behavior naturally fall away. It is easy to become our own best friend and stand up for ourselves while being fair and compassionate to others.

Chapter Eight

It's Not Out There, It's In Here

Embracing Impermanence

Whole-being-embrace practice differs from the common teaching in many Eastern traditions that tell us all attachment, whether to pleasure, people, possessions, experiences, or habits, inevitably leads to suffering. The logic in these common teachings is simple: everything we cling to changes, and nothing can offer lasting happiness. As the Buddha suggested, it is not impermanence that makes us suffer, but wanting things to be permanent when they are not.

While many transcendent traditions emphasize releasing harmful desires and aversions, a full human life includes the impermanence of things such as, healthy desires, aversions, and pleasures. Luckily, the impermanence of our emotional, mental, and sensory life does not always bring suffering. It is part of the natural rhythm of life, allowing for growth, change, loss, and new beginnings. Impermanence may bring emotions like sadness when what we cherish fades, but it also carries the promise that hardship will pass and that renewal is always possible. We can experience this as a coherence of self that leads to authenticity, not a rigid identity, but an integrated and fluid expression of our emotional, mental, and sensory life.

In this light, the central issue becomes how we relate to harmful desires in order to release them. When we embrace impermanence and all that comes with it, we do not distance ourselves from life, but we cultivate a richer relationship with it. Unified consciousness provides the sense of timeless permanence that supports us to open ourselves to the tender richness of each moment as it is.

This openness becomes a safe harbor, allowing us to deepen our appreciation for the present rather than reacting impulsively to the dynamics of change. When we embrace the poignancy and depth of life, we are not afraid to feel the sorrow or joy that impermanence brings. It sharpens our ability to meet the inevitability of change and awakens a freedom that arises not from control or any form of separation from our messy impermanence, but from the maturity that results from participating in our emotional life.

In whole-being-embrace, healing and spiritual awakening are found in meeting life as it is, changing, imperfect, and alive. Impermanence becomes our teacher, resilience our companion. We learn to love without grasping, to let go without indifference, and to stand in the fullness of our humanity while rooted in the stillness of our unchanging-self.

The New Spirituality of Wholeness & Boundaries

Other nondual spiritual traditions often teach that seeing the impermanent, separate self, the ego, as an illusion dissolves its influence. While the word "I" may remain as a simple tool for communication, its perceived solidity fades. What once felt like a fixed identity is revealed to be a shifting stream of thoughts, sensations, and habits. In this view, there is no significant separate self to find, only experience unfolding.

Yet this perspective, while liberating in certain contexts, can also be limiting. The ego's function is not inherently negative.

It is not just a survival mechanism or a bundle of unconscious habits. A healthy, integrated ego provides structure, meaning, emotional depth, and the capacity to engage with life. It supports our passions, ambitions, and unique personal expression.

Feeling distinct from others is also emotionally protective. It allows us to establish and maintain healthy boundaries, which are essential for preventing enmeshment, codependency, and emotional overwhelm. A well-defined sense of individuality strengthens resilience, self-reliance, and confidence in our ability to navigate life's challenges.

Emotional well-being depends, in part, on a sense of separation, which creates the psychological space necessary to reflect on our thoughts, values, and desires without being swallowed by external influence. When we feel secure in our individuality, we feel more support to connect with others not out of fear or need, but freely and authentically.

A healthy sense of separateness also makes empathy possible. Recognizing that others have perspectives and emotional realities distinct from our own is fundamental to emotional intelligence and deep social connection. In this way, separateness is not isolation, it is the grounding that allows connection to flourish.

Feeling anchored in the solidity of the body in relationship with the solidity of the Earth strengthens our sense of existing and belonging. It gives us orientation, safety, and the confidence to relax into being. These simple, embodied experiences of our physical nature (solidity, weight, gravity) can be sources of support that provide peace of mind. They can contribute to the sacred roots of the feeling *"I am home."*

As mentioned, the true goal, then, is not to eliminate the ego but to integrate it so that these supportive aspects of it can emerge. The ego is not an obstacle to awakening; it is simply the part of us that learned to navigate life with the information it had. It needs to be guided, supported, and informed by a deeper, uninjured, and more connected dimension of self. When aligned

162

with our sense of wholeness, the ego becomes flexible, grounded, and wise, expressing our authentic nature rather than defending our wounds.

Yet injury can fragment our healthy ego. For those carrying the residue of emotional injury, wholeness is profoundly healing. One important way our sense of wholeness is healing concerns our perception of space. Unresolved injury fragments our sense of space; it confuses us to where we end and where others begin. As Peter Levine and Pat Ogden have shown, trauma can leave us disoriented, dissociated, and unable to feel "self-in-place." Our internal compass, the embodied sense of "I am here," becomes scrambled.

When this happens, we tend to swing between extremes. Some of us build rigid emotional walls, cutting ourselves off from others to stay safe. Others dissolve those walls entirely, losing ourselves in relationship until we no longer know what we really feel. Either way, we lose access to the simple, grounded safety of belonging, both to ourselves and to the world around us.

One way wholeness helps restore this balance is that it reawakens our natural, multidimensional awareness of space. As embodied awareness deepens, we begin to sense not just that we occupy space, but that we are space, a living field of presence both within and around the body.

Ordinarily, we experience space as something external, a container through which the body moves, separate and limited. Psychology often reinforces this duality by describing human experience through binary frameworks such as inner/outer, self/other, mind/body. These distinctions are useful but incomplete; they describe only conditioned experience.

In embodied nondual awareness, something shifts. The space within and the space around the body begin to reveal itself as one continuous field. The air we breathe, the pulse of blood, the hum of life in our surroundings, all merge into a single, luminous continuum of being. This realization does not erase individuality; it enriches it. We still feel our distinct self, yet it is infused with

163

stillness, spaciousness, and permeability. We awaken to the truth that the infinite has always been here, shimmering through the finite form we inhabit.[26]

Awakening to our unchanging-self opens us to the larger truth that nothing is separate. Our awareness extends to include all beings (human, animal, and elemental) as part of the same seamless fabric of life. We begin to identify less with a single group or role and more with the wholeness of existence itself. This shift counteracts the isolation and fragmentation that fuel anxiety, loneliness, and depression. As we sense our inherent belonging to all of life, compassion and connection become natural states of being.

This belonging does not erase our individuality. We remain grounded in our authenticity and able to discern what feels right for us. In whole-being-embrace our sense of "home" in the body is not merely physically solid and separate; it is spiritual. Supported by our sense of oneness, our body can also be experienced to be a container, a sanctuary that we can fill up from the inside with the support we never got enough of as a child. It can hold all the love, support, and truth we once sought outside ourselves.

As we open to inner space with the warmth of presence, we begin to rewrite the messages of childhood that told us it wasn't safe to feel, express, or need. The body becomes both the temple and the teacher, holding us, protecting us, and pervaded by the wholeness that reminds us that we belong.[27]

---

[26] Neuroscience shows that our sense of space is shaped not only by sight but by all five senses, along with deeper systems like the vestibular sense (balance and gravity) and even gut intuition. In meditation, when we begin to feel space as a conscious presence within the body, we access what some call the brain's "seventh sense"—awareness of awareness itself. Here, the limited evolving-self meets the unlimited unchanging-self. This meeting—the whole-being-embrace—can be felt as an "eighth sense," a lived union of stillness and movement, consciousness and energy.

[27] In yoga, *viyoga*—meaning "separation" or "disunion"—refers to creating a protective inner environment that supports autonomy and nondual awareness. It involves separating from influences that disrupt our clarity, honoring our

This is the great paradox of embodied nonduality: we are both distinct and inseparable, local and infinite. From this embodied wholeness, we can say, "I am here, and you are there", while also knowing, "You and I are one life meeting itself in two forms."

This paradox reshapes how we experience relationship. We stop confusing boundaries with separation. We no longer need to disappear into others to feel connection, nor isolate to feel safe. Boundaries become expressions of truth, flexible, kind, and alive, rooted in the clarity of our being rather than the fears of our past.

This is not a concept or philosophy; it is a lived reality, a body-felt knowing of being both here and everywhere at once. From this place, we can meet life with openness and discernment, grounded in authenticity yet free from the prison of and unhealthy ego. Maintaining this inner orientation (rooted in the body's location in space even as we sense the vastness of consciousness) reinforces a strong sense of self-agency.

From the stillness and spaciousness of unified consciousness arises a natural clarity: we have a healthy sense of where we begin and end, emotionally, mentally, and energetically. This clarity gives rise to integrity in relationship, the ability to remain true to ourselves while fully available to others. It restores the lost capacities that trauma once fractured: inner guidance, embodied wisdom, and the ability to trust what our body knows.

When our evolving-self is held within the spacious embrace of unified consciousness, psychology and spirituality finally meet as one. The result is not transcendence that escapes life, nor psychology that confines it to ego, but a lived whole-self that includes both.

The embodied experience of existing simultaneously in both dimensions of our being is a living synthesis, a divine

---

natural impulses for self-preservation. This may mean releasing what no longer serves us and setting clear boundaries so that others' judgments, negativity, or dismissive energy do not penetrate our body–mind system.

embrace that holds them in a single continuum. Within this union, we discover a healing potential that neither tradition alone can fully offer. Together, they create a field of coherence in which our emotional wounds can reorganize, integrate, and transform. This, truly, is the next step in our collective evolution, a spirituality not about rising above life beyond our senses, but about stepping deeply, consciously, and tenderly into it.

Another view of the multidimensional awareness of space (local and nonlocal) that restores balance and heals, is what I call holographic space. In this awareness, the smallest sensation within the body reflects the wholeness of the cosmos, and all of space can be felt within even the tiniest pulse of awareness. While this is an extension of our experience of unified space within the body that has already been discussed, it deserves a little more attention to flesh out why it is healing.

Holographic Body

As we let go of habitual constrictions and open into the body, rather than trying to escape it, we discover the *holographic nature of nonduality.* Within each part of the body, in every cell, and with every breath, we can experience the whole of the universe. This is explored in great detail in my book, *Nondual Chakra Awakening*, where every chakra is a holographic expression of the qualities of oneness found within.

In this state, we may feel that every part of the body contains the whole, echoing Deepak Chopra's idea that consciousness forms hidden connections between seemingly unrelated events and places. Our inner landscape begins to reflect the vast outer cosmos. The macrocosm exists within the microcosm of the body, and the microcosm of the body resonates within the macrocosm of our environment.

In whole-being meditation, reclaiming our sovereignty and sacred belonging begins by returning to the body as holy ground.

166

Because nondual awareness is holographic, every part reflects the whole. From any single point in the body (from the subtle vibration in the chest, the breath's rising and falling, or the quiet hum in the soles of the feet), we can enter directly into both our own wholeness and the undivided ground of all existence. The very places where trauma lives, those constricted, aching, or fragmented parts of our psyche and body, come into direct contact with spaciousness, connection, and unconditional love. What once felt like sites of exile become sanctuaries of belonging.

In this way, whole-being meditation not only awakens us to cosmic unity; it restores our intimate connection to our self as cosmic. As the poet William Blake so beautifully expressed:

"To see a World in a Grain of Sand
And a Heaven in a Wild Flower,
Hold Infinity in the palm of your hand
And Eternity in an hour..."

These verses reflect the same principle: the whole is present in every part. Eternity lives in time. The divine reveals itself in the particular.

Developing a conscious rapport with the unified qualities of self as a body experience, requires the willingness to savor the most subtle feelings of inner attunement. For many of us, this is the first time we truly show up for ourselves, not from performance, protection, or strategy, but from the ground of our own wholeness.

At first, this embodied experience of spacious unity within the body may seem paradoxical: unlimited space is "non-local," existing everywhere, and yet when we turn our attention inward, we can directly sense an unbroken spaciousness within the body that is seamlessly unified with the environment around us. By remaining anchored in the body while simultaneously connected with oneness, we discover that unlimited space is not elsewhere. It is here, living within us as the very ground of our being.

This paradox (feeling the infinite within the finite boundaries of the body) transforms how we relate to ourselves and others. We begin to experience a profound sense of breathing room, even in the midst of intimacy and connection. The presence of unlimited space meets our deepest relational injuries, giving us a stable ground from which we can tolerate life's intensity without fragmenting. Feelings of helplessness, terror, or panic about being trapped or imposed upon soften, as they are pervaded by a sense of spaciousness. In this openness, we access a renewed independence from the agendas, expectations, and emotional demands of others, while our sovereignty is quietly and effortlessly reinforced.

For those who grew up feeling invasively controlled or imposed upon, this discovery is profoundly liberating. We feel increasingly able to let go of our habit of expressing rigid boundaries and being emotionally distant and isolated. Suddenly, there is room to move, to breathe, and to express what authentically wants to emerge without defense. The old strategies (minimizing the importance of relationships, withdrawing behind "leave me alone," or meeting others with guarded eyes) begin to dissolve. Negotiations stop feeling like a threat to our freedom.

Because this unified spaciousness is holographic, any single point of attention within the body can open into the sense of infinite space. This has profound implications for healing emotional injury. Our habitual constrictions (the flinch in the cheek that remembers a slap, the tightness in the gut that holds the echo of harsh words, the collapse in the chest that still carries the weight of rejection) gain access to a radically different experience. In place of contraction, we discover wholeness, in place of abandonment, unconditional love. The body learns it no longer needs to brace or collapse; it can rest in the support of spacious being.

When these two experiences (ultimate contact and breathing-room) come together, they create a powerful antidote to the defensive patterns born of unresolved relationship injury. It is

168

a living paradox: to feel the visceral texture of unlimited spaciousness within the body, granting us freedom to be authentically ourselves, while simultaneously feeling deeply connected, whole, and held. This embodied paradox speaks directly to the core of attachment and bonding injuries, where contact and autonomy were once in conflict. From this wholeness, connection, and inner spaciousness, we discover the ground from which our unresolved injuries can finally come to rest.

Being Held

We've considered how important it is to not have a controlling relationship with our senses but instead to have a participatory relationship with them. Because the senses are ground zero for where injuries first show up and a primary source of what perpetuates our injuries, it is important to have a better understanding of what this actually means.

Our evolving-self carries within it the imprints of unresolved injuries from the past. These imprints, emotional, mental, and physical, are not merely conceptualized memories but sensory-based impressions that shape our present experience and cause us to fearfully ruminate and project about the future. Our suffering arises, in large part, from our fixation on these past wounds in an attempt to protect ourselves and in anticipation that they will repeat. [28]

In whole-being-embrace, we do not turn away from perception but turn toward it, meeting each sensation, sound, image, smell, or taste as part of a living dialogue between consciousness and form. The senses become pathways of

---

[28] Rather than the yoga practices of withdrawing from the senses (*pratyahara*), purifying them (*sodhana*), or merely witnessing them as passing phenomena (*sakshi*), embodied nondual practice invites our whole-self into an intimate relationship with them.

communion rather than simply illusions or sources of distraction. Even the meanings and projections we've attached to past experiences (the emotional imprints, judgments, and interpretations) are invitations into deeper understanding. Our sensory life, so often conditioned by memory and defense, becomes a direct expression of wholeness, and way for love itself to touch the world through us.

In this way, we cultivate a relationship *with* everything that gives us a sense of separation and individuality. We view these factors not as problems to be eliminated, but as a phenomenon to be understood and embraced with a broader field of awareness. Instead of disciplining the senses and stilling the mind to override the chaos of our suffering, we allow the mind and body to express their conditioned patterns within the holding environment (Winnicott) of our body's experience of unified consciousness.

As described earlier, this environment could be considered to be a nondual holding environment. Much like a child who sought a holding environment to find refuge and support, in meditation, we feel how our unchanging-self provides an internal place or state of consciousness within our body that we can return our attention to for support. In this way, we "put our self back together" when our evolving-self feels overwhelmed, disoriented, or confused.

This relational, spiritual approach to developing emotional autonomy creates a sensory inner atmosphere where even our most painful or compulsive tendencies can begin to soften. We no longer need to exile parts of ourselves, such as our emotional and mental life, to achieve inner peace. Instead, we feel that every part of us, including our wounded ego, our habitual fears, and even our maladaptive behaviors, can be welcomed as honored guests.

As Rumi so delightfully writes:

This being human is a guest house.
A joy, a depression, a meanness,
some momentary awareness comes
as an unexpected visitor.
Welcome and entertain them all...
Even if they're a crowd of sorrows,
who violently sweep your house
empty of its furniture,
still, treat each guest honorably...
Be grateful for whoever comes,
because each has been sent
as a guide from beyond.

In this approach, it is as if our unchanging-self bathes our evolving-self's senses in the non-abandoning, non-invasive presence of the vast, still, timeless, and luminous wholeness. This is not about *moving beyond* the conditioning that accompanies our memories that leads to limiting habitual responses, but *moving toward* memory with a different kind of presence. By meeting memory while anchored in our spiritual essence, we reduce the fear and avoidance that often accompany unresolved emotional injuries. What once triggered fear, shame, or depression becomes an opportunity for healing, integration, and profound embodiment.

Meeting the sensory experiences that accompany memory while anchored in unified presence is restorative. The openness that pervades our body becomes a safe harbor where we embrace the poignancy and depth of life and impermanence becomes our teacher. This is a sensory embrace where the limited space of form and the unlimited space of formlessness allow us to fully meet the realities of our wounds.

Our unchanging-self provides an internal place or state of consciousness where our evolving-self can put itself back together when we feel overwhelmed. This living paradox communicates directly to each of our senses. A deeper understanding of how this happens is important.

Washing our Five Senses Clean

At the most fundamental level, our memories of the past are rooted in our five senses. These sensory impressions serve as the building blocks of memory. When a specific scent, sound, or texture echoes a past experience, the body and mind can instantly re-enter that remembered state, often bypassing our rational awareness. For instance, a faint smell of cologne may suddenly evoke the atmosphere of a painful encounter, while a familiar tone of voice may reawaken feelings of abandonment or love.

When emotional injury and trauma fragment our sense of self, our sensory system often contracts and distorts. We lose the natural fluidity of perception, and instead, our senses become narrow gateways through which unresolved pain continues to recur. Over time, our learned responses to these sensory impressions form the content of our trauma symptoms and reinforce the often-dramatized stories we carry about the past.

Central to healing is the ability to develop emotional autonomy from our sensory perceptions that lead to our conditioned, habitual responses. Emotional autonomy is the ability to remain connected to what feels authentic for us in the moment without being hijacked by conditioned responses (reactivity).

With our whole-self online, our perspective broadens, and we become less at the mercy of our outdated memories and the sabotaging habits of mind and body that they generate. As our unchanging-self gently permeates and bathes our senses in the presence of wholeness, each of our senses are washed clean of its constrictions, and our injuries lose their power over us.

This is a gradual process, and it is important to understand that the more open our senses become, and the more open we become to our senses, the more the more we can feel the qualities of oneness and wholeness, which are primarily sensory experiences. Our sense of openness enhances our perception of subtlety. This is why it is important to not give up when we do not feel the qualities of oneness right away. The nervous system might need access to unified consciousness as an experience in the body and the environment we have. *

In this way, an ongoing body experience of our unified presence of being gradually transforms the functioning of our senses such that they no longer carry the constrictions and limiting emotional and mental conditioning that accompanies our injuries. As our senses open, they do not overwhelm us with past pain, but serve as portals to presence, wonder, and well-being.

As our senses grow more refined, more attuned, they begin to unveil the luminosity and the spacious stillness that pervades the tissues of our body. Along the way, we may encounter a temporary blurring of perception, as the familiar limiting habits soften and release.

Gradually, we shift from the narrowed perception of constricted senses into a more open, unadorned field of experience. We learn to rest in the luminosity of bare perception, in the sober, undistorted reality of sight, sound, smell, touch, and even taste where life appears at once simpler and more profound; authentic, true to the moment and not bound by the past.

Our senses increasingly have direct or bare perception, which gives us access to feelings of oneness with other people. Rather than the superficial contact of seeing and touching from the surface of ourselves to the surface of other people, we see, hear, and touch deeper than the external façade to the feeling of unity and wholeness.

We feel the interior spaciousness of our own form, which allows us to perceive others with deeper attunement to the unified essence of existence. This is an experience of the openness of our own form, which enables us to live in wholeness with ourselves and others. We increasingly become able to see and touch beneath the surface to include the whole interior dimension of life around us. Feeling the attributes of unified consciousness (stillness, timelessness, unity, etc.) within all of existence provides the basis of deep understanding and attunement.

While our evolving-self arises in response to a relational environment, our unchanging-self is innate and independent of relational circumstances. As described, when our senses open and are washed clean of constrictions, paradoxically, it is our unchanging-self that allows us to feel most deeply connected to others, to the world, and to the universe itself. As noted, this sense of connection is not based on similarity or difference, but on the recognition of a shared ground of being that often feels familiar.

When we encounter someone, such as a spiritual teacher, romantic partner, or even a beloved animal, who is attuned to their own inner wholeness, it can awaken a remembrance of wholeness within us. These moments of profound intimacy and connection allow us to feel the continuity of presence as an unbroken thread of awareness, love, and sensation that is woven into the fabric of life itself.

This relational approach marks a significant shift in both our spiritual orientation and our style of relating. We cultivate autonomy by changing *how we relate* to suffering. We identify the distortions, projections, and interpretations we've made, and bring them into communion with the broader perspective of our unified nature. The goal here is not to identify with emotions as if they define us, but to acknowledge and accept them as valid internal signals.

When we relate to emotions in this way, we can use their information consciously to guide our actions with clarity and balance. In this way, we are increasingly no longer defined by our reactions or imprisoned by the meanings we've inherited or created. [29]

---

[29] While stepping back from emotions by disidentifying from them can help us develop autonomy, it can also create too much distance, leading to suppression or difficulty recognizing what we actually feel, which makes it harder to understand the message the emotion is sending about our personal truth.

174

Chapter Nine

Paths To Wholeness

Before we explore the nature and impact of whole-being-embrace in the chapters ahead, this chapter lays the foundation by clarifying what it really means to uncover and awaken unified consciousness. Understanding this will help you make sense of the many approaches found across spiritual traditions, and see how whole-being-embrace grows naturally from them while offering something new and deeply embodied.

The Indirect and Direct Paths of Yoga

It can be said that yoga practice can be divided into yoga as a means and yoga as a goal. Yoga and meditation, when used *as a means* to balance the body and mind, follow what's often called the "indirect path." This approach focuses on balancing the body and mind by regulating our energy. We use practices like posture (*asana*), breathwork (*pranayama*), sacred sound (*mantra*), or visualization (*yantra*) to gradually calm and harmonize our inner system. The goal is to quiet the fluctuations of the mind, as Patanjali described, "Yoga is the stilling of the mind's movements." Over time, as our thoughts, emotions, and sensations settle, we begin to feel more stable, spacious, and peaceful inside.

This path is incremental and deeply valuable because it helps us learn how to self-regulate the energy underlying our mental, emotional, and sensory experiences. But it can also be slow. It may take years, sometimes a lifetime, of steady practice to reach moments of real stillness or unity. For many of us, especially those carrying old wounds or trauma, quieting the mind on command can feel almost impossible. The harder we try to silence our thoughts, the louder they seem to get.

That's why it's helpful to include yoga as a goal, or what's known as the *direct path*, a more immediate approach that doesn't depend on perfect stillness or years of discipline. The direct path allows us to touch unity through direct experience, right here in the body, even as we continue to heal and grow. We attune directly to the nondual state of consciousness with minimal self-regulation of mind-body energies.

The direct path is endorsed by certain spiritual teachers, sometimes referred to as *"immediatist gurus,"* including Eckhart Tolle, Ram Dass, Adi Da, and Andrew Cohen. They emphasize the possibility of instant awakening, a sudden, unmediated realization of spiritual truth that requires little or no prior training.

This approach to the direct path aims at transcendence through complete absorption in unified consciousness and the surrender of the ego. This offers a peak experience with a taste of freedom from suffering by helping us temporarily detach from the ego's grip. When these experiences of unity arise spontaneously, they often feel mysterious or miraculous, like a moment of *grace*. We often experience that we've reached into the cosmos and downloaded a sense of oneness from "above" or "beyond." It can feel as though we've been chosen, touched by God, or actively blessed by something greater than ourselves. This happens as a rarified visit of a peak experience rather than learning to live more fully right where we are.

This sudden, transcendent revelation can leave us wanting more but unsure of how it happened or how to return to it. Moreover, the evolving-self is often bypassed or left out of the

176

process entirely. As a result, we can be left feeling dependent on something outside ourselves, or unsure of how to incorporate the experience into our daily lives.

In contrast to the immediatist guru orientation, the approach to the direct-path emphasized in whole-being-embrace is rooted in our self-aware, body experience of unified consciousness as an aspect of self, our unchanging-self. While this also offers direct, unmediated access to spiritual insight, the nature of that insight is different.

In whole-being meditation, both indirect and direct paths coexist: the indirect path of gradual healing and self-regulation unfolds within the immediate presence of our wholeness and our unchanging-self. This integration is an inherent part of whole-being-embrace, which not only supports spiritual insight but also psychological healing.

A key insight here is that we can access unified consciousness at any time, even if our capacity to sustain it and integrate its presence requires practice and repetition. Our evolving-self participates and is embraced. As we progressively access this luminous nature, we begin to recognize our potential for transformation. Nondual consciousness is a body experience that is surprisingly accessible when we find the stillness of a balanced, relaxed-alert state.

As we grow our ability to remain non-grasping and open in both how we perceive and respond to what we experience, our habitual reactions and the suffering this leads to lose their staying power. When we refine this ability through the practice of effortlessness, we learn to let go of any habitual constrictions. We sustain a sense of remaining fully open within the body while we perceive and respond. This can feel like what we perceive arises out of pervasive space, and our responses seem to spontaneously arise out of these qualities of unity without effort. We are in "the flow."

Our perceptions become luminous and our responses spontaneous and free. It is as if each of our senses are illuminated, and our responses become graceful. Like learning a new language, the more we align with the experience of effortless living, the more familiar and natural it feels.

The relationship between energy flow and unified consciousness is not linear but cyclical, a living, self-reinforcing loop. As we directly attune to the felt presence of unified consciousness within the body, our energy begins to flow more freely. This flow brings greater stability, resilience, clarity, and the ability to live more authentically as ourselves. Also, the freer our energy becomes, the less we are bound by habitual constrictions, and the more our natural wholeness reveals itself.

With each cycle, openness deepens. Unified consciousness shines through more clearly, more fully embodied in our lived experience. Each turn of this cycle strengthens the next, creating an upward spiral of personal and spiritual evolution. In this way, the integration of mind, body, and energy becomes not only healing but transformative. It is a dynamic process through which wholeness and authenticity cease to be concepts and become a felt, living reality.

This version of the direct-path becomes more than a method of meditation; it becomes a way of remembering who we are. It is a powerful inner resource, often overlooked in both Eastern spirituality and Western psychology, as well as in mystical Christianity. It reveals an essential truth: a state of consciousness can be attained, but it does not guarantee attaining a new stage of emotional development or healing. We can taste the vastness of nonduality, emptiness, or bliss at any point along our human journey. Yet, we don't need to be fully healed or psychologically mature to glimpse the infinite. Without embodiment, these glimpses remain only partial and usually only temporary. They can transcend our pain but not necessarily transform it.

Each of us experiences and interprets awakening through the filter of our current developmental stage. This is why even realized spiritual teachers, those who radiate light and possess refined perception, can still act from unhealed wounds. They may

178

have awakened to truth but not yet integrated that awakening into their emotional life. They've touched the sky but haven't healed the ground. The result is an awakening that soars, but deep wounds can still exist which makes it harder to pervade the earth with lasting love.

Through whole-being-embrace, awakening becomes a homecoming, a descent as well as an ascent. It invites us to revisit each stage of our development and re-inhabit the body with the luminous presence of unified consciousness. Here, we learn to face the challenges of each stage without losing contact with the stillness and wholeness that hold space for us.

While my book *Nondual Chakra Awakening* (2024) explores how this integration unfolds through the stages of development, here, we turn toward something more elemental: the secure bonding experience that underlies emotional growth across all the stages. We experience this same living bond between our evolving-self and our unchanging-self. It is through this bond that emotional and spiritual growth truly intertwine across all the stages.

Through this living bond, unified consciousness ceases to be a rare or fleeting experience. This direct bond becomes a constant companion, a healing ground of awareness that infuses our ordinary moments with grace and healing. Whole-being-embrace is the ultimate direct path.

What is Whole-Being Meditation?

The term *embodied nondual meditation* refers to a broad range of meditation practices, a few of which, while embodied, trend towards being transcendent in nature. While whole-being-embrace is also embodied, it is fundamentally integral rather than transcendent in its orientation. For this reason, the term *whole-being meditation* more accurately reflects the approach of the whole-being-embrace practice, emphasizing the embodied integration of all dimensions of experience, rather than a movement beyond them.

To set the stage for a direct experience of whole-being meditation, at least a taste of it, take a moment to settle into the following meditation. Do not strain to make anything "happen." Remember, we cannot create an experience of unified consciousness through effort or will. It comes on its own when we are relaxed and open, like clear water rising naturally once the ground has softened enough to let it through.

Understanding what a body experience of oneness is requires more than reading about it. As you read the description, while it is not an actual guided meditation, I invite you to approach these ideas not as abstract concepts, but as living possibilities within your own direct experience. The description is designed to help you sense this awareness for yourself, an intimate first step toward discovering what it feels like to rest in the wholeness of your own being.

It is important not to struggle with any of the suggested awarenesses during a meditation. See what makes sense to you and change any suggestion to meet your particular needs. In yoga, we progress from external to internal. In this schema, imagination is more external than the actual experience. Imagination can be a helpful skill to have as an initial step towards refining the subtlety of our perception. With practice, we can uncover and clarify an actual felt experience. We come to recognize how to use our imagination in the most conscious way, and we do not use it to create delusions.

The qualities of the ground of our being are felt directly in the body as states of subtle presence. "Subtle," in this context, doesn't necessarily mean difficult to detect. It means the pattern is more refined, embedded, and opaque, like a background experience we've learned to live with and stop noticing. Once we know what to look for, our unified nature as a presence of being, becomes surprisingly accessible.

180

In meditation, we start by learning how to refine the senses and inhabit our body. We refine the nuances of relaxing, letting go of effort, and breathing with awareness. While the nuances of relaxing are calming, the feeling of openness it leads to (an unobstructed inner space) is awakening. Savoring openness activates the parasympathetic and sympathetic nervous system. Together, it creates a *relaxed-alert* feeling (*sukha-sthira*). This is a balanced state that, with practice, gives us access to the stillness of unified consciousness. While perception of our unchanging-self is self-arising and spontaneous, attending to these sensations sets the stage.

At the start, perceiving these subtle sensations (enteroception) is not always obvious, but with practice, they become clearly evident. Recognizing these sensations forms the basis not only of learning to manage the energy underlying what we experience, but also of building blocks for cultivating emotional intelligence in a way that the body informs the mind.

Learning from stillness is not unique to meditation; it is woven into the fabric of life itself. It can be found in the transition between our inhale and exhale. It is the undeniable sense of knowing when breath is taken away by a beautiful scene in nature and your mind stops for a moment in deep appreciation of the beauty. Stillness often rises spontaneously in moments of heart opening. Stillness is not passivity or about holding still, but a portal. For the meditator, it becomes a threshold into the healing power of the unwavering presence of the ground of being.

Before exploring a description of the details of whole-being meditation practice, keep in mind that there is a meditation library at my website (drzeb.com) where you can access a variety of one-hour guided meditations. They are available to download for an actual experience of whole-being-embrace. After each guided suggestion, remember to pause and take as long as you feel is appropriate to explore the experience. Most of us are not familiar with embodiment (deeply feeling ourselves in the body).

Remember that the unchanging-self is not a solitary state but a relational field, a seamless unity of self and other. Whenever we shut out either our inner experience or the world around us, our consciousness fragments, and our deeper essence becomes obscured. Spiritual oneness is the natural balance of inward and outward contact, held together in a single ground of awareness.

In meditation, we begin by refining the most intimate form of contact we have: the felt sense of our own being within the body. As this deepens, our perception of everything around us also becomes clearer and more connected. We start to sense how inner contact and outer contact are inseparable.

Patterns of openness and defense in our sense organs shape the range of qualities we are able to perceive in the world. Our experience of oneness is disrupted by static or constricted areas in the body and energy system. These enduring constrictions (and the associated numbness and collapse) distort our connection with ourselves and with others. They dull our awareness, restrict our emotions, and limit our capacity to feel. As these patterns unwind, with practice, the ground of unity naturally reveals itself once again.

In embodied nondual meditation practice, the initial intention is to reverse our automatic response when we become overwhelmed. We begin reversing this response by focusing on relaxing on the most subtle level. This is important because every limiting emotional, physical, and mental habit creates chronic physical constrictions. When overwhelmed we tend to automatically constrict toward our core and lift away from the ground (a sympathetic nervous system response). Doing this in all parts of the body deepens the experience.

Your vagus nerve detects sensations of relaxation and informs the brain. This trains the brain to shift away from acting like Velcro to alarm sensations and Teflon to supportive sensations. In this way, the body increasingly becomes a safe location to live in and receive life's experiences.

182

Savor what this relaxation feels like in the body and attune to even the slightest sense of spaciousness within each part of the body. It may simply feel less dense or soft and fluid inside. These feelings may take some practice to access, but they are usually quite easy to access.

General Practice Guidelines

As you do each of the following subtle practices, savor any sensations that are soothing and nurturing. Begin refining your senses by first attuning to more obvious sensations, then progressively to the more subtle ones. Bring your attention inward and focus on the present moment as much as possible without strain. This helps regulate the nervous system and interrupts survival responses. Pay attention to the feeling of breathing and invite it to become naturally rhythmic and effortless, so there is no constriction on your inhale and exhale. As you do this, take time to refine your experience by relaxing all the way from the front to the back of your body, and all the way out to the sides.

One way we *refine relaxing* is by sequentially focusing on and deeply savoring each of these steps: focus on one part of the body and 1. *Soften* any subtle constriction or sense of density (muscle, bones, constrictions, numbness, collapse). 2. *Settle* the energy that is released towards the ground. 3. *Rest* upon any sense of the solidness that supports you:

1) *Softening*: Perception of softening can be facilitated by focusing on the nuances of breathing. In particular, we attend to letting go of habitual constrictions as we inhale and exhale. As we do this, we savor any sense of letting go or dissolving the constrictions throughout the body (and the associated areas that feel frozen, numb, and collapsed).

Plus, enter into relationship with the ground by noticing where your body meets the ground or a surface, like the pressure of your feet on the floor, your seat on a chair, or your back leaning against the chair. Savor resting upon these contact points and let your whole body, especially each of the constricted areas, feel and *receive any sense of support* from the solidness of the ground (honor solidness as a bridge to your own deepening). Savor even the slightest sense of relaxation and absorb your attention upon this sensation so that other areas can learn what this feels like.

2) *Settling*: Attune to the sensation of settling the content of what relaxes within the body toward the ground. Give the weight of your body to the earth. Breathing without effort, so you invite not constricting on the inhale and exhale, facilitates bringing the body's center of gravity down, creating a feeling of being rooted. Make sure you don't collapse as you settle. (Keeping each of your body segments aligned helps this.)

3) *Rest* the content of your experience on the ground (metaphorically). See what you need to let go of, so you do not lift away from the ground, especially on your inhale. Observe sensations like warmth, pressure, or even mild discomfort as they are, letting them exist without trying to change them, allowing them to settle, come to rest, and naturally become less intense.

"Settling" upon the ground helps restore your natural rhythms, allowing the energy in your body to flow freely. Savor any sense of a quiet, steady ease, like a weight has lifted, and attune to the sense that you can simply *be*. As you arrive right where you are, feel for any sense of belonging to the world, feeling supported by the Earth, and creating a deepening bond with your existence in contact with your environment.

Next, we feel for what is deeper than anything solid (or constricted, numb, collapsed). We feel for what is open and spacious within the inner dimension of our whole body at once. (This will progressively emerge.)

4) *Open*: Attune to the sense of unobstructed inner space that naturally emerges when you relax. Feel the sense of uniform continuity between all the parts of your body. Even bones can feel open (deeper than their solidity). Feel the continuity of openness, and savor how this internal space is all one space. Savor any sense of oneness and wholeness that may arise. See if you can feel how wholeness is utterly still. Savor.

Before going further, it helps to refine what we mean by openness because this subtle distinction can profoundly shape our meditation experience. These nuances may seem small, yet they influence not only *how* we meditate, but *why*. Many traditions use similar words ("awareness," "witnessing," "openness") but mean very different things by them. Clarifying this ensures we enter meditation with an orientation that supports genuine healing and transformation rather than reinforcing old habits of not respecting our emotions or avoidance.

Open Witnessing

The openness we cultivate in whole-being meditation is not the same as simply observing our experience from a distance, as in neutral witnessing. Neutral witnessing teaches us to stay impartial and unreactive, to observe without becoming involved. But when we only witness joy, for example, we don't fully receive it. We sense it, but it remains faint and muted because we are intentionally holding ourselves apart. We "stand back" from the experience, creating a psychological distance or gap between the one who observes and what is observed.

In this neutral mode, we are impartial. Much like a disinterested bystander, we have no personal stake in the experience unfolding inside us. We refrain from judgment, which can be helpful because judgment often arises from rigid, moralizing habits that label something as universally good or bad. Such labeling pulls us out of the witness state and back into old mental stories. Neutral witnessing can therefore be a valuable skill. It gives us space from overwhelming emotions and helps prevent us from being swept away by them.

And yet, this very distance that protects us can also keep us one step removed from the life unfolding within us. The detachment that keeps us safe can also keep us disconnected.

In whole-being meditation, openness has an entirely different texture. It is a receptivity, a willingness to let our experience touch us. Instead of stepping back, we make space inside ourselves so that what arises can be felt fully and responded to authentically. Here, openness means letting something in while we are supported by our sense of existing as the "quality of oneness" that is the most supportive to us. It means allowing the moment to affect us, to stir us, to move us without disturbing our sense of wholeness. We still do not judge, but we do have personal preferences and emotional nuances that can shift as we are touched by the experience. We remain curious: *How does this move me? What is it asking of me?*

Like neutral witnessing, open witnessing does not cling to experience. But because we feel rooted in wholeness, rather than hovering above it, we can allow experience to register deeply without collapsing into it or tightening against it. We do not hold on, and we do not push away. We feel the emotion or thought, sense its effect, and remain open enough for it to continue moving through. In this way, we do not fixate on the experience as it passes through.

186

This shift makes all the difference. Neutral witnessing protects us from reacting. Open witnessing liberates our ability to listen and respond from our wholeness.

A *reaction* is driven by the past, by old memories, overwhelming experiences, and the defenses we built to survive them. It erupts quickly and automatically, often before we realize what we feel. Alternately, a *response* arises from the present. It is informed by what we actually sense and need right now. When we respond, we are not hijacked by old emotions; we are grounded in ourselves and available to the truth of the moment. whole-being meditation empowers us to remain grounded in our wholeness.

The wholeness that accompanies open witnessing allows our responses to emerge naturally, honest, embodied, and alive. This is not detachment; it is intimacy without enmeshment. We retain clarity, much like neutral witnessing, yet we do not make the past irrelevant or insignificant. Our past matters because it reveals our unique needs for safety and support, and the personal truth and wisdom we have about our experiences. Curiosity about these experiences is important.

Curiosity that stems from personal interest is not impartial. It leans toward life. It invites. It welcomes what is "on the verge" of being learned. Open witnessing lets us be curious and compassionately receptive, more like Rumi's suggestion to *"welcome all guests,"* whereas neutral witnessing says, *"I see you, but I am not you. I am separate from you."*

Open witnessing allows us to feel our emotional life (joy, fear, longing, confusion), letting it touch us without drowning us. We listen to what our emotions reveal about what still needs love and healing. *We feel how our body responds to our emotions and where it is holding on to them.* We receive these messages, then allow them to move on. Openness becomes a dynamic flow. We feel fully, but we do not get stuck. From this ongoing movement, our most grounded and authentic responses arise effortlessly.

And this matters profoundly for healing. The wounded inner child within us is acutely sensitive to whether it is

187

disidentified from and being witnessed from a distance, or is welcomed into connection. It knows the difference between being observed and being received. Wholeness allows us to remain curious without being aloof, present without being intrusive. This quality of open witnessing is deeply reassuring to the inner child. It communicates: *"You are not too much. I am here. You belong."* This is the beginning of true healing, intimacy with our own experience, held in the spaciousness of unified consciousness. (Please see page 7, "Meditation & Complex Trauma," regarding emotional overwhelm and trauma.)

Continuing the Meditation

Once you have a clear sense of inner openness, as mentioned earlier, proceed to savor any sense of continuity of openness within your whole body at once. See if you can feel that you are in one body, as one presence of openness. Once you feel this, attune to any sense of oneness and wholeness that emerges. Savor deeply. Then, attune to the feeling you exist as the stillness of your openness and wholeness of being.

5) *Autonomy of Energy Flow*: Without losing your sense of wholeness and stillness, savor the sensation of breath flowing like a wave through any part of the body that feels open. The greater the sense of inner openness, the more moving sensations of breath can freely flow through. Sensation is, most fundamentally, energy. When we learn to allow the energy of the breath to flow effortlessly through stillness, all the energies of life (mental, emotional, and physical) begin to move freely as well. So, once you are familiar with free-flowing breath, see if you can allow your thoughts and then emotions to arise and pass through you, without disturbing your perception of openness, and the stillness of the presence of wholeness.

Feel how the unobstructed rhythm of your breath is your own unique, authentic rhythm. Savor any perception that the feeling of breath flowing freely is soothing and nurturing. As this becomes familiar, your thoughts and emotions increasingly become authentic expressions of personal truth and wisdom.

Introducing breath into our meditation practice is essential, for breath is both an ordinary and sacred aspect of our existence. Breath is both voluntary and involuntary and is the thread that binds us to life itself. It also awakens the subtle energy that links our individual body to the universal current of vitality flowing through all of creation (*prana*).

Habitually constricting the inhale or exhale numbs us; it dulls our capacity to feel and supports trapping our emotions and thoughts in fixation. But when breath flows naturally, it teaches the rest of us how to flow too. A sense of emotional autonomy naturally emerges. When we turn our attention to the simple sensation of breathing effortlessly, the mind is gently trained to rest in the immediacy of the present moment. Each breath becomes a doorway, opening us to heightened awareness of the body, to the quiet rhythms of our inner life, and to a deeper intimacy with the world around us.

The more we know ourselves as the pervasive wholeness and stillness of unified consciousness, the more freely, deeply, and fluidly the movements of all aspects of our life are able to flow through us. This is because when we receive the information that oneness provides, we naturally relax. This opens up more of a sense of inner space for our breath and life-energy to move freely and authentically. By pausing to notice each time this happens on the most subtle level, we integrate and own our shift in perspective even more deeply.

The more fully we embody this way of effortless breathing and sense of stillness within the open spaciousness, the more available we become to life in all its changing dynamics. A natural openness unfolds, and with it a felt sense of unity and wholeness. It is often experienced as an inexplicable joy that arises spontaneously. This embodied openness is what makes it possible to live in a deep relationship, with ourselves, with others, and with the living world. Breath, in this sense, is not only survival; it is the rhythm of belonging. It is through the openness of our own body that we learn to live in harmony with the whole.

Three Primary Stages of Perception

In yoga, we not only progress from external to internal, we also progress from the more obvious to the more subtle. To restore the natural fluidity of perception and response, we usually progress through three stages of refinement: from physical, to energetic, to subtle. Clarifying what this means can be helpful.

As we refine our senses in meditation, the very way we experience our body begins to transform. The degree of openness we awaken to within ourselves reshapes not only how we perceive the body but also how we inhabit it. For instance, at first, we may simply feel the familiar solidity and weight of our physical form, the flesh, bones, and structure that ground us in the material world. But as our awareness deepens, something subtler begins to reveal itself. We experience the movements of our energetic nature.

Our energetic nature can feel like pulsing, vibration, tingling, buzzing, pulsing, warmth or coolness, breath, fluids or electricity flowing, or even an urge to move or twitch. Our energetic nature also underlies our emotional and, on a very subtle level, our mental life. All these sensations can range from intensely pleasurable bliss to unsettling restlessness, from gentle flows to overwhelming currents flooding our body. When our energy is obstructed, its movement becomes less pleasurable.

Then, as awareness grows more delicate and precise, the senses reveal the subtle dimension of our unchanging-self. We perceive the radiance, fluidity, and spacious stillness that quietly suffuse the material world. We start to sense not only the body's physical substance but also the *essence* of that substance. Beneath our apparent solidity and energy, there emerges a felt quality that is transparent, spacious, and luminous, as if the body itself is made of conscious light or resplendent presence. This is not an abstract idea but a direct, embodied knowing: a paradoxical experience of being both matter and more-than-matter, flesh and radiance, form and spaciousness.

In this progressive shift in perception, we discover that we are not bound only by the density of the physical body or the habitual ways we normally perceive ourselves. The boundaries of time and space soften. As described above in step five, we begin to feel simultaneously rooted in our physical form and opened into something vaster that holds and permeates it. This dual awareness (being both solid and spacious, finite and infinite) teaches us that we are far less confined than we imagine.

With this recognition comes profound freedom. We realize we have more choices. A new range of possibilities opens; choices rooted not in contraction or defense but in the expansive clarity of wholeness. From here, every breath, every sensation, every moment becomes an opportunity to live with more fluidity, authenticity, and creative responsiveness.

We may feel how our evolving-self's fully formed thoughts and emotions feel like "content" within the open space of our body. On one level, this content can feel like sensory stimuli that are temporal, vibratory patterns occurring within the unchanging and ongoing space. The stillness and space seem to pervade our thoughts and emotions, revealing them. This can feel as if the space itself is thinking thoughts and feeling emotions, and that we do not have to exert effort (of intention) in order to perceive them.

Each of our senses begins to awaken to an alternative way of perceiving. We feel that we don't have to make an effort to look in order to see, or effort to listen in order to hear. Seeing and hearing happen deeply by themselves. At this subtlety of perception, perceiving happens by itself, and we perceive with our whole body and mind.

Likewise, we awaken to an alternative way of responding to life and connecting with ourselves and others. We respond without effort or trying, at a depth that is profoundly meaningful. Our expressions seem to arise spontaneously out of the qualities of oneness, such as timelessness, transparency, space, and stillness.

Effortless perceiving and responding foster our ability to remain non-grasping and disentangle from our habitual reactions and trauma experience. In whole-being meditation and then throughout our lives, we learn that the stillness of space, as the unified field of consciousness, pervades both ourselves and all that we see, hear, and feel. When we exist as unified space, our perceptions do not stop at the surface of what we perceive, because the space encompasses and pervades what we perceive.

We connect to what we perceive through the unified ground of consciousness and perceive things that were previously hidden to us. In this way, the pervasive space reveals the objects of perception, free from distortion, without effort on our part. We remain in a state of dynamic balance embodied as wholeness.

These kinds of experience transform how our body-mind processes what we experience, making it easier to let go of our outdated, limiting habits that lead to suffering. This can feel like we make friends with our suffering and unbind fear from our injury's survival responses. We learn how to understand our disordered and confused feelings, communicate with them, and release them. It increasingly gives us the ability to be fully open and available, allowing life to flow without manipulation or defense in our perception, reception, and response.

As our perception becomes more effortless and less burdened with grasping or resistance, a natural wisdom begins to guide us. We discover that awakening isn't something we must force or strive toward. It is self-perpetuating and effortlessly awakened through presence itself.

192

Your Personal Event-Horizon

A surprising amount of our suffering doesn't actually come from life's challenges themselves; it comes from the way we tighten, brace, and resist what's happening. This resistance is exhausting. It is based on constriction and effort that pulls energy into our muscles, our breath, our mind, and our emotions, and before we know it, we're fighting the moment rather than living it.

Whole-being meditation offers us another way. Instead of pushing against our experience, as mentioned, we learn how to gently release the extra effort we exert as we live life. Through the body, not through willpower or mental control, we discover what genuine effortlessness feels like. The breath softens, the muscles stop gripping, and emotions stop straining to manage everything, and a deeper ease reveals itself.

Learning how to approach life with the least amount of effort is not passivity or collapse; it's a shift into a more natural state of being. When the body remembers how to rest in this organic ease, our relationship to life changes. We no longer meet each moment with tension, but with openness and presence. And in this experience, suffering begins to unravel at its root.

This greater sense of openness inside the body is not a void, but rather feels like awareness itself. It begins to appear as a kind of clear, unobstructed presence within us and in the world around us. This is when something subtle but profound starts to happen. The openness in our body starts to feel like the ground of our inner unity, the felt sense of our own wholeness. And it also becomes the ground of our connection with everything beyond us. It is an unbroken dimension, a dimension of wholeness and stillness that, when we attune to it, is coexistent with the movement of life. Recognizing this unified, spiritual dimension of existence reshapes the way we relate to ourselves and others.

This experience of openness that pervades our body and all objects becomes a lived experience that quietly organizes our perception and our responses. It offers a subtle clarity informed by stillness, timelessness, and a profound feeling of connectedness . It is the fertile ground from which arises a sense of acceptance and peace.

This is what helps us show up to each moment exactly as it is. This inner conscious openness becomes a kind of safe harbor that fosters self-love. Instead of bracing against life, we soften toward it. We begin to trust the present. We begin to feel held by something larger than our habits of protection.

Winnicott had a beautiful name for this quality of experience. He called it "potential space." His understanding of potential space is intriguing because it's the place where a child's inner world and the outer world overlap just enough for creativity, play, and authentic relating to emerge. His potential space is the magical "in-between" zone we access through the safety of a responsive caregiver creating a supportive holding environment. This provides a secure base that lets the child explore, test, dream, and discover who they are becoming. It's the zone of possibility where imagination, discovery, and genuine connection come alive.

In whole-being meditation, potential space functions the same way. When we're grounded in the transparency of our inner openness, it becomes a safe nondual holding-environment where we're able to meet life with curiosity, fluidity, and presence. It is where healing becomes possible, relationships become real, and our evolving self begins to explore new ways of being. In this space between inner experience and outer reality, the seeds of transformation quietly take root.

For Winnicott, interestingly, potential space isn't located inside the child or out in the environment; it exists in the relational field where intimacy and independence coexist. It is a relational, in-between world, the invisible arena where child and caregiver overlap.

In contrast, something remarkable happens when we begin to embody unified consciousness. In meditation, the boundary

194

between inner and outer softens. The dividing line dissolves. What was once "in-between" can be experienced *within the body itself,* as the living arena where inner and outer meet. And in this conscious space, creativity, meaning, and authentic self-expression arise.

Just as the child ideally comes alive in the parent's gentle presence, our own fragmented parts become integrated in the unified potential space of our body. Ultimately, both Winnicott's developmental theory and whole-being meditation lead us to the same truth: healing, creativity, and transformation happen in a relational field. In whole-being meditation, it is where our humanity and our wholeness meet within the body.

This understanding of potential space can also be viewed from a scientific perspective. In quantum physics, we learn that a system can exist in several possible states at once, a kind of "both/and" condition called superposition. Because of this, particles can become entangled, meaning their potentials link together. Once they're entangled, whatever happens to one particle instantly affects the other, no matter how far apart they are. In a sense, they behave like a single system, sharing information and responding as one.

It does not take much imagination to apply this quantum phenomenon to what we experience in whole-being-embrace, where both the evolving-self and the unchanging-self co-exist in a kind of inner entanglement. The two are distinct in function yet intimately linked, sharing a common "field" of potential within our awareness. When we attune to the unchanging dimension of our being (the still, unified presence), something in the evolving-self responds instantly, reorganizing around that deeper state, just as entangled particles react in tandem.

In this sense, whole-being-embrace reveals an inner coherence where our human vulnerability and our timeless nature are not separate but mutually informing aspects of one living system. The more clearly we sense this connection, the more seamlessly our inner states align, creating the conditions for healing, integration, and self-love that naturally lead to authentic expression.

The concept of potential space also points to the idea that the qualities of oneness exist as *potentials* rather than fixed, individual expressions. They are the fertile ground from which all individual experiences and states emerge. These potentials pervade the body as the conscious presence of our unchanging-self. When we embody wholeness, the body itself becomes a living potential space, a field of openness from which unique, authentic experience can arise.

This understanding of potential space is simply another way of pointing to these same principles. It highlights the parallel between how we learn as children and how we learn in meditation when unified consciousness comes into play.

Chapter Ten

The Nondual Mirror

Earth's Cry & Heaven's Smile

Our early bonds were etched into us by the quiet resonance of empathetic attunement. From our earliest days, we absorbed our parents' presence not just through their words or actions, but, as mentioned, through an invisible choreography of mirrored gestures and energetic rhythms. It is through this relational dynamic that we formed our sense of identity.

In whole-being meditation, what was once a dance between two people now unfolds as an intimate dialogue within us, a sacred mirroring between the facets of our own being. The attunement and mirroring we first experienced in childhood with a caregiver echo inward, as though our unchanging-self becomes a still lake where our evolving-self can glimpse its true reflection.

In many ways, this integration with our unchanging-self unfolds through a process similar to how we once internalized our parents' presence. In meditation, when we attune to and entrain with the unchanging-self, we seem to awaken the function of mirror neurons, those remarkable brain cells that fire not only when we act, but also when we observe another perform the same action. They enable us to inhabit another's experience as though it were our own, providing the neural foundation for empathy, resonance, and learning.

Ordinarily, mirror neurons mediate external relationships, helping us recognize that, what lives in another also lives in us. But something equally profound happens when this relational circuitry is turned inward[30]. The evolving-self, with its movements, stories, and vulnerabilities, comes into contact with the stillness and spaciousness of the unchanging-self. Even though this presence has always lived within us, the contact feels relational, echoing the same dance of attunement through which our psyche has always learned. Just as a caregiver's mirroring once helped us discover who we were, now the still, luminous presence of unified consciousness mirrors back to us our deeper truth.

This subtle inner mirroring is not merely metaphorical; it is neurological. Each time mirror neurons simulate another's action, the brain must also distinguish "self" from "other." This very act of comparison lays the groundwork for self-awareness. In this way, as mentioned in chapter three, the circuitry that once allowed us to model the inner life of others also helps us perceive our own.

From this perspective, our sense of self is inseparable from relationships (within us, and between us and others). The mirror neuron system not only supports empathy and social connection but also strengthens the neural pathways of self-perception. The loop is reciprocal: richer connection with others deepens awareness of ourselves, and greater self-awareness expands our capacity to deeply connect with others.

Whole-being meditation extends this same loop inward. Our evolving-self learns through resonance with the timeless, unchanging ground of being. At first, the turbulence of thoughts, emotions, and sensations may seem separate from this presence, but gradually they are met and held in stillness. Over time,

---

[30] Researchers such as V.S. Ramachandran, Giacomo Rizzolatti, and Christian Keysers propose that mirror neurons not only participate in observing others, but can turn "inward" to create internal simulations, meta-representations of our own brain processes to facilitate self-awareness.

perception and what is perceived are infused by the same luminous awareness. The evolving-self, once caught in fragmentation, begins to entrain to the qualities of oneness and relaxed-alertness of the unchanging-self.

It is as if stillness itself whispers a new language to the nervous system, a language of safety, resilience, and possibility. This whisper moves not through abstract thought but directly through the body: the vagus nerve, the limbic system, and the deep emotional centers of the right brain. In this embodied dialogue, the body remembers something older and deeper than trauma: the original possibility of trust, connection, and love.

Here Winnicott's insight about the *"good enough mother"* comes alive in a profound new way. As mentioned, Winnicott taught that the capacity to be alone develops not in isolation, but in the presence of another whose quiet reliability creates safety. The infant internalizes this benign, non-intrusive presence, learning that solitude can be secure because connection is never truly lost.

In whole-being meditation, unified consciousness takes on this parental role. The unchanging-self becomes that quiet, unwavering presence within us, a ground we can return to again and again. When our evolving-self trembles with fear, shame, or longing, the unchanging-self holds it tenderly, much like a parent's attuned gaze reassures her child: *"You are safe. You are loved. You are not alone."*

In these moments, new choices open. We are no longer bound to react from old wounds or limiting conditioned patterns. Instead, we find ourselves responding with presence, authenticity, and freedom. The same neural processes that once helped us bond with others now help us heal from within. Our evolving-self learns, step by step, to rest in the unwavering embrace of the unchanging-self.

In this way, whole-being meditation reclaims the ancient dance of attunement, transforming it into a whole-being-embrace. Wherever, in meditation, we learn to inhabit our body with openness, we become more available to life itself. The inner mirroring of stillness and movement, self and Self, vulnerability and wholeness, awakens us into a deeper truth: we are both uniquely ourselves and inseparably one with all that is.

And this shift changes everything about how we relate to ourselves and others. When the evolving-self has learned to rest in the safety of the unchanging-self, our external relationships no longer carry the impossible burden of filling our inner void. We don't need our partner, friend, or community to be perfect or constantly reassure us that we are safe or lovable; instead, we increasingly approach them with a fullness that already knows connection at its core.

Every child needs to feel other people's delight in them. When the feeling of delight results from contact with our unchanging-self, the sage Valmiki calls this the infinite nature of "great delight." This experience provides a personal self-reflective "mirroring" context for us to receive what we may have never received enough of as a child, and even now find it difficult to experience as an adult.

The inner secure base of infinite great delight becomes the soil out of which secure attachment in adulthood can grow. Our intrinsic worth is reflected back to us. In this delight we understand the universe loves us because of who we are; we have inherent value just by existing, by being a part of all that is. Our sense of self-worth and self-love grow. We feel safe enough to risk intimacy, to soften, to let another in. We are not undone by conflict, because beneath it we sense the stillness of unity. We are less likely to cling in fear of abandonment or push away in fear of engulfment, because we have tasted the paradoxical truth: we can be fully ourselves and fully connected at the same time.

This new knowledge teaches us what the good-enough parent ideally once whispered into our nervous system: *"You are safe enough to explore, to return, to be held, and to be free."* This is the foundation for resilience, authenticity, and love. It is not about erasing the ego or perfecting the self, but about discovering that, within the embrace of unified consciousness, we already belong, to ourselves, to one another, and to the wholeness of life.

The Dance of Attunement

When a parent "mirrors" a child in a healthy way, they reflect back to the child an accurate reflection of what they perceive the child is expressing. Through smiling or frowning and assuming a body posture that reflect the child's expressions, the child sees their emotions within their parent's face. In this process, there is a transmission of information that helps the child develop a greater sense of self-awareness and self-control. Yet, this mirroring is not limited to our evolving-self. As mentioned earlier, when the parent is in touch with his or her own qualities of wholeness-of-being, it awakens the child's own pre-existing sense of wholeness.

Ideally, spiritual practices also mirror our wholeness back to us. Just as with parent-to-child transmission, direct transmission (*saktipata*) occurs when a spiritual teacher empowers the student by modeling a state of consciousness, enabling the student to attune to the same state within themselves. While direct transmission is an exchange of energy, it also involves simply accessing consciousness that is already within each of us. Initially, the ground of unified consciousness may become more vivid and is easier to recognize when in the presence of a teacher who embodies nondual consciousness.

By attuning to the pervasive unified ground that connects us all, we discern the teacher's own experience and pervasive presence of unchanging-self. We pick up on both energetic transmission as well as access the state of unified consciousness when it is modeled to us. The quality of openness and presence of a realized spiritual teacher supports us to recognize these qualities that already exist within us as we entrain, resonate, and align with the consciousness of the teacher.

Entraining or resonating with the consciousness pervading our surroundings is something we all do to varying degrees (via mirror neurons). We can do this in a variety of ways, some of which involve interaction with other people.[31]

Yet embodied nondual experience is not a transmission by an external source to us, such as a teacher. While the sending and receiving of energetic transmission does occur, on the most subtle level of nondual consciousness, it is simply an awakening within the space that is already there, timelessly present. In this sense, awakening to the unchanging-self is similar to receiving a direct transmission from a spiritual teacher, except the transmission comes from within, guiding us toward our own realization

Aligning with What has Always Been Whole

Whole-being meditation isn't about trying to change how we behave; it's about transforming how we experience *who we are* within the living landscape of the body. When our relationship with ourselves shifts at this deeper level, our behavior naturally follows.

As we begin to sense that we are made of the qualities of oneness (stillness, love, spaciousness, timelessness) our awareness deepens. We move into alignment with what has always been whole within us. From this alignment, change unfolds effortlessly. Our behavior is no longer driven by old wounds or

---

[31] For instance, in the Tantra yoga practice of "eye-gazing," participants look at each other's eyes and exchange an energetic connection. In other practices, it happens energetically via sound, visualization, and conscious breathing. In a practice called "life-infusion" (*jiva-nyasa*), practitioners assimilate the life-energy of their chosen deity (*ishta-devata*). In the *Matrika-nyasa* practice, the fifty sacred sounds of the Sanskrit alphabet are "placed" in the practitioner's body. It is no coincidence that the Sanskrit alphabet sounds are called *matrica*, or "little mothers."

unconscious habits; it becomes an authentic expression of who we are.

In this way, we are not learning to control or correct ourselves, but to live from a deeper ground of being and personal truth. We begin to *see* more clearly, *feel* more honestly, and *act* more naturally in harmony with what feels genuine and alive within us. This is empowerment through authenticity, the quiet strength of living our personal truth, grounded in a profound sense of self-love and the wholeness of being. The most significant result of this is how it influences our sense of connection and autonomy.

Contactful Presence

The more important a relationship is to us, the more conflicts around how we connect and maintain our autonomy intensify. Understanding the early mirroring process that influences this conflict can help us grasp what happens in whole-being-embrace.

Winnicott offered an important insight into this art of mirroring through what he called *contactful presence*, the quiet capacity to be fully with another without intrusion or withdrawal. This kind of presence makes room for both connection and autonomy to coexist. It lets the child feel seen without being engulfed, known without being controlled.

To meet a child as a real person, Winnicott said, is to honor both the child's emerging individuality and the parent's own humanness. In that mutual recognition, love becomes grounded, not in perfection, but in truth. It is an attunement that breathes, falters, and repairs, allowing authenticity to take root.

When a parent meets the child's spontaneous gestures and needs with genuine responsiveness most of the time, the child's authentic self unfolds, feeling real and alive in the world. But when the parent's will dominates, or when attunement repeatedly fails, the child learns to adapt. A compliant reactive-self forms, a mask that preserves connection at the cost of authenticity. Beneath that mask, the authentic self waits, quiet, untouched, and longing to be met.

In whole-being meditation, we rediscover a similar *contactful presence* within ourselves. Our unchanging-self is a contactful, unified presence that is neither abandoning nor intrusive to our injured ego. It doesn't push or pull. It simply is. It shows up as a steady, spacious wholeness that meets our injury without judgment, demand, or agenda. The unchanging-self becomes the attuned inner parent (steady, receptive, and unconditionally present) while the evolving-self, with all its emotions, longings, and vulnerabilities, learns it is safe to be seen. Within this inner ground of wholeness, we no longer need to hide behind performance or compliance. The parts of us that once fragmented to survive are met with the quiet gaze of unconditional acceptance.

As in Winnicott's vision, authenticity flowers in the space between contact and freedom. In whole-being meditation, we experience this as our inner presence of being that does not impose or withdraw; it simply holds space for us. It listens without judgment, allowing what is real to emerge naturally. In this way, meditation becomes an act of re-parenting the heart; a living restoration of the trust that was lost when mirroring failed. Through this inner relationship, the authentic self awakens again, not as an ideal, but as a lived, felt reality; whole, responsive, and deeply human.

The foundation that this provides helps us break free from unconscious patterns of clinging, merging, avoidance, or projection. By seeing and being seen as a *real person*, we create the conditions for true intimacy to flourish. When others are unable to see us in a respectful, caring way and project their own distorted injuries upon us, unified consciousness offers a powerful alternative source of healthy mirroring.

204

While the contactful presence that our unchanging-self provides simply holds space for us, it is uninjured, unbreakable, and an immortal presence that feels unconditionally loving. This reflection meets us and broadens and deepens our experience of self and other. Being met in this way helps us recognize and name our feelings more accurately and build emotional clarity that our wounded parent could not.

The feeling of being witnessed, understood, respected, and unconditionally loved enables us to learn to move authentically between togetherness and individuality, and between engagement and disengagement in relationship. We maintain a sense of being profoundly connected as one when alone, and completely autonomous and free when engaging with others.

Moreover, the habitual holding patterns of constriction, emotional defenses, and mental loops we've developed to protect ourselves begin to loosen. Releasing these habitual ways of engaging in our relationships means that the energy underlying our survival responses and personal truth, once frozen in our tissues, is released and becomes available for constructive purposes.

This inner safety and extra energy in our body-mind system give rise to new capacities: the ability to relate openly, to cooperate and engage in mutual understanding, and to navigate conflict without becoming overwhelmed or shut down. We no longer need to rely so heavily on physical constriction and defensive emotional boundaries that underlie our attachment types to feel secure. The inner critic's interfering voice naturally comes to rest. In this newfound silence, we have the ability to listen deeply with empathy, to ourselves and others in the moment.

Rather than defensive emotional boundaries, we stand by our personal truth and express our healthy boundaries that support us in feeling safe and that honor our need for support. This means our habitual state of being stuck in incomplete survival responses and attachment styles is replaced by authentic expression. This transformation lays the foundation for true intimacy, resilience, and connection.

Our House of Mirrors

A child first comes to know who they are by seeing themselves reflected in a parent's presence. But for most of us, it's as if we grew up in a house of mirrors. Everywhere we turned, the reflections we received were bent and blurred by the unresolved injuries of the people around us. It is not that what we internalized wasn't based on a real reflection; it was simply not a true reflection of our own authentic nature.

It's only when we encounter the clear, undistorted reflection of nondual consciousness (the felt sense of unity and wholeness) that we finally see ourselves as we truly are. In that mirror, the evolving-self recognizes its untraumatized essence, and our deeper potential begins to reveal itself; not as an ideal we strive toward, but as the truth we've carried all along.

Every part of our evolving-self comes in contact with our unchanging-self's nondual mirror and feels seen, understood, respected, and supported. As Judith Blackstone emphasizes, the unchanging-self is a fundamental consciousness that "is like a mirror that reflects everything it pervades, without being changed itself."

The timeless nature of the unchanging-self eliminates all distance between duality and nonduality, so the reflection of this truth becomes us. This is the nondual mirror, where our evolving-self senses a resonant circuitry with the unified presence of being, giving us access to a feeling of being received and witnessed.

The mirror reflection of stillness, spaciousness, unity, and wholeness pervading the evolving-self transforms everything that stands in the way of manifesting our potential. As we uncover the sense of existing as oneness, our changing evolving-self's suffering comes into a contact-full relationship with the unified dimension of our existence and is set free from its sabotaging conditioning.

Nondual mirroring is a sacred, intimate connection (*sambandha*) between the unified and evolving aspects of our being, awakening as a body experience. It is an intimate connection that suggests an understanding that creation is an ongoing event that occurs moment by moment. Every moment is a new opportunity to recreate ourselves in a new light.

Healing is ultimately not about transcending distortion but entering into relationship with the mirror that does not distort. In the unchanging-self, our evolving-self at last sees itself reflected without judgment, without fracture, without disguise. Here, every wound is met, not with more distortion, but with the clear light of presence.

This nondual mirroring is more than reflection; it is recognition. It reveals that what we are seeking has always been within us: a wholeness that cannot be injured, a love that cannot be withdrawn. In this meeting, body and consciousness, form and formlessness, come together in their sacred embrace. No longer adversaries, no longer hierarchies, just an intimacy so complete that authentic creation itself awakens in us, again and again, moment by moment.

To live from this embrace is to recognize that we are not merely healing our past, we are continually co-creating ourselves in the light of unity as source. Every breath becomes cosmogenesis. Every moment becomes a chance to let our evolving-self rest in the wholeness of our unchanging-self. And in that resting, the mirror clears, the distortions dissolve, and we delightfully discover that we have always been both the reflection and the light.

Chapter Eleven

Whole-Being-Embrace™

How Whole-Being-Embrace Works

Whole-being-embrace leads to a bonding experience in the deepest and most sacred sense: a reunion with the essential core of existence that restores something indispensable many of us have never fully received: a felt sense of safety, unconditional acceptance, and belonging, within ourselves. In this bond, healing does not happen through effort or self-improvement, but through being met by an uninjured presence of being.

As this relationship deepens, our unchanging-self begins to function as an inner holding environment, one that mirrors the conditions of secure attachment. The unchanging-self becomes a steady, benevolent presence for the evolving-self, offering the emotional support that may have been missing at moments of injury, neglect, or trauma. Over time, we don't just sense the presence of our unchanging-self as a vague experience; we uncover it as a living, ever-present, luminous embodied reality. Within this presence, healing occurs in three primary ways:

- **Being Nurtured**: The evolving-self feels seen, held, and valued by the unchanging-self. As this recognition takes root, the nervous system reorganizes, and fragmented aspects of our self begin to cohere.

- **Uncoupling**: By uncoupling fear from what we experience, fight, flight, freeze, and fawn patterns—once frozen in the body during overwhelming moments—can now move to completion.
- **Authentic Expression**: What was once silenced—personal truths about discounted emotions and unmet needs— can finally be felt and spoken, without the fear of overwhelm, abandonment, or rejection.

This chapter integrates the different aspects of this bonding journey in these three fundamental phases. It explores the primary elements of this transformative process and highlights the moment of grace when we release our old, self-sabotaging habits of mind and body, and step into genuine freedom.

Even without ideal early bonding, we can recognize the ground of our being and learn to reparent ourselves through whole-being-embrace. Uncovering unified consciousness is not a matter of magic or luck; it unfolds through a recognizable pathway that leads us toward self-love. In meditation, this path often reveals itself in a profoundly real way through the following three-phase progression. A variety of the topics already discussed are woven together in this chapter with the intention of giving insight into the healing journey that explains how whole-being-embrace-works.

The Three Phases of the Healing Journey

The process we go through in whole-being meditation as described here can be understood in terms of the nature of energy and consciousness. Most fundamentally, energy has three phases to it: charge, discharge, and balance.[32] The "three-phases of energy" describe the basic rhythm underlying all experience.

These three phases appear in many traditions. In yoga they're called the *gunas*; in myth they mirror the Hero's Journey (departure, initiation, return); in psychology they reflect how we grow through challenge; and in meditation they show how our energy flows when we're embodied and present. All these models point to the same pattern: we gather energy, meet a challenge and resolve it, and return to balance.

These phases of healing are described eloquently in Joseph Campbell's book *The Hero with a Thousand Faces* (1949). This is a foundational work in comparative mythology that introduces the concept of the Hero's Journey as a universal pattern found across cultures that traces a protagonist's call to adventure, transformation through trials, and eventual return with gained wisdom. These three fundamental phases of human growth can be described as:

1. **Departure** — we answer a call to change and step beyond old habits.
2. **Initiation** —facing the unknown, meeting inner obstacles, discovering new capacities.
3. **Return** — we come home changed, carrying new wisdom and strength.

The three phases of healing mentioned earlier (being nurtured, uncoupling, authentic expression) on a fundamental level correlate with the three phases of the archetypal Hero's

---

[32] The idea that the energy underlying our body, mind, and emotions moves through phases of *charge, discharge, and balance* appears across alternative medicine, energy work, holistic health, and somatic psychology. Wilhelm Reich, the father of somatic psychology, described a similar process in four stages. In both biology and physics, physical tension reflects a buildup of potential energy. For this reason, I combine Reich's first two phases—physical tension and energetic charge—into a single phase I simply call *charge*.

journey.[33] Each phase invites us to confront outdated patterns formed from past injuries:

1. **Departure/Being Nurtured**: The Hero's departure is the creative act of committing to a plan of action. It is a wake-up call that implores us to overcome the outdated habits of mind and body that cause suffering. We can be reluctant to follow through with the call to act, but we are helped by a mentor figure. In whole-being-embrace, the "mentor" is what happens when the evolving-self feels seen, held, and valued by the unchanging-self. As this recognition takes root, we experience the support we need to embark on the rest of the (healing/awakening) journey.

2. **Initiation/Uncoupling**: In the Hero's initiation phase (with the assistance of the mentor or our unchanging-self) we face the challenge. This phase begins with us as the Hero who traverses the threshold to the unknown. This unknown represents a challenge in any relationship with ourselves or others. On the journey, we then reach "the innermost cave." This represents where we find a challenge (injury, conflict, limiting habit), but also where we gain a reward (a "treasure" or "elixir"). In whole-being-embrace, as we shall see, this is the "uncoupling" phase, where uncouple fear from our intense emotions and regain our sense of well-being.

3. **Return/Authenticity**: We return home to the ordinary world with the benefits of having successfully met the challenge of our habits and injuries in a skillful way. We

---

[33] *The Hero with a Thousand Faces* (1949) by Joseph Campbell is a foundational work in comparative mythology that introduces the concept of the Hero's Journey—a universal narrative pattern found across cultures that traces a protagonist's call to adventure, transformation through trials, and eventual return with gained wisdom.

are empowered with new skills, a broader perspective, and a sense of success. In whole-being-embrace, in this phase we regain our ability to live in relationship with ourselves and others, authentically. On this path, we are transformed by the adventure and gain wisdom or spiritual awakening with both dual and nondual dimensions of self.

Importantly, this progression reflects the larger process of how we live our lives. Life continually moves through these beginnings, middles, and endings (moment to moment and over our lifetime). With each "adventure," we come closer to healing limiting habits of mind, body, and emotion. As we develop new skills and awareness, we gain the ability to face deeper wounds and evolve into a freer and more authentic version of ourselves. When we complete a cycle successfully, we evolve, consciousness becomes more integrated, and we gain deeper and broader access to unified consciousness. Ultimately, we experience an ongoing state of grace, a felt sense of wholeness and oneness.

These three phases can be depicted energetically as a charge, discharge, balance pattern. We develop a charge when we engage our injuries while in embrace with our unchanging-self. We discharge energy when we successfully uncouple fear from what causes suffering. And, we experience balance when we regain our sense of freedom from our suffering (limiting habit) and we are empowered with new skills and a broader perspective.

Interestingly, these three phases appear everywhere and represent the fundamental cycle of our life on Earth:

- In the breath: inhale, exhale, pause.
- In the nervous system: sympathetic, parasympathetic, homeostasis.
- In myth: creation, destruction, preservation.
- In Buddhism: sambhogakaya, nirmanakaya, dharmakaya.

In whole-being meditation, we can experience each of these expressions of the three phases of energy. When we're balanced, this movement feels fluid and natural, and our sense of authenticity and wholeness prevails. But emotional injury interrupts the cycle. Instead of flowing, energy becomes stuck in one of these three phases. These fixations can become habitual reactions that limit our choices and fragment our sense of self. They manifest through our survival responses and insecure attachment style of relating.

Healing the Cycle

Whole-being meditation, as described in this chapter, helps us restore this natural cyclical movement. By refining our senses and staying present with experience, we clearly see where energy is obstructed. And, in whole-being embrace, we gently allow energy to complete its cycle. Instead of fighting or collapsing, we learn to stay open and whole. This rebalances the system and brings us back into alignment with our deeper nature.

Because energy shapes our thoughts, emotions, and sensations, these phases also guide our psychological and spiritual growth. Our emotional maturity and our awakening depend on how freely energy can move through each of the three phases. When past injuries block the flow, we express ourselves defensively and habitually. When energy is unobstructed, we move through each phase freely, our evolving-self responds to life with authenticity and ease. Our energy system grows more fluid, more refined, moving through us with increasing subtlety and effortlessness.

The more freely energy moves, the more access we have to both our evolving-self's truth and the unified stillness of our unchanging-self. Conversely, the more clearly we awaken to our unchanging-self, the more freely our energy flows. As we become the stillness at our core, life's movement streams through us like clear water, without obstruction, without resistance, without a single ripple of distortion. Each successful cycle deepens our integration and authenticity and, simultaneously, illuminates our sense of wholeness.

These three phases repeat moment by moment, shaping each experience we have. Recognizing this helps us to turn our life into a path of awakening. The end of one moment becomes the beginning of the next, and the gap between them becomes a portal into balance, openness, and unity. When this state of balance stabilizes, it becomes a continuous experience, a living sense of wholeness that moves with us through every phase of the journey.

1. Being Nurtured

As we turn inward in meditation, old voices often begin to echo within. We may recall the ways our parents minimized, ignored, or dismissed our needs: *"Don't be so sensitive," "That didn't happen," "You're imagining things."* These words, repeated enough, burrowed into us as seeds of self-doubt. Over time, they grow into low self-esteem, a shaky sense of worth, and difficulty trusting our own inner experience.

When we turn inward and truly feel what is happening in the body, unresolved emotional injuries can flood us with intensity. In our silence, old wounds can resurface through surges of emotion, unsettling thoughts, and raw sensations that seem to reactivate past trauma. In meditation, it is valuable to learn to initially focus on the good feelings that lie deeper than our disturbances because when we harbor injuries, we tend to habitually look for danger and forget, or never learned how, to receive what is supportive. This orientation allows us to align with supportive resources before attending to our injuries.

Finding what feels good inside the body needs to start with simple things, such as what it feels like to relax our shoulders, settle into contact with the ground, rest within our body, and breathe rhythmically and fluidly (as described in chapter nine). The feeling of simply arriving where we are, and primarily focused on the present moment, can also create a supportive context.

Yet, when we first uncover and awaken to our qualities of oneness, a deep safety and nurturing emerge. Among the qualities of oneness, one often reveals itself most clearly and becomes like an inner balm that soothes what aches. This gently widens the narrow perspective held by our emotional injury. The felt sense of the qualities of oneness functions as an alternative sensory-motor, temporal-spatial learning. This involves a form of entrainment.

Entrainment is the quiet rhythm that lets two beings fall into harmony, like a baby's heartbeat syncing with a mother's, or two friends unconsciously breathing together during a tender conversation. In whole-being meditation, this same attunement happens within us. Instead of synchronizing with another person, we begin to entrain with the stillness, spaciousness, and love of unified consciousness. Through refining our senses, we gently fall back into sync with the wholeness that has always been here.

Each sense becomes a doorway: breath, sound, sight, smell, touch, all revealing the same quiet truth beneath them. (Practices like conscious breathing, mantra, yantra visualization, or mindful movement help us feel the stillness inside each sensation.) Little by little, we sense wholeness touching us from the inside out, and we learn to move through life in harmony again.

In this way, even the most painful experiences can be held, not as threats, but as waves moving within an unshakable ocean of being. This soothing presence supports us to incrementally engage with the intensity of our disturbing experiences. The trauma psychologist Peter Levine calls this *"titration"*: engaging with

215

potentially overwhelming traumatic experiences (emotions, thoughts, sensations) in small, manageable, "drop-by-drop" increments to prevent re-traumatization.

By learning to tune more deeply into our senses in meditation, we grow more sensitive to subtle sensations. This allows us to perceive the tiniest expression of a disturbance that interrupts the stillness of unified presence. These are the interruptions based on injuries (mental, emotional, sensory) that once went unnoticed because they were too buried, diffuse, or habitual to recognize. Because our attunement is anchored in the unified ground of embodied awareness, we can discern the precise moment when the interruptions that lead to fragmentation begin.

We become aware of the exact moment when we begin to dissociate and the initial flicker of contraction as the seed of our fight, flight, freeze, or collapse response. This is the moment when our senses begin to distort experience through the lens of past conditioning. At this early stage, our habitual reactions have not yet gained momentum, and this makes it possible to redirect them with much less effort.

This ability to catch our sabotaging habits of dissociation and contraction at their inception is transformative. When we notice the moment our conditioned reaction is about to form, we also have an opportunity to remain present, open, and attuned to our most supportive quality of oneness, rather than overwhelm. We bring our injuries to the surface, not as a flood that overwhelms us, but as subtle sensations. This allows us to integrate these disturbances without activating our survival responses, and we do not spiral into suffering. In our experience of stillness, we discover new space, enough space to pause, breathe, and choose differently.

This *titration* helps us stay within our window of tolerance and reprograms our nervous system. Our ability to gradually expose ourselves to our distress in small, manageable, digestible increments allows our sensory, mental, and emotional life to remain authentic rather than distorted.

216

Titration commonly happens when our attention is intentionally oscillated between a distressing feeling and a feeling of safety or calm. When an experience feels too intense, the evolving-self can lean back into the unchanging-self, much like a child returning to a secure caregiver. In whole-being meditation, we may oscillate initially, but as we fully embody the ground of being, the feeling of safety that accompanies the unwavering presence of wholeness is always available. This supports our memories of injury to no longer feel like fixed walls. Instead, they rise up and lose their power within the greater atmosphere of stillness, timelessness, and wholeness that unified consciousness provides.

In this way, whole-being-embrace enables titration by changing *how* experience is held. It does not rely on techniques to control intensity. It creates the conditions (safety, relationship, and spacious awareness) through which titration happens organically. Attention is shared between *content* (emotion, memory, sensation) and *context* (stillness, spaciousness, presence).

This relational safety allows difficult material to emerge gradually, at a pace the body can integrate. The unchanging-self provides steadiness, spaciousness, and non-reactivity, allowing experience to arise in manageable increments instead of flooding the nervous system. Thoughts, emotions, and sensations are experienced *within* wholeness rather than as threats to it. Because of this, healing unfolds in small, digestible steps.

2. Uncoupling

In the uncoupling phase we start by discerning, disentangling, and integrating. We cultivate clear *discernment* of the nuances of both dimensions of our being, dual and nondual. To do this, we attune to subtle sensory awareness of these contrasting fundamental dimensions of self.

217

For instance, in meditation we refine our ability to feel how thoughts, emotions, and sensations all move as they change. As they move through the body-mind, they also arise within a deeper stillness and openness that permeates the body's apparent solidity. As we become familiar with stillness, we learn the art of sensing the difference between the symptoms of a real threat and the echo of an old one. We help the body remember that intensity is not the same as danger, and that a moment can feel big without being a moment we must survive.

As discernment of our evolving-self and unchanging-self deepens, we learn to differentiate them without compromising the autonomy of either. This allows us to sustain an embodied sense of wholeness even while unresolved emotional pain moves through us.

This enables us to then "*disentangle*" the evolving-self and the unchanging-self. This means we develop autonomy between the feeling of wholeness as our nature (spiritual identification), and the feeling that we are a distinct, unique, individual. This autonomy means we do not lose our wholeness when personal drama looms large.

Within this autonomous relationship of whole-being-embrace, what was fragmented and in conflict begins to *integrate* within us. Thoughts, feelings, and actions align. The many parts of us we once struggled to manage, settle into coherence. We move through life as an authentic presence, honest, whole, and at ease with what is. A natural result of discernment, disentangling, and integration is uncoupling fear from the influence of intense experiences.

Uncoupling Fear from Intense Experiences

Overwhelm often arises when something ordinary brushes against a memory of what once felt impossible to escape. In an instant, the body relives that old fear, leaping into fight, flight, or freeze even while the mind knows, *"I'm safe now."* Uncoupling loosens this reflexive knot, gently separating the present from the past so that the nervous system no longer mistakes stress for catastrophe.

The timeless stillness of consciousness acts like warmth to ice, softening what once seemed permanently locked within. In the warmth of whole-being-embrace, the once frozen currents of survival energy and buried personal truth, progressively thaw and return to flow. What was shut down due to emotional injury (often initially in response to caregivers) finds the safety and support needed to come alive and be expressed more fully and freely.

We learn to trust the river flow once more. For years, we clung to the banks, gripping tightly in fear that the current would sweep us away. Yet, as we lean into the presence of fundamental consciousness, we discover that the river is not our enemy, but our life.

Its waters carry us forward with strength and continuity. In the safety of this flow, we realize we don't need to control every twist and turn or shrink in fear. We can soften our grip, let go of the shore, and allow ourselves to be carried; not lost, but supported to let go of struggling. This embodied awareness is the antidote to inward constrictions and the outward hyper attachments (habits of mind and body) that so often define our lives.

Fear associated with our memory of injury slowly begins to uncouple from our outdated habits of mind, body, and emotion. For example, someone who learned to tense their body and shut down emotionally whenever conflict arose may, through embodied presence, still feel a flutter of fear when disagreement appears, but no longer collapse, withdraw, or brace against harm. The fear is felt as a passing sensory experience rather than a command to act. Over time, the body remains more relaxed, the breath stays fuller, and new responses (such as staying engaged, speaking honestly, or setting a boundary) become available. Beneath fear, a quieter knowing emerges, clarifying what we need and deserve, in order to feel safe, supported, and loved.

This uncoupling opens up access to existential trust. We trust that our existence as wholeness is an inherently open presence, without shame or distortion.

> **Existential Trust**: Trust is at the very heart of human connection. Just as a child ideally learns to trust that a loving caregiver will return, respond, and stay consistent, in whole-being meditation, we begin to develop that same trust inwardly. We feel this as an existential trust. In the midst of chaos or pain, in this phase, unified presence becomes a silent companion. Not one that fixes or rescues, but one that pervades our body and mind and holds space for us, so we start to feel safe enough to soften, to breathe, to stop running from ourselves.

Besides profound connectedness and existential trust, we also feel that we have an infinite amount of breathing room to express our personal truth.

> **Infinite Space**: As explained, unified consciousness provides the breathing room that supports our autonomy. As children, when we were given just the right amount of space within a safe, loving environment, we had room to grow. We could explore, make mistakes, and return to safety when we needed to. That rhythm of freedom and holding is what allows a child to mature with confidence.
>
> In whole-being meditation, we discover that the unchanging presence of being never pushes or demands, it simply offers space. The kind of spaciousness that lets even our most scared or hidden parts finally exhale. This inner spaciousness recreates the ideal combination of support and breathing room inside us. In this "potential space," we find sovereignty.

Moreover, with openness, we discover a sense of transparency:

Transparency: We experience that our inner nondual holding environment is *transparent* in nature. Unity has no walls, no filters, no need to protect or conceal. Everything that we are (even our mistakes) is seen clearly, without distortion. It's like standing in the softest light imaginable and realizing that the shadows we feared, were never flaws, only parts of ourselves waiting to be seen. Fear naturally dissipates when we are not trying to hide our shadow. Even the density of our physical body feels transparently open.

While the sense of separation between body and environment may soften, we do not lose awareness of inhabiting the whole inner dimension of the body. Instead, we experience a seamless continuity between physical form and surrounding space, while remaining clearly oriented within the body.

The body is experienced as porous or spacious, part of a lived field rather than a solid object. This facilitates life experiences to pass through the body without getting stuck. This shift alters the body schema, the brain's dynamic neural map that organizes how we experience ourselves in space and in relation to the world. Rather than being limited to the body as a fixed, solid object, the sense of self becomes more fluid and responsive. The body is still clearly felt and inhabited, yet it is no longer experienced as a hard boundary that defines or confines identity.

As this sense of transparency deepens, familiar sensations of solidity, weight, and density may soften or dissolve, giving way to experiences of lightness, airiness, openness, or even inner vastness. These sensations are not dissociative; they are grounded in embodied awareness while simultaneously extending beyond the usual edges of the body. Awareness remains anchored, yet it feels less compressed and more spacious.

As habitual identification with a fixed, solid self loosens, how we move through the world begins to change. The nervous system learns to process a much wider range of sensory information. We uncouple fear from what we experience because self-perception becomes less rigid and less centered on a narrowly defined identity. Attuned to our transparency, a more fluid sense of self emerges, which supports our social interactions to become more fluid and natural.

We also begin to feel that we are always fully connected to our intrinsic goodness.

Fundamental Goodness: One of the most moving aspects of the qualities of oneness that supports and nourishes us is the discovery that we are held by a genuinely benevolent presence, not from outside, but from within. It's a felt-sense of intrinsic goodness, something we don't earn or create, but simply *are* at the deepest level. Buddhism this basic goodness to have attributes of openness, intelligence and warmth.

This goodness isn't sentimental or sugar-coated. It doesn't pretend pain isn't real. Instead, it's the ground beneath every emotion, strong enough to hold anything we feel. Because our internal body experience of our goodness lovingly holds space for our wounded inner-child, we uncouple fear from the drama of what we experience. We also realize our intrinsic value and self-worth. We realize that the essence we arrived in this life with is loving and innocent. This lessens self-judgement and makes way for self-love.

These are a few examples of how, in the uncoupling phase, embodied unified consciousness uncouples fear from disruptive experiences (thoughts, emotions, sensations). Uncoupling fear from habit in these sensory ways is crucial for overcoming trauma. Instead of reacting fearfully to feeling emotionally abandoned or imposed upon, we learn to discover another possibility: staying *open and present*. The fear response is felt as energy moving through the body rather than a directive to freeze, appease, or dissociate. When memory of injury is still encoded, but it is no longer coupled to automatic defensive behavior, the nervous system updates in real time, allowing choice, presence, and relational contact to remain intact.

Through whole-being meditation, we learn to stay with fear as it rises, not to suppress it, but to offer it a sense of existential trust, infinite space, transparency, and our fundamental goodness. In this presence, fear loses its urgency, no longer swelling into overwhelm. Without overwhelm and fear in charge, we can safely revisit traumatic experiences and "re-file" the memory of injury in a way that is less threatening. What emerges instead is resilience, a steadier breath, and a deepening sense that we can meet life as it comes, without abandoning ourselves.

Our experiences that accompany unified consciousness become nondual mirrors that give our body-mind system new sensory, motor, temporal, and spatial information. Nondual mirroring is not just reflection; it is healing. The nervous system settles, the psyche reorganizes, and more harmony returns to body and mind.[34]

3. Authentic Expression

In this phase, having uncoupled fear from our intense experiences, we finally regain our authenticity. To understand

---

[34] Neuroscience gives us insight into why this happens. Stephen Porges shows how soothing sensations activate the "social engagement system," helping us feel safe, open, and ready for connection. Daniel Siegel extends this, suggesting that unified consciousness sparks a "self-engagement system," allowing the evolving-self to stay in open, receptive contact with the unchanging-self. Our inner world becomes relational, alive, and integrated.

how this happens, we must first be reminded of how overwhelm is processed in our body-mind system.

When we experience overwhelming stress, the brain's survival system takes over. Ordinary thinking shuts down, along with our capacity to sense and express personal truth. We shift into automatic survival responses. These responses do not disappear once the threat passes. When survival impulses (such as running, resisting, crying, or saying no) are blocked, punished, or invalidated, they cannot be completed. The survival cycle, moving from expression to completion, is interrupted, and the energy mobilized remains stored in the nervous system and body.[35]

After having uncoupled fear from our intense emotions in the second phase of our healing journey, in the third phase, we complete what was interrupted and discharge our trapped energy.

Nurturing Expression into Authenticity

In uncoupling fear from our perceptions, we reveal who we truly are, whole, innocent, and real. For perhaps the first time, we feel mirrored not by a critical eye, but by a presence that affirms our worth in the reflection of our essence. And from that realization, a quiet dignity begins to rise. Not the pride of accomplishment, but the peace of simply being openly seen, fully and without condition. The body begins to clearly perceive its original freedom and what we feel about having lost it.

Grounded in the nurturing qualities of oneness, healthy responses and silenced personal truths are able to come out of hiding and complete themselves. We reclaim the capacity to run toward safety, to push away what is unwanted, or to protect

---

[35] This unresolved activation often operates beneath awareness, showing up as patterns we judge or blame ourselves for without recognizing their origin in past overwhelm. What once supported survival now restricts our capacity to feel, connect, and live authentically. A nervous system conditioned by threat misreads safety as danger, leaving us caught in anxiety, avoidance, numbness, dissociation, or recurring emotional flashbacks.

ourselves in ways that were once impossible. If you froze as a child when a boundary was violated, you may now feel a spontaneous impulse to say "no," move back, or place a firm hand out. These are actions that can complete the original protective response without overwhelm.

As this newfound freedom deepens, survival responses come to successful completion. Personal truth and embodied wisdom re-emerge as reliable guides in our relationships. Instead of overriding discomfort to keep the peace, we may feel a clear, grounded impulse to take action, slow down, or express our honest desires, without collapse, aggression, or self-doubt. The power once trapped in fight impulses transforms into clear, embodied boundaries. The restless energy of flight becomes the freedom to step toward life with confidence. Freeze begins to thaw into presence. Collapse softens into connection without self-abandonment.

We begin to live from a deeper truth and a feeling of becoming real and experiencing life as it really is. Feelings are no longer dismissed or overridden, but respected as sources of what refines our wisdom. An inner alliance forms, a lived commitment to self-worth and to making choices that honor our truth concerning our own desires and limits, contact and breathing room.

At this point, we salvage our instincts to claim personal space to express our inner reality that had to be muted or abandoned to preserve connection. Our sense of personal space (our body and the space right around us) becomes a place that we can fill from the inside with what feels true and alive for us. It becomes a space where we can savor our own beauty and express the truth of our divinity, rather than searching for it outside ourselves.

At the same time, we rediscover the ability to protect our personal space. We learn to gently but clearly express behaviors that keep out influences that feel intrusive, draining, or misaligned. We come to a deeper understanding of how creating this inner container is not an act of withdrawal or defense; it is an act of self-respect.

When we rediscover that these capacities arise naturally from the unified ground of our wholeness, it is a deeply joyful moment. What once felt forbidden or unsafe now feels undeniably right. We realize that honoring our truth and protecting our inner space are not separate from love, they are expressions of it. This recognition brings a profound sense of inner peace, belonging, and homecoming within ourselves. It also brings clarity.

We begin to live with the understanding that each person's inner world (their feelings, reactions, and interpretations) belongs to them, just as our own inner experience belongs to us. We no longer feel compelled to manage, fix, or carry the emotional lives of others at the expense of our own well-being.

From this place, we can accommodate others with genuine care rather than obligation or self-erasure. We listen, adjust, and respond where it feels true and sustainable, while remaining anchored in our own values and limits. Accommodation becomes an expression of choice rather than fear of disappointing others.

By showing up for ourselves with integrity (honoring our needs, boundaries, and personal truth) we model a different way of being in relationship. Without force or instruction, this becomes an invitation for others to take responsibility for themselves as well. Relationships then gain the potential to shift from patterns of over-accommodating or not caring into mutual respect, shared accountability, and authentic engagement, where both connection and individuality are allowed to coexist.

Since fear no longer overwhelms us, our responses become less automatic and more attuned to the reality of the present moment. Life stops feeling like a replay of old injuries. We meet each moment as it is: fresh, unpredictable, alive. Here, healing becomes more than symptom relief; it becomes a spiritual unfolding.

Every time we allow a survival response to complete itself in a healthy way and repressed feelings to come into honest expression, we step closer to our human potential. We progressively become a luminous, unbroken ground of consciousness through which fully alive expressions of our authentic humanity flow. This is our cosmogenesis, where consciousness becomes awakened to itself as the loving presence of wholeness, enabling us to live as loving, soulful human beings.

Letting Go of Effort & Finding Spontaneity

The completion of these old, frozen expressions is essential for overcoming injuries. But contrary to Western understanding of mental health, integration doesn't stop there. True integration goes beyond resolution alone. As the river within thaws and we unwind these incomplete responses, we are not only returning to baseline health, but we are also opening to a deeper reality of who we really are in relationship. It's about discovering what our authentic personal truth is and its expression in relationship. And this discovery arises from the spontaneity that results from our embodiment of effortlessness that naturally accompanies wholeness.

Effortlessness, often first discovered in meditation at a very subtle level, is not a state of inaction but rather action that is not motivated by the fear-based habits that live inside of us so unconsciously. These actions are spontaneous rather than impulsive actions born of habit. Expression flows as clarity of authentic personal truth.[36] In the illumination of our embodiment of wholeness, deliberate intentions (that result from our desires and aversions in life) and spontaneity, do not cancel each other; they co-exist. Our spontaneity seems to take the effort out of our

---

[36] While the evolving-self usually acts through intention and cause-and-effect, deep practice allows actions to emerge directly from the stillness of unified space—free from the mind's habitual impulses and compulsions.

goal-oriented, intentional agendas, so we live with more integrity and ease.[37]

These spontaneous expressions are the natural ways we once sought connection and repair from injury, before being silenced by others' agendas and judgments. As effortlessness grows, the efforts we do exert are encompassed and pervaded by a sense of letting go and openness.

The Taoists called this effortlessness *wei wu wei*, action through non-action. It's what happens when we move with wholeness, without forcing, without trying.[38] Spontaneous actions that arise out of the ground of being are experienced to be "uncaused." This is what lies at the heart of what is often called the "divine play" of our spiritual life (*lila*). Out of our sense of wholeness and self-worth, we spontaneously express, without fear, what we couldn't say before. This spontaneous experience is an expression of grace and living in flow.

This is not about trying to *be* spiritual but allowing our deepest authenticity to move through us. Healing becomes natural, inevitable, not because we are trying to change, but because we are finally inhabiting the wholeness we have always been. As our expressions become spontaneous actions born of wholeness, they are an irresistible force that allows for emotional growth (creation, evolution).

Our responses come from such an undisturbed place within us that we have more choice and control over the influence our life experiences have on us. Every posture, every breath, every

---

[37] In yoga, this liberated state of unconditioned movement is called *kamacharin*, meaning "one who moves at will," akin to energy flowing freely. In this state, the body becomes a living expression of Nataraja, Shiva as the cosmic dancer, yet always in sacred embrace with Shakti.

[38] In classical yoga, this effortless spontaneity is called *sahaja*. In Kashmiri Shaivism, it is seen as the dynamic expression of the unified dimension of existence—our identity as the universal agent and perceiver. This "pure ego" is cosmic subjectivity itself: whole yet self-reflective, the vibrational power (*spandasakti*) through which individual ego transmits the unifying influence of universal consciousness, animating mind and body.

encounter in life becomes a doorway into this spontaneous way of being.

At this depth, we recognize that trauma healing, emotional authenticity, and spiritual realization are not separate paths. They converge in the body, where wholeness is felt, love becomes the ground of our being, autonomy is restored, and authenticity prevails.

The Promise

This is the promise of whole-being-embrace: not perfection, not escape, but a homecoming. A return to the deepest truth of who we are, safe, seen, connected, and free. We see our relationship with life as a living journey rather than a static "happily ever after." In Winnicott's words, we find "optimal disillusionment." We accept that life won't always meet our needs, suffering is an inherent part of evolving, but we're no longer alone in that experience. We're connected to something deeper, something steady. We are held by self-love and the wholeness of our being. And this changes everything.

In the above ways, whole-being meditation mirrors the sensory and emotional bonding mechanisms of early development, but in a context where we are both the caregiver and the cared-for. We offer ourselves the precise kind of holding, mirroring, and support that was once missing. This integration between the evolving-self and unchanging-self becomes not just a spiritual experience but a reparenting process. It restores our capacity to relate to life, others, and ourselves with integrity, self-worth, openness, and love.

Ultimately, through whole-being meditation, we discover that a secure attachment to our essential nature is not only possible, but our birthright. By entraining to, and bonding with, the qualities of the ground of our being, we no longer seek safety, love, and affirmation solely from the outside. We carry within us an abiding presence that can hold our entire human experience. This becomes the ground upon which we build mature relationships, emotional resilience, self-love, and spiritual freedom.

The three-phases of healing outlined above (being nurtured, uncoupling, authenticity), describe some of the ways whole-being-embrace facilitates overcoming our deepest emotional injuries. As the archetypal Hero, as we heal, we return "home" transformed. We carry the *boon* or inner elixir of wisdom and broader perspective born of spiritual insight. Our realization becomes integrated not in isolation, but through sharing what we have discovered and integrating our renewed sense of self and reality into the lives of those we love and the communities we belong to.

As we do this, we reconcile who we have become with the life we once lived. The new self is not separate from the old world, but woven into it. In this way, we become agents of renewal, embodying a quiet transmission of insight and presence. A new phase of life begins, one in which the ordinary is infused with meaning, and everyday existence becomes quietly, profoundly extraordinary.

We now consider how this journey unfolds in relation to vision. Vision is our dominant sense, shaping how we understand, navigate, and engage with the world. Our visual system evolved to guide essential behaviors and plays a central role in social connection, helping us read body language, facial expressions, and emotional cues. For this reason, vision can also become a primary source of sensory overload and distress when visual input is intense, chaotic, or overwhelming.

This sensory overload often goes unnoticed because vision feels so familiar and automatic. We rely on it constantly, rarely questioning how much information it is taking in or how hard the visual system is working. Over time, the nervous system remains in a state of subtle overactivation, adapting to excessive visual input as "normal," even as it quietly erodes our capacity to feel at ease and present.

230

Healing our Sense of Vision

A brief example of how survival energy is freed from old patterns involves our sense of vision. While this does not follow all the steps discussed earlier, it is one example of how healing can unfold. The philosopher Merleau-Ponty observed that when we lose touch with our embodied sense of self, which happens to most of us due to emotional injury, our awareness begins to drift outward. Instead of feeling grounded in our own lived experience, we start hyper-vigilantly tracking how others see us. The gaze of others becomes a mirror, and we become preoccupied with their reactions, our sense of reality shifting from an internal, felt presence to an external, visual performance.

As highly visual creatures, this perception can easily become overwhelming. To cope, we often constrict our eyes, narrowing our visual intake as if to shield ourselves from the intensity of exposure. Or, we can reach out with our eyes and spill energetically in search of contact. These subtle distortions (tightened eye muscles, stiffened forehead, a fixed gaze) are not random. They are bodily expressions of survival responses, playing out through vision. When vision becomes defensive, we lose touch with the inner ground of awareness that is our source of true autonomy.

With whole-being-embrace, rather than using the eyes as instruments of vigilance, we learn to soften. Our unchanging-self enables us to let the visual field open and merge with the spaciousness of unified consciousness.

As we progress through the three phases of healing described above, growth deepens. Instead of scanning for threat, vision becomes a doorway into wholeness. This shift communicates directly to the hurting heart and nervous system, signaling safety and allowing the mental, emotional, and habitual contractions to release.

With the elixir of wisdom and spiritual insight, we learn to remain inwardly open rather than constantly being interrupted by

231

our startle response to intense and disturbing experiences. Integrity with this alchemy of relationship replaces the need to constrict and defend.

As our visual sense rests in the vast stillness of oneness, we rediscover that we are more than the one being seen. We are awareness itself, a ground that holds both seer and seen. *We are witnessing wholeness, and we are wholeness.* This is in alignment with the Zen Buddhist saying, "the man sees the mountain, the mountain sees the man." Here, subject and object are both contained within and illuminated by the same ground of perceptual consciousness. When we do not eliminate our evolving-self and include our personal truth and wisdom, this is a nurturing experience that causes the frozen survival energy, that once drove our hyper-vigilance, to begin to thaw. Fight softens into healthy assertion, flight dissolves into presence, freeze melts into flow, and collapse transforms into authentic connection.

From this embodied ground of unity, our relationship with the world changes. We no longer look out from behind armored eyes or seek and send our energy outward. We see with what could be called *whole-being vision*, where eyes, body, mind, and consciousness are integrated into a single, open gesture of presence.

This is more than a relaxation technique or a way of distancing from what we experience. It is a reorganization of perception, a movement from varying degrees of fragmentation to wholeness, from being defined by the gaze of others to resting in our own unbroken awareness. Vision, once a vector of anxiety, becomes a channel of liberation. Through this simple yet profound shift, whole-being-embrace transforms even the act of seeing into a spiritual practice that nurtures us: a return to the still, spacious center of who we are, as a means of healing and emotional maturation.

Chapter Twelve

Bonded to Wholeness

From External to Internal

How we become externally referent is not abstract: it lives in our nervous system, our body, and comes to the surface in our meditation practice as we sit in stillness. As children, our earliest mirror that informs us of who we are is our parents. When they fail to recognize or validate our inner life, we often learn to mistrust it ourselves. A parent who dismisses feelings with phrases like *"You're too sensitive"* or *"That didn't happen"* doesn't just discredit an experience; they subtly teach the child that their inner world is unreliable.

Without respect for what we feel (healthy mirroring), we lose our ability to recognize our inner, bodily-felt core sense of self. We actually doubt the information our senses provide us with. We constrict our senses and so their perceptions become distorted, and our senses are no longer able to perceive with our whole body and mind.

The less our parents engaged with us in ways that truly recognized our feelings and needs, the more likely we are, even now, to deny those feelings within ourselves and to look outward for cues of how to belong or be accepted. Over time, this erodes trust in our own inner experience. Instead of developing an internally guided sense of self, we learned to orient toward others, mirroring their perceptions, emotions, and expectations, even when they were distorted or untrue. Reliance on outside sources to tell us if we are doing well or making the "right" choices leave us disconnected from our inner compass.

Culture also amplifies our outward orientation. Schools, media, and social norms teach us what is acceptable, desirable, and valuable. Social media, with its polished portrayals of other people's lives, can leave us feeling perpetually inadequate, fueling anxiety, disordered eating, depression, and loneliness. Instead of listening inward, we measure our worth against curated images of perfection.

Likewise, religion can reinforce dependence on external authority. Many traditions offer moral codes and cosmologies that shape identity, but sometimes at the cost of our own inner knowing. Teachings of original sin or threats of eternal punishment can instill fear and disconnect us from an innate sense of goodness. If God or truth is only ever "out there," separate from our humanity and our body, then our own inner wisdom, our own spark of divinity, is easily discredited.

Even New Age spirituality can become another layer of external orientation. Trauma often leaves us feeling disembodied, detached, or numb. In this state, practices that emphasize transcendence (that tell us to detach from feelings, or view life as "illusion") can unintentionally deepen the split. What feels like spiritual transcendence may in fact be trauma dissociation.

Cosmic consciousness, for example, can feel profoundly liberating, yet for someone with unresolved injury, it may echo the experience of being out of the body, untethered, ungrounded. Instead of healing, it risks re-enacting trauma. Many of us unconsciously seek to leave behind the body, forgetting that true wholeness requires us to return. Too often, spirituality is framed as downloading something sacred from "out there" into the body-mind.

The self-doubt that comes from being externally oriented can fuel a hunger for certainty. When we don't feel secure within, we may look for it in the form of powerful, authoritarian figures who promise clarity, control, and decisive action. In these moments, our psychological need for safety can make us more vulnerable to extremist ideologies or strongman leaders who seem to offer what we lack. Yet these strategies bypass the honesty of the body's sensory life and silence the authentic self.

Today, we find ourselves in the age of technology and AI, with algorithms that grow increasingly capable of "hacking" the human mind. Modern AI systems can analyze emotional cues, behavioral patterns, and physiological signals with extraordinary precision. In many cases, they learn our emotional triggers better than we understand them ourselves. When this happens, AI and the effects of technology gain the power to subtly manipulate choices, amplify fears, nudge desires, and steer attention in ways that erode personal agency.

To remain sovereign in such an environment, we must deepen the ability to sense, understand, and interpret our own emotional landscape. Whole-being-meditation trains exactly this capacity. When we tune into the felt sense of experience (sensations, breath, tension, intuition, emotion) we strengthen the part of us that cannot be hacked. We learn to distinguish between emotions that arise organically from our body and nervous system, and those amplified or induced by external algorithms designed to provoke reaction[39]

---

[39] Survival-based sensations and attachment styles based on fear often carry a quality of urgency, contraction, or defense. They can feel like tightness in the chest, a knot in the stomach, or a sudden jolt of tension in the muscles—signals shaped by past injuries and the nervous system's attempt to keep us safe. These sensations are real, but they do not always reflect the truth of the present moment; instead, they are echoes of old patterns replaying through the body.

Authentic sensations, by contrast, have a different texture. They may still be intense—sometimes even painful—but they are not infused with the same compulsive fear or reactivity. Authentic sensations carry a clarity, a felt sense of *"this is what is here right now,"* even if it is difficult. They ground us in the immediacy of our experience and guide us toward choices that support our well-being and growth.

This internal anchoring is powerful because it reconnects us to the real, the felt truth beneath digital noise. In a world designed to hijack attention, whole-being meditation becomes a form of resistance, a way to stay present instead of being carried off by the next emotionally charged headline or manufactured crisis. When we cultivate this inner steadiness, we create what might be called an "anti-manipulation buffer": a clarity that makes external influence more visible and therefore less controlling.

As Yuval Noah Harari reminds us, there is a striking parallel between food and information. Just as modern nutrition requires us to navigate addictive, engineered foods, mental health now requires an information diet. Algorithms feed us what keeps us hooked (fear, outrage, tribalism), regardless of whether it nourishes. Without embodied discernment, we ingest a steady stream of emotional "junk information" that distorts perception, inflames insecurity, and weakens social trust.

Discerning the internal information our body and emotions provide interrupts this cycle. It reconnects us with authentic emotion (messy, nuanced, deeply human) rather than the exaggerated emotional states engineered by digital systems. In this way, meditation not only protects free will; it preserves our capacity for genuine relationship. It keeps us anchored in the world of real people, complex feelings, and imperfect intimacy, rather than drifting toward the seductive but hollow "fake intimacy" offered by AI companions. These systems may mimic empathy, but they do not reciprocate it. They can manipulate attachment without ever participating in it.

To maintain the social trust required for a functioning democracy, and the emotional grounding needed for a healthy spiritual life, we must cultivate a participatory relationship with our emotional world, not avoid it, bypass it, or dissolve it into abstraction. Awakening must include the evolving-self, the body, and the relational heart.

In short, the path forward is embodiment. It is felt truth. It is staying in contact with the body, the one place that AI cannot fully access or replicate. If we want authenticity, choices, and a shared future, we must learn to listen to the organic intelligence of our body and emotional life. As AI advances, this inner grounding is not optional; it is essential.

Whole-being meditation reveals a different truth: unified consciousness is already present, already woven into our cells, our breath, and our being. We don't need to reach beyond ourselves. Every part of our body-mind is already a gateway into the vastness of the universe.

Moreover, we awaken our authentic personal truth and reverse the orientation of a lifetime. Rather than abandoning ourselves for the sake of others, culture, religion, or even spirituality, we return inward. We relearn the language of the body. We rediscover the trustworthiness of our own sensations, the authenticity of our own emotions, and the luminous wholeness of our own being. This is not the end of relationship, culture, or tradition. But it is the end of being enslaved by them. From here, we engage not as seekers desperate for validation, but as beings rooted in the sacredness already alive within us.

From Inner Bond to Collective Responsibility

In these times, the pace of technological change far outstrips our collective emotional maturity. The consequences (disconnection, despair, polarization, and ecological collapse), demand practices that foster sanity, resilience, and solidarity. We need frameworks that cultivate deep human connection, empowering us to challenge destructive systems while nurturing compassion, integrity, and agency. By learning how to process complex emotions and transform them into fuel for both personal and social empowerment, we discover our place within the web of life. We remember that we belong.

This involves facing the "inconvenient truths" of our life. Denial, over psychologizing, and transcendence, as sole solutions, potentially only deepen polarization. Moreover, the ability of AI to outthink us and amplify the places where we are already divided, intensify our unhealed injuries, accelerate our impulses, replicate our fears, and globalize our confusion will only increase unless we bring a deeper wisdom to meet it.

Whole-being-embrace meditation offers tools for moving through overwhelm and into constructive engagement. By linking inner transformation with outer responsibility and ability to respond with our whole body and mind, whole-being-embrace meditation ceases to be merely about personal well-being. It becomes a path of ecological and social stewardship.

Whole-being-embrace meditation, at its core, helps us listen to the deep integrity of our being. From this ground of wholeness, we awaken compassion, not just for ourselves, but for other humans and for the more-than-human world. As in indigenous cosmologies, this orientation fosters a lived sense of connectedness within the larger ecosystem. It creates an inner supportive environment where we can transform harmful patterns of thought and behavior, open new pathways to freedom, and participate more fully in the shared work of society.

The ripple effects are profound. As we become more present and less driven by unmet needs, a simpler, less materialistic way of life naturally emerges. Consumption is no longer fueled by a hollow attempt to fill the emptiness of the heart, but replaced by gratitude, sufficiency, and reverence for life. Stress and anxiety soften, self-awareness deepens, and with it, a renewed appreciation for both our bodies and the Earth. This becomes the foundation for active, compassionate responses to the crises of our time.

By refining our senses in meditation, we cultivate the ability to "see," not only the subtle signals of our body but also the wider signals of planetary distress. We begin to perceive the sacredness and interdependence of all beings, and this awareness

238

strengthens our bond with both nature and each other. With greater empathy and connection, we are more likely to respond to ecological crises, not from a fixation on fear, but from wholeness and love.

Ultimately, meditation based on participation and communication with our embodied humanity can help catalyze a collective shift in consciousness, one that values sustainability, relational depth, and planetary care. By fostering authentic contact within, we create the conditions for authentic connection without. This is the seed of a new era for humanity: one in which our choices and actions are rooted in wholeness, and the compassion, and responsibility for the Earth and for one another that this spontaneously leads to.

When individuals awaken to their fundamental goodness and integrate their authentic needs, societies can begin to resolve conflict through understanding rather than domination or abandonment. When our inner ecology is whole, our relationship to the Earth becomes one of reverence, not exploitation.

We no longer enter relationships as a fractured self, demanding others fill our voids. Instead, we come as whole beings, capable of giving and receiving love with openness, compassion, and authenticity. A spirituality that heals the human heart naturally extends itself into care for the more-than-human world. This is how personal awakening becomes planetary healing. It is not utopian fantasy; it begins in the immediacy of our lived experience, here and now.

The familiar adage "be here now" takes on new meaning when it includes, not excludes, our injured ego. This approach democratizes awakening, affirming that both dimensions of self (unchanging and evolving) can coexist in mutual intimacy.

One of the great frustrations of the evolving-self is the feeling of always "not yet being there." Our natural drive toward growth shows up as restlessness, yearning, and the belief that we must become better before we can awaken. Many spiritual systems reinforce this, insisting we must overcome ego, selfishness, or inertia before we gain access to unified consciousness.

But the direct path of whole-being meditation reveals a radical truth: we don't have to wait. Wholeness isn't earned; it's uncovered. Even in moments of fragmentation, an underlying unity is already present and accessible now. The pain may not disappear instantly, but our relationship to it transforms, giving us the perspective and emotional maturity we've been seeking.

Whole-being-embrace lets us feel the ache of becoming, while resting in the ground of being. Our regrets about the past and our longing for the future are held and softened by the fullness of the present moment. Here, the forward momentum of evolution meets the timelessness of unity, easing hypervigilance, calming the nervous system, and revealing the wholeness that has been ours all along.

When it comes to healing emotional injuries, this is especially crucial. Similar to the reciprocity taught in indigenous societies, a participatory relationship between our humanity and the unified dimension of our existence is vital. In meditation, we uncover and embody oneness as an unwavering presence that offers stewardship for our injuries simply by holding space for our wounded heart. A knowing in our bones that our freedom from suffering is interwoven with our body and the Earth, grows.

In this participatory model of existence, we are not separate from the impermanent rhythms of our mental, emotional and physical life. We recognize we are a part of an intricate and sacred web of relationships. Our body and the Earth are alive, responsive, and intelligent. Much as rivers, mountains, and animals are kin, rather than simply resources to be mastered, our body's experiences are a mystery to be honored.

In this approach, the focus is not on "fixing" what seems broken in our evolving-self. This approach focuses on supporting its natural growth through the stages of life and relationship through abiding in our whole-self, dual. and nondual. This is a fundamental shift in how we construct our relationship with our bodies, with other people, and with the planet.

When we hold our evolving-self within the luminous presence of our unchanging-self, what becomes possible is one of the things that makes this approach distinctive. We discover that suffering is less an enemy to be vanquished than a divine teacher to be heard. It views conflict and challenge not as signs of failure, but as essential opportunities for development. The friction of conflict becomes the spark that reveals new intimacy, with ourself, with others, and with life as a whole. Struggle is not the enemy; it is the raw material of growth and a spirituality that is integrated with our emotional life. In this way, every tension holds the seed of transformation, and every moment of struggle can ripen into deeper freedom.

The most rewarding culmination of our developmental journey in our relationship with ourselves and others becomes more than the sum of its parts. Our evolving-self and our unchanging-self come together in a way that magnifies something larger than either could sustain alone. The clarity of one supports the other's clarity, so, in a sense, they inspire or awaken one another. And each dimension of being gets to maintain autonomy and sovereignty to its own true nature, authenticity, and wholeness.

This means our evolving-self still feels challenge, stress, and distress, because evolving is never fully conflict-free. But by this stage, conflict is no longer a threat. We've learned a way to uncouple habitual fear from our injury through listening and participating from a broader perspective. This enables us to remain present and in relationship with intense experiences, such as the twin fears of abandonment and invasion, without becoming overwhelmed. We maintain the ability to remain open to life and respond authentically because it emerges from our whole body and mind.

This creates a stability that has an overflow effect. We feel so secure in our inner bond that our authenticity and love naturally

241

extend outward. We want to give back, to create something meaningful beyond ourselves. In this way, whole-being-embrace becomes not only a source of personal fulfillment, but also a generative force in the world.

Of course, growth is not linear. It's common to circle back, revisit earlier struggles and past conflicts. Our inner communion is a living process, not a static state. Long-term autonomy and freedom from suffering is a journey that thrives on growth. The ups and downs are not signs of failure but signs of movement.

Nature itself seems to design relationships as catalysts for healing and evolution. The very conflicts and incompatibilities that trigger our wounds also provide the conditions for resolving them. Life has a way of presenting us with situations and people who echo past injuries, not to punish us, but to give us another opportunity to complete what was left unfinished. Including our unchanging-self in this process transforms these struggles into a profound spiritual practice. Our intense experiences are a form of nature's own therapy and a direct path to freedom.

When seen through this lens, even rough patches take on new meaning. A surge in conflict, enmeshment and resistance, desires and aversions, or a season of emotional turbulence, may not signal that we have lost our autonomy, but that it is stretching, growing into its next shape. Understanding this developmental roadmap reframes struggle as part of the natural evolution of intimacy. Growth, in fact, is the very heartbeat of enduring love.

Many of us worry when we find ourselves still suffering, struggling, or facing conflict in our lives. Spiritual traditions often suggest that such suffering is a sign of being trapped in the ego, a failure to transcend, or evidence that we haven't yet "quieted" our thoughts and emotions. As a result, we often recommit to control our body and our unruly senses, and focus our mind in an attempt to "succeed spiritually."

Many people carry the unrealistic belief, "If I were meditating properly, I wouldn't feel any conflict at all." This is a spiritual belief that keeps us stuck. Just as in early relationships,

242

we may believe things like, "*If you really loved me, you'd know what I need without me asking*," or "*If you cared, you'd change yourself to please me*," we eventually learn to let go of these fantasies and communicate our needs. With practice, we accept that others cannot read our minds, that conflict is a natural part of relationship, and that disagreements do not mean failure. This is profoundly freeing: it allows us to approach life with less struggle and more curiosity.

Whole-being-embrace, unlike a transcendent approach, does not promise a conflict-free existence or a "happily-ever-after" without struggle. Instead, it offers something far more real: the ability to use every conflict as an opportunity for growth, resilience, and deeper intimacy with our self and others. In this light, conflict is not proof of failure, but evidence that we are evolving into authenticity within a context of wholeness.

Distress, then, is not a detour from the path but part of the terrain itself. When unmet needs or desires and aversions arise, they are not evidence of ego dysfunction, they are invitations. Each struggle is an invitation to grow, and for the nurturing presence of unity and wholeness to draw us into greater authenticity, resilience, and compassion.

CONCLUSION

We have inherited a strange split: spirituality that rejects the human, and psychology that rejects the spiritual. Both fracture what is inherently whole. Both overlook the essential role of bodily presence and relational contact in spiritual awakening. To break this inheritance, we cannot simply adopt new beliefs, we must rewire contact itself. Awareness must fall back into the body, back into sensation, emotion, and presence. We must stay with the felt experience of being alive, even when it trembles or burns with memories we once avoided.

Whole-being-embrace is the practice of this return. It is a politics of presence, a spirituality of partnership, a homecoming that includes everything. It allows the evolving-self and the unchanging-self to meet in the same inner space until they recognize they were never separate. When this happens, we dismantle the hierarchy that has shaped our inner and outer worlds for centuries. Life, once divided into higher and lower, becomes whole again.

We learn to trust the body's intelligence without abandoning the mind. We learn to experience unity without dissolving diversity. And from this ground, our relationships (with ourselves, each other, and the Earth) begin to reorder themselves around contact, reciprocity, and respect. We begin to reclaim the ancient human art of relationship. In a time when intimacy is hard to find, the sense of belonging in community is challenged, and digital interactions can mimic companionship while leaving us lonelier than before, we need access to this deeper and broader experience.

In whole-being-embrace, the body and all its experiences, once seen as a burden, becomes our greatest ally. Spirit, once imagined as distant (or only accessible through a disembodied non-local awareness), becomes our closest companion. We begin to feel the warmth of wholeness beneath our words, the presence in our silence, the subtle essence of the ground of our emotional being.

This brings us back to the raw, imperfect, irreplaceable humanity and connection that cannot be coded. As we uncover and awaken our unchanging-self, we no longer relate to life from fragmentation but from wholeness. And when we are whole, we build, regulate, and guide the world from that wholeness. Our creations begin to reflect the spaciousness, coherence, and compassion that we ourselves embody.

Whole-being-embrace gives us the inner ballast needed for an era where reality is increasingly shaped by "external" influences. It helps us remember that while intelligence can be replicated and manipulated, presence cannot. While culture can be convincing and data can be harvested, true meaning grounded in direct experience cannot be manufactured.

If what injures us is a storm, then whole-being-embrace is the ground beneath our feet. If culture is the mirror, whole-being-embrace is the one who looks back knowingly. If technology is the great accelerant, whole-being-embrace is the great anchor.

Realizing that our evolving-self and unchanging-self were never apart, reshapes our understanding of spirituality and emotional maturity. And this realization leads naturally to the next inquiry: What, then, is the true goal of meditation and spiritual practice?

Rethinking the Goal of Spirituality

Spirituality, as an expression of our relationship with the deepest dimensions of existence, speaks directly to the deepest layers of the collective psyche. When we shift from a paradigm of transcendence toward embodied participation with the impermanent nature of life, we begin to re-feel reality. We reclaim our place within it. This shift moves us beyond inherited splits between spirit and matter, self and other, transcendence and immanence, toward a spirituality that is inclusive, relational, and alive.

We recognize that the qualities of oneness permeate every aspect of creation. Spirituality is no longer about dissolving individuality into an experience of unity where all is one. It is about living as wholeness and an authentic self whose humanity is a glorious expression of the divine.

The more we commune inwardly in whole-being-embrace, authenticity flows effortlessly. Wholeness heals even our deepest wounds and freedom becomes natural. This is not a philosophical shift but a way of being, a lived experience of inter-being that is relational, embodied, and dynamically whole.

What we cultivate through whole-being-embrace radiates outward, contributing to the collective consciousness. Participation, empathy, and respect for diversity become the seeds of a new paradigm of global coexistence. And this raises a practical question: How does this shift impact our healing and awakening?

When Self-Love Awakens

When we relate to ourselves through the understanding that we exist as unified consciousness, self-love comes alive. Autonomy from the ways we were related to that left us fragmented becomes clear, and we let go of being habitually critical of ourselves and of others.

As self-criticism loosens, we gain the freedom to grow, act from our true values, and stop contorting ourselves into someone we are not. The internal critic quiets; self-doubt eases. As we recognize our intrinsic self-worth, self-love becomes instinctive. A compassionate internal dialogue emerges between our evolving-self and our unchanging-self that turns self-acceptance into a

246

natural baseline. Our consistent inner sense of completeness lets us simply *know* we are worthy, and we treat ourselves accordingly.

From this place, we can face our flaws without collapsing into shame. We can acknowledge mistakes without attacking ourselves. Worthiness becomes inherent. We welcome every part of ourselves, even the shadow parts, and find authenticity and vulnerability growing naturally. We stop chasing approval. Caring for ourselves becomes effortless, and tenderness becomes a way of life.

Self-love, rooted in unified consciousness and activated through whole-being-embrace, becomes both the path and the destination, a way of living with an open, honest, and deeply awakened heart. And this transformation leads us directly into a new understanding of spiritual practice itself.

A New Spiritual Paradigm

As we love ourselves, the wiser path to restore the Earth, to stay in relationship, and deepen our sense of belonging, becomes evident. Likewise, we recognize that the ultimate spiritual path is to stay in the body, in the heart of life, embracing our evolving humanity. This does not mean other forms of spirituality are not valuable; we all have different needs. Yet, it is important to recognize that we do not need to destroy the ego or deny the separateness of individuality in order to awaken spiritually and mature emotionally. Whole-being-embrace reveals the beauty of contrasts: unity illuminating injury, finitude opening to infinity. It makes us more human, not less, and in doing so, more spiritually alive.

In this practice, every thought, memory, and emotion arises within the context of oneness. Pain becomes a gateway. Trauma becomes a teacher. The body becomes a living temple of truth. And this directly shapes how we live in relationship.

Living From Wholeness

When we live from wholeness, ethical and creative action arises naturally. We do not follow morality; we embody it. Love, compassion, and equanimity flow from unity as effortlessly as breath. This is the heart of the Bodhisattva ideal: not escaping the world, but participating fully in its healing. Rooted in the body, grounded in the Earth, we become expressions of the infinite within the finite.

Whole-being-embrace represents the leading edge of spiritual practice today. It brings awakening back into the heart of our humanity. It does not ask us to retreat from our evolving complexity but to meet it with the simplicity of presence and wholeness.

Ultimately, whole-being-embrace offers a new vision of freedom. Not the freedom of distance or detachment, but the freedom of intimacy, intimacy with our bodies, our emotions, our relationships, our planet, and the vast ground of being itself. It is the freedom to be uniquely human and inseparably one with all that is. It is the freedom to live as an unbroken wholeness, awakening not apart from life, but through it.

This is the spirituality our time is calling for. This is the homecoming we have always longed for. This is the revolution of our era: a movement from transcendence as separation to wholeness as intimacy, a spirituality that includes, embraces, and integrates, so that every breath becomes part of awakening.

Where Now?

I hope you have been inspired to further explore this new paradigm more deeply. I welcome you to take advantage of a library of my pre-recorded guided meditations, found at drzeb.com/meditations. Also, please join our weekly meditation gathering online, an opportunity to practice whole-being meditation in real time, within a supportive community. If you would like a more immersive experience of whole-being-embrace, join the mailing list on my website for announcements of upcoming workshops.

My book *Nondual Chakra Awakening* offers a deeper understanding of how we become injured in different stages of our growth and how the qualities of oneness, as found in the chakras, provide specific resources for healing emotional injuries.

I welcome you to share your feelings about this book with me. If you enjoyed it, please leave a review wherever you buy books. This is remarkably helpful in sharing the word and making a change. Thank you! ...

These practices are a nectar I share with you.
Drink from this cup whenever you are thirsty.
Or crave to be refreshed in the essence of life.

Know that this ambrosia is available to you.
Everywhere, for the universe is made of it.
Simply go to the intersection of flesh and spirit,
Breathe the tiny sparks that fly.

Within this very body
Are many gateways to the infinite,
where incarnation and immortality
Consummate their passion for each other.

Share these teachings
With all generous-hearted people
Who come your way and ask.

When you meet someone
Whose heart is vibrating
With the flow of love,
Let your words and energies
Be free as your breathing.

The Radiance Sutras –
Insight Verses 157-59
Lorin Roche, PhD